GW00502906

CIMA

Paper E1

Organisational Management

Study Text

Published by: Kaplan Publishing UK

Unit 2 The Business Centre, Molly Millars Lane, Wokingham, Berkshire RG41 2QZ

Copyright © 2014 Kaplan Financial Limited. All rights reserved.

No part of this publication may be reproduced, stored in a retrieval system or transmitted in any form or by any means electronic, mechanical, photocopying, recording or otherwise without the prior written permission of the publisher.

Acknowledgements

We are grateful to the CIMA for permission to reproduce past examination questions. The answers to CIMA Exams have been prepared by Kaplan Publishing, except in the case of the CIMA November 2010 and subsequent CIMA Exam answers where the official CIMA answers have been reproduced.

Notice

The text in this material and any others made available by any Kaplan Group company does not amount to advice on a particular matter and should not be taken as such. No reliance should be placed on the content as the basis for any investment or other decision or in connection with any advice given to third parties. Please consult your appropriate professional adviser as necessary. Kaplan Publishing Limited and all other Kaplan group companies expressly disclaim all liability to any person in respect of any losses or other claims, whether direct, indirect, incidental, consequential or otherwise arising in relation to the use of such materials.

Kaplan is not responsible for the content of external websites. The inclusion of a link to a third party website in this text should not be taken as an endorsement.

British Library Cataloguing in Publication Data

A catalogue record for this book is available from the British Library.

ISBN: 978-1-78415-123-2

Printed and bound in Great Britain.

Contents

Introduction

How to use the materials

These official CIMA learning materials have been carefully designed to make your learning experience as easy as possible and to give you the best chances of success in your Objective Test Examination.

The product range contains a number of features to help you in the study process. They include:

- a detailed explanation of all syllabus areas;
- extensive 'practical' materials;
- generous question practice, together with full solutions.

This Study Text has been designed with the needs of home study and distance learning candidates in mind. Such students require very full coverage of the syllabus topics, and also the facility to undertake extensive question practice. However, the Study Text is also ideal for fully taught courses.

The main body of the text is divided into a number of chapters, each of which is organised on the following pattern:

- **Detailed learning outcomes.** These describe the knowledge expected after your studies of the chapter are complete. You should assimilate these before beginning detailed work on the chapter, so that you can appreciate where your studies are leading.

- **Step-by-step topic coverage.** This is the heart of each chapter, containing detailed explanatory text supported where appropriate by worked examples and exercises. You should work carefully through this section, ensuring that you understand the material being explained and can tackle the examples and exercises successfully. Remember that in many cases knowledge is cumulative: if you fail to digest earlier material thoroughly, you may struggle to understand later chapters.

- **Activities.** Some chapters are illustrated by more practical elements, such as comments and questions designed to stimulate discussion.

- **Question practice.** The test of how well you have learned the material is your ability to tackle exam standard questions. Make a serious attempt at each question, but at this stage do not be too concerned about attempting the questions in Objective Test Examination conditions. It is more important to absorb the material thoroughly than to observe the time limits that would apply in the actual Objective Test Examination.

- **Solutions.** Avoid the temptation merely to 'audit' the solutions provided. It is an illusion to think that this provides the same benefits as you would gain from a serious attempt of your own. However, if you are struggling to get started on a question you should read the introductory guidance provided at the beginning of the solution, where provided, and then make your own attempt before referring back to the full solution.

If you work conscientiously through this Official CIMA Study Text according to the guidelines above you will be giving yourself an excellent chance of success in your Objective Test Examination. Good luck with your studies!

Quality and accuracy are of the utmost importance to us so if you spot an error in any of our products, please send an email to mykaplanreporting@kaplan.com with full details, or follow the link to the feedback form in MyKaplan.

Our Quality Co-ordinator will work with our technical team to verify the error and take action to ensure it is corrected in future editions.

Icon Explanations

Definition – These sections explain important areas of knowledge which must be understood and reproduced in an assessment environment.

Key point – Identifies topics which are key to success and are often examined.

Supplementary reading – These sections will help to provide a deeper understanding of core areas. The supplementary reading is **NOT** optional reading. It is vital to provide you with the breadth of knowledge you will need to address the wide range of topics within your syllabus that could feature in an assessment question. **Reference to this text is vital when self studying**.

Test your understanding – Following key points and definitions are exercises which give the opportunity to assess the understanding of these core areas.

Illustration – To help develop an understanding of particular topics. The illustrative examples are useful in preparing for the Test your understanding exercises.

Exclamation mark – This symbol signifies a topic which can be more difficult to understand. When reviewing these areas, care should be taken.

Study technique

Passing exams is partly a matter of intellectual ability, but however accomplished you are in that respect you can improve your chances significantly by the use of appropriate study and revision techniques. In this section we briefly outline some tips for effective study during the earlier stages of your approach to the Objective Test Examination. We also mention some techniques that you will find useful at the revision stage.

Planning

To begin with, formal planning is essential to get the best return from the time you spend studying. Estimate how much time in total you are going to need for each subject you are studying. Remember that you need to allow time for revision as well as for initial study of the material. You may find it helpful to read 'Pass First Time!' second edition by David R. Harris ISBN: 978-1-85617-798-6. This book will help you develop proven study and examination techniques. Chapter by chapter it covers the building blocks of successful learning and examination techniques. This is the ultimate guide to passing your CIMA exams, written by a CIMA examiner and shows you how to earn all the marks you deserve, and explains how to avoid the most common pitfalls.

You may also find 'The E Word: Kaplan's Guide to Passing Exams' by Stuart Pedley-Smith ISBN: 978-0-85732-205-0 helpful. Stuart Pedley-Smith is a senior lecturer at Kaplan Financial and a qualified accountant specialising in financial management. His natural curiosity and wider interests have led him to look beyond the technical content of financial management to the processes and journey that we call education. He has become fascinated by the whole process of learning and the exam skills and techniques that contribute towards success in the classroom. This book is for anyone who has to sit an exam and wants to give themselves a better chance of passing. It is easy to read, written in a common sense style and full of anecdotes, facts, and practical tips. It also contains synopses of interviews with people involved in the learning and examining process.

With your study material before you, decide which chapters you are going to study in each week, and which weeks you will devote to revision and final question practice.

Prepare a written schedule summarising the above and stick to it!

It is essential to know your syllabus. As your studies progress you will become more familiar with how long it takes to cover topics in sufficient depth. Your timetable may need to be adapted to allocate enough time for the whole syllabus.

Students are advised to refer to the notice of examinable legislation published regularly in CIMA's magazine (Financial Management), the students e-newsletter (Velocity) and on the CIMA website, to ensure they are up-to-date.

The amount of space allocated to a topic in the Study Text is not a very good guide as to how long it will take you. The syllabus weighting is the better guide as to how long you should spend on a syllabus topic.

Tips for effective studying

(1) Aim to find a quiet and undisturbed location for your study, and plan as far as possible to use the same period of time each day. Getting into a routine helps to avoid wasting time. Make sure that you have all the materials you need before you begin so as to minimise interruptions.

(2) Store all your materials in one place, so that you do not waste time searching for items every time you want to begin studying. If you have to pack everything away after each study period, keep your study materials in a box, or even a suitcase, which will not be disturbed until the next time.

(3) Limit distractions. To make the most effective use of your study periods you should be able to apply total concentration, so turn off all entertainment equipment, set your phones to message mode, and put up your 'do not disturb' sign.

(4) Your timetable will tell you which topic to study. However, before diving in and becoming engrossed in the finer points, make sure you have an overall picture of all the areas that need to be covered by the end of that session. After an hour, allow yourself a short break and move away from your Study Text. With experience, you will learn to assess the pace you need to work at. Each study session should focus on component learning outcomes – the basis for all questions.

(5) Work carefully through a chapter, making notes as you go. When you have covered a suitable amount of material, vary the pattern by attempting a practice question. When you have finished your attempt, make notes of any mistakes you made, or any areas that you failed to cover or covered more briefly. Be aware that all component learning outcomes will be tested in each examination.

(6) Make notes as you study, and discover the techniques that work best for you. Your notes may be in the form of lists, bullet points, diagrams, summaries, 'mind maps', or the written word, but remember that you will need to refer back to them at a later date, so they must be intelligible. If you are on a taught course, make sure you highlight any issues you would like to follow up with your lecturer.

(7) Organise your notes. Make sure that all your notes, calculations etc. can be effectively filed and easily retrieved later.

Objective Test

Objective Test questions require you to choose or provide a response to a question whose correct answer is predetermined.

The most common types of Objective Test question you will see are:

- Multiple choice, where you have to choose the correct answer from a list of four possible answers. This could either be numbers or text.

- Multiple choice with more choices and answers, for example, choosing two correct answers from a list of eight possible answers. This could either be numbers or text.

- Single numeric entry, where you give your numeric answer, for example, profit is $10,000.

- Multiple entry, where you give several numeric answers.

- True/false questions, where you state whether a statement is true or false.

- Matching pairs of text, for example, matching a technical term with the correct definition.

- Other types could be matching text with graphs and labelling graphs/diagrams.

In every chapter of this Study Text we have introduced these types of questions, but obviously we have had to label answers A, B, C etc rather than using click boxes. For convenience we have retained quite a few questions where an initial scenario leads to a number of sub-questions. There will be questions of this type in the Objective Test Examination but they will rarely have more than three sub-questions.

Guidance re CIMA on-screen calculator

As part of the CIMA Objective Test software, candidates are now provided with a calculator. This calculator is on-screen and is available for the duration of the assessment. The calculator is available in each of the Objective Test Examinations and is accessed by clicking the calculator button in the top left hand corner of the screen at any time during the assessment.

All candidates must complete a 15-minute tutorial before the assessment begins and will have the opportunity to familiarise themselves with the calculator and practise using it, although they can also use a physical calculator.

Candidates may practise using the calculator by downloading and installing the practice exam at http://www.vue.com/athena/. The calculator can be accessed from the fourth sample question (of 12).

Please note that the practice exam and tutorial provided by Pearson VUE at http://www.vue.com/athena/ is not specific to CIMA and includes the full range of question types the Pearson VUE software supports, some of which CIMA does not currently use.

Fundamentals of Objective Tests

The Objective Tests are 90-minute assessments comprising 60 compulsory questions, with one or more parts. There will be no choice and all questions should be attempted.

Structure of subjects and learning outcomes

Each subject within the syllabus is divided into a number of broad syllabus topics. The topics contain one or more lead learning outcomes, related component learning outcomes and indicative knowledge content.

A learning outcome has two main purposes:

(a) To define the skill or ability that a well prepared candidate should be able to exhibit in the examination.

(b) To demonstrate the approach likely to be taken in examination questions.

The learning outcomes are part of a hierarchy of learning objectives. The verbs used at the beginning of each learning outcome relate to a specific learning objective, e.g.

Calculate the break-even point, profit target, margin of safety and profit/volume ratio for a single product or service.

The verb '**calculate**' indicates a level three learning objective. The following tables list the verbs that appear in the syllabus learning outcomes and examination questions.

CIMA VERB HIERARCHY

CIMA place great importance on the definition of verbs in structuring Objective Test Examinations. It is therefore crucial that you understand the verbs in order to appreciate the depth and breadth of a topic and the level of skill required. The Objective Tests will focus on levels one, two and three of the CIMA hierarchy of verbs. However they will also test levels four and five, especially at the management and strategic levels. You can therefore expect to be tested on knowledge, comprehension, application, analysis and evaluation in these examinations.

Level 1: KNOWLEDGE

What you are expected to know.

VERBS USED	DEFINITION
List	Make a list of.
State	Express, fully or clearly, the details of/facts of.
Define	Give the exact meaning of.

For example you could be asked to make a list of the advantages of a particular information system by selecting all options that apply from a given set of possibilities. Or you could be required to define relationship marketing by selecting the most appropriate option from a list.

Level 2: COMPREHENSION

What you are expected to understand.

VERBS USED	DEFINITION
Describe	Communicate the key features of.
Distinguish	Highlight the differences between.
Explain	Make clear or intelligible/state the meaning or purpose of.
Identify	Recognise, establish or select after consideration.
Illustrate	Use an example to describe or explain something.

For example you may be asked to distinguish between different aspects of the global business environment by dragging external factors and dropping into a PEST analysis.

Level 3: APPLICATION

How you are expected to apply your knowledge.

VERBS USED	DEFINITION
Apply	Put to practical use.
Calculate	Ascertain or reckon mathematically.
Demonstrate	Prove with certainty or exhibit by practical means.
Prepare	Make or get ready for use.
Reconcile	Make or prove consistent/compatible.
Solve	Find an answer to.
Tabulate	Arrange in a table.

For example you may need to calculate the projected revenue or costs for a given set of circumstances.

Level 4: ANALYSIS

How you are expected to analyse the detail of what you have learned.

VERBS USED	DEFINITION
Analyse	Examine in detail the structure of.
Categorise	Place into a defined class or division.
Compare/ contrast	Show the similarities and/or differences between.
Construct	Build up or compile.
Discuss	Examine in detail by argument.
Interpret	Translate into intelligible or familiar terms.
Prioritise	Place in order of priority or sequence for action.
Produce	Create or bring into existence.

For example you may be required to interpret an inventory ratio by selecting the most appropriate statement for a given set of circumstances and data.

Level 5: EVALUATION

How you are expected to use your learning to evaluate, make decisions or recommendations.

VERBS USED	DEFINITION
Advise	Counsel, inform or notify.
Evaluate	Appraise or assess the value of.
Recommend	Propose a course of action.

For example you may be asked to recommend and select an appropriate course of action based on a short scenario.

E1
ORGANISATIONAL MANAGEMENT

Syllabus overview

E1 focuses on the structuring of organisations. It covers the structure and principles underpinning the operational functions of the organisation, their efficient management and effective interaction in enabling the organisation to achieve its strategic objectives. It lays the foundation for gaining further insight into both the immediate operating environment and long-term strategic future of organisations, which are covered in E2 and E3.

Summary of syllabus

Weight	Syllabus topic
25%	**A.** Introduction to organisations
15%	**B.** Managing the finance function
15%	**C.** Managing technology and information
15%	**D.** Operations management
15%	**E.** Marketing
15%	**F.** Managing human resources

E1 – A. INTRODUCTION TO ORGANISATIONS (25%)

Learning outcomes

On completion of their studies, students should be able to:

Lead	Component	Indicative syllabus content
1 discuss the different types of structure that an organisation may adopt.	(a) discuss the different purposes of organisations	<ul><li>Ownership: – private sector, public sector.</li><li>Motive: – for-profit, non-profit.</li><li>Mission and vision: – shared values and beliefs.</li><li>Creating value for stakeholders: – control and coordination of resources to achieve goals and outcomes – efficient production of goods and services – facilitating innovation.</li></ul>
	(b) explain the different structures organisations may adopt	<ul><li>Organisational configuration (Mintzberg): – technical core – technical support – administrative support – top and middle management.</li><li>Organisational configuration, contextual dimensions, the effect of: – technology – environment – culture.</li><li>Structural dimensions, influence of: – size – formalisation – specialisation – organisation type e.g. sole-trader, partnership, company, multinational.</li><li>Structural organisation: – functional – divisional – matrix – geographical.</li></ul>

Lead		Component	Indicative syllabus content
	(c)	explain the various forms and functional boundaries of the organisation including externalisation, shared service centres (SSC) and business process outsourcing (BPO).	• Closed and open systems. • Vertical and horizontal structures. • Outsourcing. • Alliances. • Virtual network structure.
2 discuss relationships between internal and external sources of governance, regulation and professional behaviour.	(a)	discuss the purpose and principles of good corporate governance, the ethical responsibilities of the organisation and individuals, and ways of achieving corporate social responsibility.	• Corporate governance, including expectations of stakeholders and the role of government. • Creating an ethical organisation. • Principles of corporate social responsibility (CSR). • Developing business-government relations. • The impact of regulation on the organisation. • Role of institutions and governance in economic growth. • Personal business ethics and the fundamental principles (Part A) of the CIMA Code of Ethics for Professional Accountants.

E1 – B. MANAGING THE FINANCE FUNCTION (15%)

Learning outcomes
On completion of their studies, students should be able to:

Lead	Component	Indicative syllabus content
1 discuss the purpose of the finance function and its relationships with other parts of the organisation.	(a) demonstrate the contribution the finance function makes to the sustainable delivery of the organisation's strategies in a range of contexts	• Stewardship and control of physical and financial resources within the organisation. • Interpreting and reporting the financial position of the organisation for external stakeholders (including statutory requirements) and internal management. • Collating and providing information to enable efficient asset management and cost effective operation of the organisation. • Comparing the current position with forecast/budget expectations and indicating where and how differences have occurred. Providing this in a timely and accurate manner. • Assisting and interacting with other functions in providing solutions to variances.
	(b) analyse the components of the finance function (financial and management accounting, treasury, company secretarial and internal audit)	• Financial accounting – ensuring accurate asset values, efficient working capital management, statutory reporting. • Management accounting – operational reporting (profit and loss) cost control, variance analysis. • Treasury management – sourcing finance, currency management, effective taxation administration. • Company secretarial. • Internal audit – ensuring compliance, fraud detection and avoidance.

	(c) discuss the potential for conflict within the role of the finance function.	• Potential conflicts:
		  – interdependence/independence.
		  – short-term/long-term.
		  – capital/revenue.

Learning outcomes

On completion of their studies, students should be able to:

Lead	Component	Indicative syllabus content
2 explain how the finance function supports the organisation's strategies and operations.	(a) explain the activities fundamental to the role of the finance function (accounting operations, analysis, planning, decision making and control)	<ul><li>Preparation of statutory reports.</li><li>Preparation of plans, forecasts, budgets.</li><li>Working capital reporting and control, inventories, receivables, payables, cash.</li><li>Provision of analysis to support decisions.</li><li>Performance reporting, budget/actuals.</li><li>Cost reporting, product/process.</li><li>Ensuring systems in place to provide timely and accurate control information.</li></ul>
	(b) explain the contemporary transformation of the finance function.	<ul><li>Reconfiguration: – bureaucratic to market oriented.</li><li>Shared services: – outsourced market orientation.</li><li>Business Process Re-engineering: – roles of process working.</li><li>Relocation: – retained/near-shore/off-shore.</li><li>Segregation of the finance function: – transactional/transformational activities.</li><li>Business partners: – support involvement.</li></ul>

E1 – C. MANAGING TECHNOLOGY AND INFORMATION (15%)

Learning outcomes
On completion of their studies, students should be able to:

Lead	Component	Indicative syllabus content
1 demonstrate the purpose of the technology and information function and its relationships with other parts of the organisation.	(a) demonstrate the value of information systems in organisations	• The role of information systems in organisations. • Emerging information system trends in organisations. The networked enterprise, organisational benefits, customer relationship management systems.
	(b) demonstrate ways of organising and managing information systems in the context of the wider organisation.	• Information technology – enabling transformation; the emergence of new, more virtual forms of organisation, technology infrastructure. • Geographically dispersed (virtual) teams; role of information systems in virtual teams and challenges for virtual collaboration. • Managing knowledge, enhancing internal and external relationships. • Ethical and social issues associated with information systems.

2 explain how information systems support the organisation's strategies and operations.	(a) explain the technical components and options for information technology system design	• Evaluating costs and benefits of information systems.
		• The internet, intranet, wireless technology, cloud technologies.
		• Privacy and security.
		• Overview of systems architecture and data flows.
		• Big Data information management:
		  – large volumes of data
		  – complexity and variety of data
		  – velocity, real time data.

	(b) explain the role of emerging technologies e.g. Big Data, digitisation and their uses.	• Enhancing decision making support using Big Data and analytics:
		  – identifying business value
		  – relating to customer requirements
		  – developing organisational blueprint
		  – building capabilities on business priorities
		  – ensuring measurable outcomes.

Learning outcomes

On completion of their studies, students should be able to:

Lead	Component	Indicative syllabus content
		• Information system implementation as a change management process; avoiding problems of non-usage and resistance.
		• System changeover methods (i.e. direct, parallel, pilot and phased).
		• Information system outsourcing (different types of sourcing strategies; client-vendor relationships).
		• E-commerce, digital markets, social media, digital goods.
		• Remote working, hot desking.
		• Big Data and digitisation: – addressing customer needs – effective and speedy decisions.

E1 – D. OPERATIONS MANAGEMENT (15%)

Learning outcomes
On completion of their studies, students should be able to:

Lead	Component	Indicative syllabus content
1 demonstrate the purpose of the operations function and its relationships with other parts of the organisation.	(a) demonstrate the contribution of operations management to the efficient production and delivery of fit-for-purpose goods and services	• Overview of operations strategy and its importance to the firm.
	(b) demonstrate how supply chains can be established and managed.	• Procurement as a strategic process in supply chain management. • Development of relationships with suppliers, including the use of supply portfolios. • Supply chains in competition with each other; role of supply networks; demand networks as an evolution of supply chains. • Design of products/services and processes and how this relates to operations and supply. • The concept of CSR and sustainability in operations management.

2 apply tools and techniques of operations management.	(a) apply the tools and concepts of operations management to deliver sustainable performance	• Process design.
		• Product and service design.
		• Supply network design.
		• Forecasting.
		• Layout and flow.
		• Process technology:
		  – CNC, Robots, AGV, FMS, CIM
		  – decision support systems
		  – expert systems.
		• Work study.
		• Capacity planning and control, inventory control.

Learning outcomes

On completion of their studies, students should be able to:

Lead		Indicative syllabus content
	Component	• Supply chain planning and control:
	(b) explain how relationships within the supply chain can be managed.	– lean synchronisation – contractual/relational approaches – material requirement planning – quality planning and control – statistical process control – operational improvement, total quality management (TQM), Kaizen, Six Sigma, Lean thinking – reverse logistics.

E1 – E. MARKETING (15%)

Learning outcomes
On completion of their studies, students should be able to:

Lead	Component	Indicative syllabus content
1 demonstrate the purpose of the marketing function and its relationships with other parts of the organisation.	(a) apply the marketing concept and principles in a range of organisational contexts	• The marketing concept as a business philosophy. • The marketing environment, including societal, economic, technological, political and legal factors affecting marketing (PESTEL). • The role of marketing in the business plan of the organisation. • Marketing in public sector and not-for-profit organisations e.g. charities, non-governmental organisations, etc.

	(b) apply the elements of the marketing mix.	• The 7 Ps:
		  – product
		  – place
		  – price
		  – promotion
		  – processes
		  – people
		  – physical evidence.
		• Theories of consumer behaviour (e.g. social interaction theory), as well as factors affecting buying decisions, types of buying behaviour and stages in the buying process.
		• Social marketing and CSR.
		• Social media and its effect on the organisation.

Learning outcomes

On completion of their studies, students should be able to:

Lead	Component	Indicative syllabus content
2 apply tools and techniques to formulate the organisation's marketing strategies, including the collection, analysis and application of Big Data.	(a) apply the main techniques of marketing	• Market research, including data gathering techniques and methods of analysis. • Segmentation and targeting of markets, and positioning of products within markets. • How business to business (B2B) and business to government (B2G) marketing differs from business to consumer (B2C) marketing in its different forms: – consumer marketing – services marketing – direct marketing – interactive marketing – E-marketing – internal marketing. • Promotional tools and the promotion mix. • The 'service extension' to the marketing mix. • Devising and implementing a pricing strategy. • Internal marketing as the process of training and motivating employees to support the firm's external marketing activities. • Relationship marketing. • Not-for-profit marketing. • Experiential marketing. • Postmodern marketing.

Learning outcomes

On completion of their studies, students should be able to:

Lead	Component	Indicative syllabus content

	(b) explain the role of emerging technologies and media in marketing.	• Big Data analytics and its use in the marketing process:
		  – predicting customer demand
		  – improving the customer experience
		  – monitoring multi-channel transactions
		  – identifying customer preferences.
		• Marketing communications, including viral, guerrilla and other indirect forms of marketing.
		• Distribution channels and methods for marketing campaigns, including digital marketing.
		• Brand image and brand value.
		• Product development and product/service life-cycles.
		• The differences and similarities in the marketing of products, services and experiences.
		• Product portfolios and the product mix.
		• Marketing sustainability and ethics.

E1 – F. MANAGING HUMAN RESOURCES (15%)

Learning outcomes
On completion of their studies, students should be able to:

Lead	Component	Indicative syllabus content
1 demonstrate the purpose of the HR function and its relationships with other parts of the organisation.	(a) explain the contribution of HR to the sustainable delivery of the organisation's strategies	• The concept of HRM and its influence on organisational processes and performance. • The psychological contract and its importance to retention. • The relationship of the employee to other elements of the business. • HR in different organisational forms, project based, virtual or networked firms and different organisational contexts.

	(b) apply the elements of the HR cycle.	• Acquisition:
		  – identify staffing requirement
		  – recruitment
		  – selection.
		• Development:
		  – training
		  – evaluation
		  – progression.
		• Maintenance:
		  – monetary and non-monetary benefits.
		• Separation:
		  – voluntary and involuntary.

2 apply the tools and techniques of HRM.	(a) demonstrate the HR activities associated with developing employees	• Practices associated with recruiting and developing appropriate abilities including recruitment and selection of staff using different recruitment channels:
		  – interviews
		  – assessment centres, intelligence tests, aptitude tests
		  – psychometric tests
		  – competency frameworks.

Learning outcomes
On completion of their studies, students should be able to:

Lead	Component	Indicative syllabus content

		• Issues relating to fair and legal employment practices (e.g. recruitment, dismissal, redundancy, and ways of managing these).
		
		• The distinction between training and development, and the tools available to develop and train staff.
		
		• The design and implementation of induction programmes.
		
		• Practices related to motivation including issues in the design of reward systems:
		  – the role of incentives
		  – the utility of performance-related pay
		  – arrangements for knowledge workers
		  – flexible work arrangements.

	(b) demonstrate the role of the line manager in the implementation of HR practices.	• The importance of appraisals, their conduct and their relationship to the reward system. • Practices related to the creation of opportunities for employees to contribute to the organisation including; job design, communications, involvement procedures and principles of negotiation. • Problems in implementing HR plans appropriate to a team and ways to manage this. • Preparation of an HR plan. Forecasting personnel requirements: retention, absence and leave, employee turnover. • Ethical code and the interface with HR practice.

PRESENT VALUE TABLE

Present value of 1.00 unit of currency, that is $(1+r)^{-n}$ where r = interest rate; n = number of periods until payment or receipt.

Periods (n)	Interest rates (r)									
	1%	2%	3%	4%	5%	6%	7%	8%	9%	10%
1	0.990	0.980	0.971	0.962	0.952	0.943	0.935	0.926	0.917	0.909
2	0.980	0.961	0.943	0.925	0.907	0.890	0.873	0.857	0.842	0.826
3	0.971	0.942	0.915	0.889	0.864	0.840	0.816	0.794	0.772	0.751
4	0.961	0.924	0.888	0.855	0.823	0.792	0.763	0.735	0.708	0.683
5	0.951	0.906	0.863	0.822	0.784	0.747	0.713	0.681	0.650	0.621
6	0.942	0.888	0.837	0.790	0.746	0.705	0.666	0.630	0.596	0.564
7	0.933	0.871	0.813	0.760	0.711	0.665	0.623	0.583	0.547	0.513
8	0.923	0.853	0.789	0.731	0.677	0.627	0.582	0.540	0.502	0.467
9	0.914	0.837	0.766	0.703	0.645	0.592	0.544	0.500	0.460	0.424
10	0.905	0.820	0.744	0.676	0.614	0.558	0.508	0.463	0.422	0.386
11	0.896	0.804	0.722	0.650	0.585	0.527	0.475	0.429	0.388	0.350
12	0.887	0.788	0.701	0.625	0.557	0.497	0.444	0.397	0.356	0.319
13	0.879	0.773	0.681	0.601	0.530	0.469	0.415	0.368	0.326	0.290
14	0.870	0.758	0.661	0.577	0.505	0.442	0.388	0.340	0.299	0.263
15	0.861	0.743	0.642	0.555	0.481	0.417	0.362	0.315	0.275	0.239
16	0.853	0.728	0.623	0.534	0.458	0.394	0.339	0.292	0.252	0.218
17	0.844	0.714	0.605	0.513	0.436	0.371	0.317	0.270	0.231	0.198
18	0.836	0.700	0.587	0.494	0.416	0.350	0.296	0.250	0.212	0.180
19	0.828	0.686	0.570	0.475	0.396	0.331	0.277	0.232	0.194	0.164
20	0.820	0.673	0.554	0.456	0.377	0.312	0.258	0.215	0.178	0.149

Periods (n)	Interest rates (r)									
	11%	12%	13%	14%	15%	16%	17%	18%	19%	20%
1	0.901	0.893	0.885	0.877	0.870	0.862	0.855	0.847	0.840	0.833
2	0.812	0.797	0.783	0.769	0.756	0.743	0.731	0.718	0.706	0.694
3	0.731	0.712	0.693	0.675	0.658	0.641	0.624	0.609	0.593	0.579
4	0.659	0.636	0.613	0.592	0.572	0.552	0.534	0.516	0.499	0.482
5	0.593	0.567	0.543	0.519	0.497	0.476	0.456	0.437	0.419	0.402
6	0.535	0.507	0.480	0.456	0.432	0.410	0.390	0.370	0.352	0.335
7	0.482	0.452	0.425	0.400	0.376	0.354	0.333	0.314	0.296	0.279
8	0.434	0.404	0.376	0.351	0.327	0.305	0.285	0.266	0.249	0.233
9	0.391	0.361	0.333	0.308	0.284	0.263	0.243	0.225	0.209	0.194
10	0.352	0.322	0.295	0.270	0.247	0.227	0.208	0.191	0.176	0.162
11	0.317	0.287	0.261	0.237	0.215	0.195	0.178	0.162	0.148	0.135
12	0.286	0.257	0.231	0.208	0.187	0.168	0.152	0.137	0.124	0.112
13	0.258	0.229	0.204	0.182	0.163	0.145	0.130	0.116	0.104	0.093
14	0.232	0.205	0.181	0.160	0.141	0.125	0.111	0.099	0.088	0.078
15	0.209	0.183	0.160	0.140	0.123	0.108	0.095	0.084	0.079	0.065
16	0.188	0.163	0.141	0.123	0.107	0.093	0.081	0.071	0.062	0.054
17	0.170	0.146	0.125	0.108	0.093	0.080	0.069	0.060	0.052	0.045
18	0.153	0.130	0.111	0.095	0.081	0.069	0.059	0.051	0.044	0.038
19	0.138	0.116	0.098	0.083	0.070	0.060	0.051	0.043	0.037	0.031
20	0.124	0.104	0.087	0.073	0.061	0.051	0.043	0.037	0.031	0.026

Please check the CIMA website for the latest version of the maths tables and formulae sheets in advance of sitting your live assessment.

Cumulative present value of 1.00 unit of currency per annum, Receivable or Payable at the end of each year for n years $\frac{1-(1+r)^{-n}}{r}$

Periods (n)	Interest rates (r)									
	1%	2%	3%	4%	5%	6%	7%	8%	9%	10%
1	0.990	0.980	0.971	0.962	0.952	0.943	0.935	0.926	0.917	0.909
2	1.970	1.942	1.913	1.886	1.859	1.833	1.808	1.783	1.759	1.736
3	2.941	2.884	2.829	2.775	2.723	2.673	2.624	2.577	2.531	2.487
4	3.902	3.808	3.717	3.630	3.546	3.465	3.387	3.312	3.240	3.170
5	4.853	4.713	4.580	4.452	4.329	4.212	4.100	3.993	3.890	3.791
6	5.795	5.601	5.417	5.242	5.076	4.917	4.767	4.623	4.486	4.355
7	6.728	6.472	6.230	6.002	5.786	5.582	5.389	5.206	5.033	4.868
8	7.652	7.325	7.020	6.733	6.463	6.210	5.971	5.747	5.535	5.335
9	8.566	8.162	7.786	7.435	7.108	6.802	6.515	6.247	5.995	5.759
10	9.471	8.983	8.530	8.111	7.722	7.360	7.024	6.710	6.418	6.145
11	10.368	9.787	9.253	8.760	8.306	7.887	7.499	7.139	6.805	6.495
12	11.255	10.575	9.954	9.385	8.863	8.384	7.943	7.536	7.161	6.814
13	12.134	11.348	10.635	9.986	9.394	8.853	8.358	7.904	7.487	7.103
14	13.004	12.106	11.296	10.563	9.899	9.295	8.745	8.244	7.786	7.367
15	13.865	12.849	11.938	11.118	10.380	9.712	9.108	8.559	8.061	7.606
16	14.718	13.578	12.561	11.652	10.838	10.106	9.447	8.851	8.313	7.824
17	15.562	14.292	13.166	12.166	11.274	10.477	9.763	9.122	8.544	8.022
18	16.398	14.992	13.754	12.659	11.690	10.828	10.059	9.372	8.756	8.201
19	17.226	15.679	14.324	13.134	12.085	11.158	10.336	9.604	8.950	8.365
20	18.046	16.351	14.878	13.590	12.462	11.470	10.594	9.818	9.129	8.514

Periods (n)	Interest rates (r)									
	11%	12%	13%	14%	15%	16%	17%	18%	19%	20%
1	0.901	0.893	0.885	0.877	0.870	0.862	0.855	0.847	0.840	0.833
2	1.713	1.690	1.668	1.647	1.626	1.605	1.585	1.566	1.547	1.528
3	2.444	2.402	2.361	2.322	2.283	2.246	2.210	2.174	2.140	2.106
4	3.102	3.037	2.974	2.914	2.855	2.798	2.743	2.690	2.639	2.589
5	3.696	3.605	3.517	3.433	3.352	3.274	3.199	3.127	3.058	2.991
6	4.231	4.111	3.998	3.889	3.784	3.685	3.589	3.498	3.410	3.326
7	4.712	4.564	4.423	4.288	4.160	4.039	3.922	3.812	3.706	3.605
8	5.146	4.968	4.799	4.639	4.487	4.344	4.207	4.078	3.954	3.837
9	5.537	5.328	5.132	4.946	4.772	4.607	4.451	4.303	4.163	4.031
10	5.889	5.650	5.426	5.216	5.019	4.833	4.659	4.494	4.339	4.192
11	6.207	5.938	5.687	5.453	5.234	5.029	4.836	4.656	4.486	4.327
12	6.492	6.194	5.918	5.660	5.421	5.197	4.988	4.793	4.611	4.439
13	6.750	6.424	6.122	5.842	5.583	5.342	5.118	4.910	4.715	4.533
14	6.982	6.628	6.302	6.002	5.724	5.468	5.229	5.008	4.802	4.611
15	7.191	6.811	6.462	6.142	5.847	5.575	5.324	5.092	4.876	4.675
16	7.379	6.974	6.604	6.265	5.954	5.668	5.405	5.162	4.938	4.730
17	7.549	7.120	6.729	6.373	6.047	5.749	5.475	5.222	4.990	4.775
18	7.702	7.250	6.840	6.467	6.128	5.818	5.534	5.273	5.033	4.812
19	7.839	7.366	6.938	6.550	6.198	5.877	5.584	5.316	5.070	4.843
20	7.963	7.469	7.025	6.623	6.259	5.929	5.628	5.353	5.101	4.870

This page is blank

This page is blank

1

The Different Purposes of Organisations

Chapter learning objectives

Lead	Component
A1. Discuss the different types of structure that an organisation may adopt.	(a) Discuss the different purposes of organisations.

1 Introduction

Chapters 1 to 3 focus on Section A of the syllabus, 'Introduction to Organisations'.

All organisations will have a unique set of goals and we are going to introduce this syllabus area by focusing on the different purposes of organisations. In chapter 2, we go on to explain the different structures that organisations may adopt in pursuit of the goals set and in chapter 3 we will discuss governance, regulation, ethics and corporate social responsibility.

2 Organisations and the Reasons they are Formed

2.1 What is an organisation?

Defining an organisation is difficult as there are many types of organisations which are set up to meet a variety of needs, such as clubs, schools companies, charities and hospitals.

What they all have in common is summarised in the definition produced by **Buchanan and Huczynski**.

'Organisations are social arrangements for the controlled performance of collective goals.'

What is an organisation?

Consider the three aspects of Buchanan and Huczynski's definition in more detail:

(a) 'Collective goals' – organisations are defined by their goals. The main goal of a school is to educate pupils. It will therefore be organised differently to a company that aims to make profits.

(b) 'Social arrangements' – someone working alone cannot be classed as an organisation. Organisations are structured to allow people to work together towards a common goal. Usually, the larger the organisation, the more formal its structures.

(c) 'Controlled performance' – an organisation will have systems and procedures in place to ensure that group goals are achieved. For a company this could involve setting sales targets, or periodically assessing the performance of staff members.

It is worth noting that a major similarity between most organisations is that they are mainly concerned with taking inputs and transforming them into outputs.

For a manufacturing company, this could involve taking raw materials and transforming them into a finished product that can be sold onto its customers.

An accountancy training firm will also take inputs (students and syllabuses) and transform them into outputs (qualified accountants).

Illustration 1 – Football team

A football team can be described as an organisation because:

- It has a number of players who have come together to play a game.

- The team has an objective (to score more goals than its opponent).

- To do their job properly, the members have to maintain an internal system of control to get the team to work together. In training they work out tactics so that in play they can rely on the ball being passed to those who can score goals.

- Each member of the team is part of the organisational structure and is skilled in a different task: the goalkeeper has more experience in stopping goals being scored than those in the forward line of the team.

- In addition, there must be team spirit, so that everyone works together. Players are encouraged to do their best, both on and off the field.

2.2 Why do we need organisations?

Organisations enable people to:

- **Share skills and knowledge** – this can enable people to perform tasks that they would be unable to achieve on their own. Knowledge can also be shared between all the people within the organisation.

- **Specialise** – individual workers can concentrate on a limited type of activity. This allows them to build up a greater level of skill and knowledge than they would have if they attempted to be good at everything.

- **Pool resources** – whether money or time.

This results in **synergy** where organisations can achieve more than the individuals could on their own.

Objective test questions

E1 will be examined in a computerised objective test (OT) exam. A large number of objective test questions (OTQs) have been included in this text. It is important to practise as many questions as possible. The actual exam questions will be in a range of different formats. The main types will be multiple choice, multiple response, number entry, drag and drop, hot spot and drop down.

Test your understanding 1 – OTQ

Jared is organising a social event. Which of the following would be benefits of him forming a committee to manage the planning process and the event itself?

(i) It would help to overcome his limitations, by bringing on board other people with different skills to him.

(ii) It would save time through the joint efforts of everyone on the committee.

(iii) It would help to satisfy Jared's social needs.

(iv) All members of the committee would have to be skilled in all aspects of managing the social event.

A (i), (ii) and (iii) only

B (i), (iii) and (iv) only

C All of the above

D None of the above

3 Different Types of Organisation

As we have discussed, different organisations have different goals. We can therefore classify them into several different categories.

3.1 Profit versus not-for-profit (NFP)

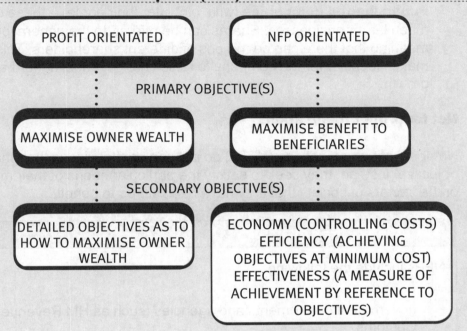

Profit-seeking organisations

Profit-seeking (or commercial) organisations see their main objective as maximising the wealth of their owners.

There are three common forms that a commercial company can take:

- **Sole traders** – the organisation is owned and run by one person.
- **Partnerships** – the organisation is owned and run by two or more individuals.

Note that in both of these organisations, the owner of the business is not legally separate from the business itself. If a partnership is sued by a customer, the customer is actually suing the owner of the business.

- **Limited liability companies** – a company has a separate legal identity to its owners (who are known as shareholders). The owner's liability is limited to the amount they have invested into the company.

In the UK, there are two types of limited company:

Private limited companies (with 'Ltd' after their name) – these tend to be smaller businesses, often owned by a few shareholders. Shares cannot be offered to the general public.

Public limited companies (with 'plc' after their name) – these can be much larger businesses. Shares can be offered to the general public, meaning that there can be millions of different shareholders. This makes it easier for the company to raise finance, enabling further growth.

Not for profit organisations

Not-for-profit organisations (NFPs) do not see profitability as their main objective. Instead, they seek to satisfy the particular needs of their members or the sectors of society that they have been set up to benefit.

Illustration 2 – NFP examples
NFPs include the following: • government departments and agencies (such as HM Revenue and Customs)   • schools   • hospitals   • charities (such as the Red Cross, Oxfam and Doctors Without Borders)   • clubs.

The objectives of different NFPs will vary significantly:

- Hospitals exist to treat patients.
- Councils may see their mission as caring for their communities.
- Government organisations usually exist to implement government policy.
- A charity may have 'provision of relief to victims of disasters' as its main objective.

3.2 Public versus private sector organisations

Public sector organisations

The public sector is the part of the economy that is concerned with providing basic government services and is controlled by government organisations.

> **Illustration 3 – Public sector organisations**
>
> The organisations that make up the public sector vary from country to country, but generally include:
>
> - police
> - military
> - public transport
> - primary education
> - healthcare for the poor

Private sector organisations

The private sector consists of organisations that are run by private individuals and groups rather than the government.

> **Illustration 4 – Private sector**
>
> The private sector will therefore normally include:
>
> - businesses
> - non-governmental organisations
> - charities and
> - clubs.
>
> Within these will be both profit-seeking and not-for-profit organisations.

Note on question style

A number of the test your understandings included in this text do not represent the style of question that you will be presented with in the operational level exams (i.e. either OTQs or case style questions). However, they are included for learning purposes and should serve to enhance your knowledge and understanding of the subject. It is important to work through these questions before sitting the exam.

Test your understanding 2

Many schools run fund-raising events such as fêtes, where the intention is to make a profit. This makes them 'profit-seeking'.

Is this statement:

A   True

B   False

Non-governmental organisations (NGOs)

A non-governmental organisation is one which does not have profit as its primary goal and is not directly linked to the national government.

NGOs often promote political, social or environmental change within the countries they operate.

Illustration 5 – NGOs

Some of the largest NGOs operate in the humanitarian sphere and include:

- Oxfam

- the Red Cross

- World Vision

- Amnesty International.

Expenditure by these NGOs can exceed the GDP of some countries.

NGOs could operate as partners with firms in lobbying government for change or as opponents if the firm's activities are at odds with the NGO's mission.

There are two types of NGO:

- **Operational NGOs** – seek to achieve change directly through projects such as community development. Oxfam is an example of an operational NGO.

- **Campaigning NGOs** – seek to achieve change indirectly through the use of lobbying and public relations (PR) programmes to influence government. Amnesty International is an example of a campaigning NGO.

3.3 Co-operatives

Co-operatives are organisations that are owned and democratically controlled by their members – the people who buy their goods or services.

They are organised solely to meet the needs of the member-owners, who usually share any profits.

Illustration 6 – Co-operatives
In the UK, the largest example of a co-operative is the Co-operative Group, which has over 5.5 million members and operates in diverse markets, such as banking, travel and groceries.

Test your understanding 3 – OTQ
Which of the following are usually seen as the primary objectives of companies?

(i)   To maximise the wealth of shareholders

(ii) To protect the environment

(iii) To make a profit

A   (i), (ii) and (iii)

B   (i) and (ii) only

C   (ii) and (iii) only

D   (i) and (iii) only

Which one of the following organisations is most likely to be classified as part of the public sector?

A   A charity

B   A social club

C   A school

D   A public limited company

4 Mission, Vision and Objectives

We have already discussed the different objectives of organisations. We are now going to introduce two important terms regarding objectives.

4.1 Mission

Mission is the most generalised type of objective and can be seen as an expression of the **organisation's reason for being**.

Mission is neither quantifiable or within time-constrained targets.

Elements of mission

- **Purpose** – **why** does the organisation exist and **who** does it exist for?
- **Strategy** – **what** does the organisation provide (goods/services) and how are these provided?
- **Policies and culture** – **how** does the organisation expect its staff to behave/act?
- **Values** – **What** are the core principles of the organisation?

Illustration 7 – Examples of mission

'Our mission is:

- to refresh the world in mind, body and spirit,
- to inspire moments of optimism through our brands and actions and
- to create value and make a difference everywhere we engage.'

(Coca Cola)

'To produce cars and trucks that people will want to buy, enjoy driving and will want to buy again.'

(Chrysler)

'To create lasting solutions to poverty, hunger and social injustice.'

(Oxfam)

'To make Merseyside a safer, stronger and healthier community.'

(Merseyside Fire and Rescue Service)

Test your understanding 5

What are the potential benefits and drawbacks to an organisation of setting a mission statement?

4.2 Vision

An organisation may also have a vision which sets out **how they see the organisation in the future**. This is closely linked to the mission of the organisation.

Illustration 8 – Examples of Vision

'A personal computer in every home running Microsoft software.'

(Microsoft)

'To be the company that best understands and satisfies the product, service and self-fulfilment needs of women-globally.'

(Avon)

> ### Distinction between mission and vision
>
> Vision and mission should not be confused. The terms are often used interchangeably but mission statements are present-based statements designed to convey a sense of why the organisation exists to all of its interested parties. Vision statements, on the other hand, are future-based and meant to inspire and give direction to the employees of the organisation, not those outside the organisation.

4.3 Objectives

The mission establishes what the organisation wants to achieve overall. However, in order to achieve the mission, an organisation should establish a number of detailed objectives. Objectives should be SMART, i.e. **s**pecific, **m**easurable, **a**chievable, **r**elevant and **t**ime-constrained.

5 Creating Value for Stakeholders

5.1 Introduction

An organisation has many different interested parties or stakeholders, each with different objectives and degrees of influence. Stakeholders are virtually everybody who has anything to do with an organisation.

It is vital for managers to understand the varying needs of the different stakeholders in the organisation. Failure to do so could mean that important stakeholders do not have their needs met, which could be disastrous for the organisation.

Value for stakeholders can be created in a number of ways, including notably:

* control and co-ordination of resources to achieve goals and outcomes
* efficient production of goods and services
* facilitating innovation.

5.2 Control and co-ordination of resources to achieve goals and outcomes

Controls are activities undertaken within an organisation that will increase the chance of an organisation achieving its objectives.

They monitor whether the organisation is on track to achieve its goals and if not, corrective action can be taken.

Typical controls include:

- **direct supervision** of staff
- **planning** processes
- **targets**
- the **culture** of the organisation
- **self-control** by employees

Co-ordination

Co-ordination means bringing together all the activities of an organisation. The capacity of an organisation to co-ordinate human resources and physical, financial and technological resources is linked to its overall effectiveness and achievement of goals.

Test your understanding 6

Explain the benefits of co-ordination for an organisation.

5.3 Efficient production of goods and services

In producing goods and providing services an organisation should strive to minimise the wastage of resources.

The concept of **lean** production was developed by the Japanese car manufacturer, Toyota. It is a philosophy that aims to systematically reduce waste, i.e. through minimising:

- inventory
- waiting (idle time)
- defective units
- effort
- transportation
- over-processing and
- over-production.

The efficient production of goods and services can be facilitated through the use of technology and innovation. Technology will enable an organisation to **maximise asset usage**. For example:

- There has been a move towards a paperless office in the service industry (i.e. a work environment in which the use of paper is eliminated or greatly reduced). This has been done by converting documents into digital forms thus boosting productivity, saving space, making documentation sharing easier and helping the environment.

- Although it is nothing new to put robots on the assembly line, technology innovation has resulted in more recent steps to revolutionise the role of robots. Robots are now working alongside humans on car production lines.

Illustration 9 – Use of robots at BMW

In the United States, BMW's factory in Spartanburg employs more than 7,000 people, making an average of about 1,000 vehicles each day. It also employs robots, which work alongside humans, to help make car doors. BMW says the plan isn't to replace people on the assembly line, but instead to keep the skilled workforce healthy and in work for longer; an important consideration given the increase in the retirement age in the United States (and many other countries).

5.4 Facilitating innovation

In the modern business environment, the ability to innovate is becoming a competency in itself. The idea that 'what is good today, will not be tomorrow' has never been so relevant.

Innovation can be used to:

- reduce costs
- provide a basis for differentiation.

An organisation will need to exploit its creative ideas. This can be done via certain organisational dimensions:

- **Structure** – a flexible structure to avoid the stifling of innovation.

- **Culture** – sees failure as a learning experience to be expected.

- **Leadership** – to lead the organisation via communication and the creation of vision.

- **People** – a team-based approach creating ownership and participation.

- **Communication** – creating awareness within the organisation of the ideas created.

Illustration 10 – Innovation at Google

The most successful internet company of our time, Google, is known for its deceptively simple search function but the company continues to pursue projects that could reinvent the company and society. Many of its current projects aim to be life changing, for example:

- **Calico** – a spin-off company working to extend human lifespan.

- **Glass** – which is making wearables the next computer trend.

- **Shopping Express** – an experiment in same-day delivery with national and local retailers.

- **Google Now** – which reminds users when their favourite band or author has a new release and when the last train is leaving – before it's too late.

6 Chapter Summary

```
                    ┌──────────────────────────┐
                    │   The different purposes  │
                    │     of organisations      │
                    └──────────────────────────┘
```

Organisations and the reasons they are formed
- what is an organisation?
- why do we need organisations?

Different types of organisation
- profit versus not-for-profit
- public versus private sector
- co-operatives

Mission, vision and objectives
- mission
- vision
- objectives

Creating value for stakeholders
- control and co-ordination
- efficient production
- facilitating innovation

7 Practice Questions

Question 1 – OTQ

The public sector is normally concerned with:

A   making profit from the sale of goods

B   providing services to specific groups funded from charitable donations

C   the provision of basic government services

D   raising funds by subscriptions from members to provide common services

Question 2 – OTQ

Which one of the following statements regarding limited companies is correct?

A   Public limited companies have access to a wider pool of finance than partnerships or sole traders

B   Both public and private limited companies are allowed to sell shares to the public

C   Companies are always owned by many different investors

D   Shareholders are liable for any debts the company may incur

Question 3 – OTQ

Consider the following list of different organisations:

(i) Government departments

(ii) Partnerships

(iii) Charities

(iv) Companies

Which of these organisations would normally be classified as BOTH a not-for-profit organisation AND a private sector organisation?

A   (i) and (iii) only

B   (iii) only

C   (i) only

D   (ii) and (iii) only

Question 4 – OTQ

Westeros is an organisation which imports computers into country A and sells them to the public in order to make a profit. It is owned by ten individual investors, each of whom owns an equal number of shares in Westeros. Westeros is not a public limited company.

Which of the following is likely to be the most appropriate source of finance for Westeros?

A   Central government funding

B   The existing owners of Westeros

C   Issue of shares to the public

D   Donations from the public

Note on case style questions

The E1 text includes a number of 'case style' questions. These are longer questions with a time guidance and are aimed at giving a flavour of the types of areas that may be examined in the operational level case study. These questions will serve as excellent question practise before sitting the case study but will also enhance your knowledge and understanding which will be of benefit when sitting the OT exam.

Question 5 – C (Case style)

Background

C is a company which is engaged in synthetic fibre production. It is situated in Home country where it operates two production plants. C pipes raw material from an oil refinery (which it does not own) to its own production plant where it manufactures a single product which is a special grade of polymer. The polymer is then transferred to a second production site which produces two products, 'Synfib' and 'Thetfib'. As the polymer is of a special grade and manufactured specifically for the production of Synfib and Thetfib, there is no intermediate market for it. The transfer price for the polymer has been set at $40 per litre.

Mission and objectives

C's Chairman has declared that the firm's mission is to 'provide its customers with the highest quality product at a reasonable price'. The organisational objectives are to:

- satisfy the demands of the shareholders

- reduce pollution to a minimum

- maintain secure employment and

- to sell a product of high quality which satisfies customer requirements.

The objectives also make reference to maximisation of shareholder wealth while at the same time keeping the shareholders' exposure to financial risk to a minimum.

Approximately 75% of the shares are held by large financial institutions. The remainder are held by individual investors including employees and the Directors.

Task:

Produce a critical appraisal of the content of the mission statement and objectives of C as they are presented to you in the scenario. Recommend what changes should be made to their content.

(20 minutes)

Test your understanding answers

Test your understanding 1 – OTQ

The correct answer is A

Statement (iv) would not be true, as organisations (which this committee could be classified as) allow for specialisation. Not all of the members would have to be skilled at performing all of the necessary tasks.

Test your understanding 2

The correct answer is B – False

Schools run fund-raising activities to help pay for extra books, e.g. to improve the quality of education given to pupils. The primary objective is educational, not profit. The money made at the fête is thus a means not an end.

Test your understanding 3 – OTQ

The correct answer is D

While protecting the environment is to be encouraged and is reinforced within statute to some degree, it is not a primary objective of the company. Companies exist primarily to maximise the return to their owners.

Test your understanding 4 – OTQ

The correct answer is C

Public sector organisations will be controlled by the central government. This is unlikely to be a charity, a company or a social club – which are typical examples of the private sector.

Note that a privately owned and operated school could be part of the private sector, but schools are still the most likely from the list to be public.

Test your understanding 5

Benefits	Drawbacks
• Provides strategic direction thereby assisting in the formation of acceptable policies.	• They may be unclear or vague.
• Provides a framework within which managerial decisions can be made.	• They may be unrealistic.
• Assists in communicating key cultural values to employees and other stakeholders.	• There may be inconsistencies between the different elements of the mission statement.
• Helps to prevent potential misinterpretations of the organisation's reason for being.	• They may be inconsistent with management action.
• Assists in resolving conflict between stakeholder groups.	• They may lack sufficient external focus.

Test your understanding 6

Co-ordination is necessary for a number of reasons:

- **It makes optimum utilisation of resources** – co-ordination brings together different organisational resources and focuses on minimising wastage in order to achieve organisational goals.

- **It encourages team spirit** by arranging work in such a way to minimise conflicts and rivalries.

- It gives **proper direction** to all departments of an organisation.

- It encourages employees to show **initiative** thus increasing motivation.

- It helps **achieve objectives quickly** by minimising conflicts, rivalries, wastage, delays and other organisational problems.

- It **improves relations between different levels** within the organisation.

Question 1 – OTQ

The correct answer is C

C is the correct answer because this is the main activity in the public sector. Options A and B relate to the private sector and D to a mutual organisation.

Question 2 – OTQ

The correct answer is A

As public limited companies are able to sell their shares to the public, they will often find it easier to raise large amounts of capital for growth, if needed. This may be much harder for partnerships and sole traders. Only public companies can sell shares to the public, companies may be owned by only one shareholder and shareholders enjoy limited liability.

Question 3 – OTQ

The correct answer is B

Partnerships and companies would both usually be profit seeking. While government departments are likely to be not-for-profit, they would be part of the public sector. Therefore only charities would be likely to be both public AND not-for-profit.

Question 4 – OTQ

The correct answer is B

Westeros is a profit-seeking organisation – given that its ten owners own 'shares', it must be a private limited company. As such, only B is likely to be appropriate from the options provided. Central government funding is usually for public sector organisations, donations would usually be the major source of funding for charities and Westeros cannot issues shares to the public as it is a private limited company.

Question 5 – C (Case style)

A mission statement is directed primarily towards the employees of an organisation, and should help the company towards achieving its objectives. It might provide a statement of the company's culture, and also state the aims of the company and the business areas within which the company will operate. An alternative view is that a mission statement should include a statement of the business areas in which the company will operate and in addition, its reason for existence and the stakeholder groups who will be served by the company.

The mission statement of C is 'to provide its customers with the highest quality product at a reasonable price'.

This can be **criticised** as a mission statement for a number of reasons.

- It does not state the business areas in which the company intends to operate. Presumably, the company means synthetic fibre products, but the statement does not make this clear.

- It does not give a reason for the company's existence. In particular, the statement fails to give any indication why the company will be better than its competitors in what it does.

- It appears to focus on customer requirements only, and has nothing to say about other groups, particularly employees and shareholders. It does not actually define who its customers are or who it wants its customers to be.

- It is dull. Short mission statements should be inspiring.

- The terms 'highest quality' and 'reasonable price' are unclear in their meaning. It is not clear what is meant by 'quality', nor what 'reasonable' is in terms of price. Assuming that it will be expensive to achieve the highest quality, how high might a reasonable price be?

Objectives might be phrased in general terms, as in the case of C, but to be of much value they should be more specific.

It has been suggested that objectives should be 'SMART', i.e. specific, measurable, achievable, relevant and time-constrained. From the information provided, it seems that the objectives of C fail to meet these criteria.

- The stated aim is to 'satisfy the demands' of shareholders. Although there is reference to maximising shareholder wealth, and to setting limits to acceptable risk, there is no clear statement of what these objectives mean. They must be stated more specifically and put within a time frame. For example, an objective might be to increase profits and dividends over the next five years at the rate of at least x% each year. The risk limits would also have to be specified.

- The aim of reducing pollution to a minimum is also inadequate, because it fails to state what 'minimum' means or the time frame within which the objective should be met.

- The objective of maintaining secure employment is also vague and meaningless, except perhaps to indicate that the company will be reluctant to make members of its work force redundant, and this might be an unrealistic target. Again, a more specific objective is required.

- The objective of selling a high quality product to satisfy customer requirements has a link to the mission statement, but is also vague and so meaningless. Actual achievements cannot be monitored against such a vague objective.

Both the mission statement and the objectives should therefore be re-formulated along the guidelines suggested above.

Organisational Structure

Chapter learning objectives

Lead	Component
A1. Discuss the different types of structure that an organisation may adopt.	(b) Explain the different structures organisations may adopt. (c) Explain the various forms and functional boundaries of the organisation including externalisation, shared service centres (SSC) and business process outsourcing (BPO).

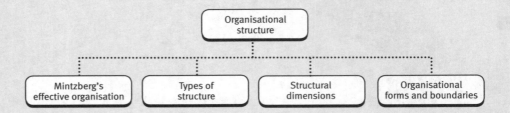

1 Introduction

A structure is necessary in order to facilitate the achievement of objectives.

Organisational structure is concerned with the way in which the work is divided up and allocated. It outlines the roles and responsibilities of individuals and groups within the organisation.

2 Mintzberg's Effective Organisation

Mintzberg suggested that an organisation is made up of five parts (building blocks). It is important that an organisation considers the relative balance of these elements in order to achieve their organisational goals and secure optimal competitiveness.

Co-ordinating mechanisms should be put in place to integrate the building blocks into one cohesive unit.

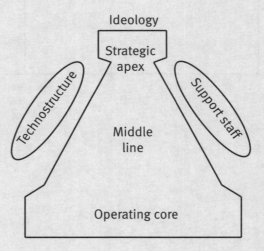

Operating core

Refers to those individuals who perform the task of producing the product or providing the service. In a small organisation this will represent nearly all of the organisation, but larger organisations will require more complex arrangements.

Strategic apex

Those individuals who formulate and implement strategy, and ensure that the organisation executes its mission, in order to serve the owners of the organisation.

Middle line

As an organisation grows there will be a need for multiple managers of workers, plus a manager to manage the managers. This creates the middle line which is the hierarchy of authority from strategic apex to front line supervisors. Links the strategic apex to the operating core and includes middle and lower level management.

Technostructure

As the organisation grows larger, it typically develops a separate group of people who decide what the organisation's technology and procedures should be. Concerned with co-ordinating the work by standardising processes, outputs and skills. Includes human resource (HR) managers (who will standardise skills), accountants (who will standardise outputs) and industrial engineers (who will standardise processes).

Support staff

The organisation may add other administrative units to provide services to itself. The support staff provide assistance outside of operational workflow such as catering services, legal advice and press relations.

Ideology

This is the organisation's values and beliefs (culture) and can be discerned by examining norms or observable behaviour in the workplace.

Test your understanding 1

Many organisations are now actively seeking flatter hierarchies, better quality and ways of contracting out of non-core activities.

Required:

Briefly discuss the implications of this on Mintzberg's organisation.

Linking mechanisms

The detailed configuration of the organisation is also made up of linking (co-ordinating) mechanisms:

- a formally determined hierarchy of decision levels, power and responsibility

- a formal flow of information around the organisation

- an informal communication network, the 'grapevine'

- formal work constellations whereby sections of the organisation set up and operate formal co-ordinating mechanisms such as work parties and committees

- a system of ad hoc decision processes whereby the organisation responds in a particular manner when it faces a problem.

Main configurations

Mintzberg identified six successful organisational structures. Different types of organisation will place varying levels of emphasis on each of the building blocks and will have differing co-ordination mechanisms in place.

- **Simple structure**. The strategic apex, possibly consisting of a single owner-manager in a small business, exercises direct control over the operating core, and other functions are pared down to a minimum. There is little or no middle line, and technostructure or support staff are also absent. Co-ordination is achieved by direct supervision, so that this structure is flexible, and suited to dynamic environments.

- **Machine bureaucracy**, which arises from the power of the technostructure. The emphasis is on regulation: bureaucratic processes govern all activities within the organisation. This means that speedy reaction to change is impracticable, and this arrangement is best suited to simple, static environments.

- **Professional bureaucracy**, which arises from the predominance of the operating core. This type of structure commonly arises in organisations where many members of staff have a high degree of professional qualification (for example, the medical staff in a hospital or the analysts and programmers in a software developer).

- **Divisionalised form**, which is characterised by a powerful middle line in which a large class of middle managers each takes charge of a more or less autonomous division. Depending on the extent of their autonomy, managers will be able to restrict interference from the strategic apex to a minimum.

- **The 'adhocracy'**, a complex and disorderly structure is which procedures or processes are not formalised and core activities are carried out by project teams. This structure is suited to a complex and dynamic environment. There are two types of adhocracy:

  - operating adhocracy which innovates and solves problems directly on behalf of its clients. Admin work and operating work are blended together (consultancy firm, advertising agency)

  - administrative adhocracy which undertakes projects to serve itself, so it has its own operating core (research and development, hi-tech companies).

- **Missionary organisations** are formed on the basis of a common set of beliefs and values shared by all workers in the organisation. Firm belief in such norms implies an unwillingness to compromise or change, and this means that such organisations are only likely to prosper in simple, static environments.

Supplementary reading

	Environment, i.e. nature of external influences	Internal factors including size and importance of technology	Key building block	Key co-ordinating mechanism
Simple structure	Simple/dynamic	Small, young, Simple tasks	Strategic apex	Direct supervision between entrepreneur and employees
Machine bureaucracy	Complex/ static	Large, old regulated tasks	Techno structure	Standardisation of work using specified operating procedures
Professional bureaucracy	Complex/ static	Professional, simple systems	Operating core	Standardisation of skills - identification of training needs and necessary skills to do work
Divisionalised	Simple/Static diverse	Very large, old, divisible tasks	Middle line	Standardisation of outputs, i.e. product/ service specification
Adhocracy	Complex/ dynamic	Young, complex tasks	Operating core/Support staff	Mutual adjustment, i.e. co-ordination through informal contact.
Missionary	Simple/ static	Middle-aged simple systems	Ideology	Standardisation of norms

---

Test your understanding 2 – OTQ

The Technostructure:

A   is dedicated to the technical side of product and process development

B   is the board of directors who decide on the financial structure and technicalities of a business

C   are departments such as accounting and personnel which provide support for technical structures by co-ordinating and standardising work

D   are functions to purchase materials and process them for distribution

---

3 Types of Structure

The structure of most organisations will change over time as the company grows. A typical pattern of structural change would be as follows:

- entrepreneurial structure

- functional structure

- divisional structure

- matrix structure.

Each of these will be reviewed in turn.

3.1 Entrepreneurial structure

This structure is built around the owner manager and is **typical of small businesses in the early stages of their development**.

It is also often found where the entrepreneur has specialist knowledge of the product or service that the organisation offers.

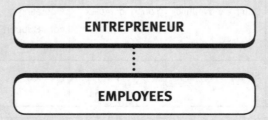

Advantages	Disadvantages
• Fast decision making.	• Lack of career structure.
• More responsive to market.	• Dependent on the capabilities of the manager/owner.
• Goal congruence.	• Cannot cope with diversification/growth.
• Good control.	
• Close bond to workforce.	

Advantages & disadvantages of entrepreneurial structures

Advantages

- There is only one person making decisions – this should lead to decisions being made quickly.

- As soon as an element of the market alters, the entrepreneur should recognise it and act quickly.

- A lack of a chain of command and the small size of the organisation should mean that the entrepreneur has control over the workforce and all decisions within the organisation, leading to better goal congruence.

Disadvantages

- This type of structure is usually suited to small companies where due to the size there is no career path for the employees.

- If the organisation grows, one person will not be able to cope with the increased volume of decisions etc.

3.2 Functional (departmental structure)

Functional organisations group together employees that undertake similar tasks into **departments**.

This type of structure is often found in organisations that have outgrown the entrepreneurial structure.

It is most appropriate for small organisations which have relatively few products or locations and which exist in a relatively stable environment.

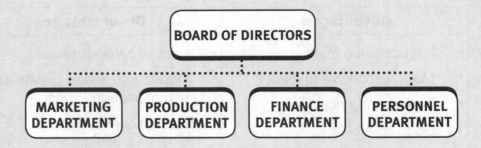

Advantages	Disadvantages
• Economies of scale.	• Empire building.
• Standardisation.	• Slow.
• Specialists more comfortable.	• Conflicts between functions.
• Career opportunities.	• Cannot cope with diversification.

Advantages & disadvantages of functional structures

Advantages

• Rather than duplicating roles in different parts of the company, similar activities are grouped together, leading to:
  – lower costs
  – standardisation of output/systems, etc.
  – people with similar skills being grouped together and so not feeling isolated.

• Due to the larger size of the organisation and the grouping into functions, there is a career path for employees – they can work their way up through the function.

Disadvantages

• Managers of the functions may try to make decisions to increase their own power or are just in the best interests of their function, rather that working in the best interest of the company overall. This leads to empire building and conflicts between the functions.

• Due to the longer chain of command, decisions will be made more slowly.

• This style of structure is not suited to an organisation which is rapidly growing and diversifying. For example, the specialists in one organisation's production function may not be able to cope with making, say, gas fires and radios.

3.3 Divisional structure

This structure occurs where an organisation is split into several **divisions** – each one autonomously overseeing a **product** (i.e. separate divisions for cars and motor bikes), a **geographic section** (i.e. separate divisions for US and Europe) or even by customer (i.e. separate divisions that look after corporate clients and private clients).

Each division is likely to have a functional structure, with all the departments it needs in order to operate in its particular market segment.

Divisions are likely to be run as profit centres, with their own revenues, expenditure and capital investments. Each division is a separately identifiable part of the overall organisation, which is often referred to as a **strategic business unit** (SBU).

Product based divisional structure

A separate division exists for each product.

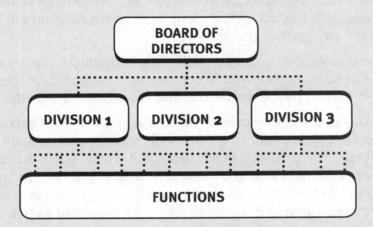

Illustration 1 – Divisional structure

A Ltd is a company that manufactures two different products – toasters and televisions. The products require different components and require different advertising and sales.

A Ltd therefore operates a divisional structure, with a toasters division and a television division. Each division has its own sales, purchasing, HR and advertising divisions.

The finance department, however, is still operated centrally.

Advantages	Disadvantages
• Enables growth.	• Duplication.
• Clear responsibility for products/divisions.	• Sub-optimisation.
• Training of general managers.	• Potential loss of control.
• Easily adapted for further diversification.	• Allocation of central costs can be a problem.
• Top management free to concentrate on strategic matters.	• Specialists may feel isolated.

Advantages & disadvantages of divisional structures

Advantages

- If an organisation wants to grow and diversify, the functional structure cannot cope, so instead the divisional structure should be adopted. Should the company want to diversify further, it is easy to 'bolt on' another division.

- It encourages growth and diversity of products, e.g. by adding additional flavours etc to capture other segments of the market. This in turn promotes the use of specialised equipment and facilities.

- Due to the breakdown of the company's activities into the divisions, it should mean that the divisional managers can clearly see where their area of responsibility lies and it should leave the top management free to concentrate on strategic matters, rather than to get involved in the day to day operations of each division – although this can lead to a lack of control over the activities of the division and possible lack of goal congruence.

- The focus of attention is on product performance and profitability. By placing responsibility for product profitability at the division level, they are able to react and make decisions quickly on a day to day basis.

- The role of the general manager has less concentration upon specialisation. This promotes a wider view of the company's operations.

Disadvantages

- Duplication of business functions – each division must have its own finance, personnel and sales manager. This results in more managers than if the company were centralised

- Potential for sub optimisation as the divisions take decisions to benefit themselves, possibly to the detriment of the overall company

- Increased cost arising from extra administration and the development and maintenance of the control system

- The design of the control system poses serious problems with regard to creating goal congruence between investment decisions made by managers and decisions which may be made to improve their own personal reward package – the risk of short-termist action or suboptimal behaviour

- Loss of operational and tactical control requires increasing elements of formality which can stifle the operation of the divisionalised concept;

- Designing a transfer pricing system where divisions are interdependent

- Specialists may feel isolated.

Geographical based divisional structure

This is similar to the divisional structure, but involves each division covering a specific location.

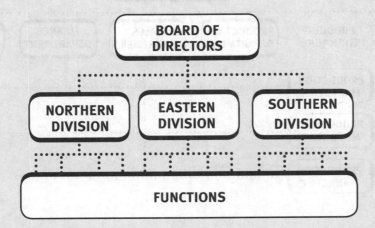

Advantages	Disadvantages
• Enables geographic growth. • Allows local decision-making. • Clear responsibility for areas. • Training of general managers. • Top management free to concentrate on strategic matters.	• As for divisional structure above.

Product v geographic divisional structure

Product divisionalisation is generally preferred over say geographic divisionalisation when the product is relatively complex and requires a high cost of capital equipment, skilled operators, etc., e.g. the car industry.

3.4 Matrix structure

Matrix structures are a combination of the functional and divisional structures.

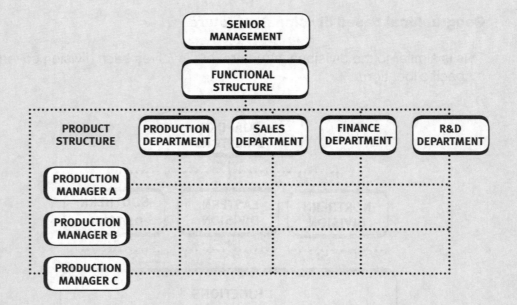

The matrix requires dual reporting to two different managers. For example, looking at the diagram above, an employee manufacturing product A would have to report to the manager of the production department **and** the manager in charge of product A.

Matrix structures are widely used for project management.

The aim of the matrix structure is to combine the benefits of both the divisional and functional structures.

Advantages	Disadvantages
• Advantages of both functional and divisional structures. • Flexibility. • Customer orientation. • Encourage teamwork and the exchange of opinions and expertise	• Dual command and conflict. • Dilution of functional authority. • Time-consuming meetings. • Higher admin costs.

Advantages and disadvantages of matrix structures

Advantages

- In today's rapidly changing environment, there is a need for effective coordination in very complex situations. If a car manufacturer wants to design, produce and market a new model, the process involves most parts of the organisation and a flexible system is needed to achieve the objectives. The more rigid structure experienced in a divisional company would not have the flexibility to be able to coordinate the tasks and the people, whereas the matrix structure can cope.

- The production managers could be replaced with customer managers, in which case the whole team will be focussed on meeting the needs of the customer.

Disadvantages

- Where the matrix structure can cause difficulty is in the lines of control. These may become ambiguous and conflict with each other. A team member may be answerable to the product manager **and** to a functional head, and this may cause confusion and stress. Time consuming meetings may be required to resolve the conflict, so resulting in higher administration costs.

Test your understanding 3 – OTQ

Consider the following statements:

(i) Under the functional structure, each department operates as a strategic business unit.

(ii) The matrix structure will enable rapid decision-making within the organisation.

Which of the statements is/are correct?

A   (i) only

B   (ii) only

C   Both

D   Neither

Test your understanding 4 – OTQ

M plc is a large company that operates in country G. It manufactures several different products, each of which is highly complex and extremely specialised. Its sales have grown significantly over the last several years, with each of its products producing a roughly equal amount of M's overall revenue.

Which organisational structure is most likely to be appropriate for M?

A   Geographic

B   Divisional

C   Functional

D   Entrepreneurial

4 Structural Dimensions

Given the many choices of structure, how should an organisation decide upon which structure is the most appropriate? There are a number of factors that influence organisational structure. These include:

- **Size** – it may be argued that size is the most important factor influencing the structure of organisations. A small organisation could be paralysed by too much **specialisation**.

In larger organisations, on the other hand, there may be economies of scale that can be gained by maintaining functionally specialist departments and teams. In addition, a large organisation has more complex decision making needs and some decision making responsibilities are likely to be devolved or **decentralised**.

> **Test your understanding 5**
>
> Discuss the advantages and disadvantages of decentralisation of decision making to those at lower levels of the hierarchy.

In larger organisations, the frequency of recurrent events and the repetition of decision making will make **formalisation** and standardisation preferable. Formal documents may include written procedures, job descriptions, regulations and policy manuals.

- **Strategy** – the organisation design must support its strategy. For example, a hierarchical structure will not work for an innovative organisation where as an organisation with a strategy based on low cost, high volume delivery will require a rigid structure with tight controls in place.

- **Organisational type** – this factor is closely related to size. For example, a large multinational company may benefit from a matrix structure (and a number of layers of management) where as a small partnership may find an entrepreneurial or functional structure (with few layers of management) more suited to its needs.

- **Technological change** – technology has affected organisational structure in a number of ways:
  - Some administrative and managerial roles have been replaced by more effective IT systems.
  - Some production roles have been replaced by the use of robots and automated production lines. This has also reduced the need for as many supervisors.
  - Improved communication (e.g. using email and wireless networks) has meant that employees can work out of the office/ at home allowing for more flexible working arrangements.

5 Organisational Forms and Boundaries

5.1 Closed and open systems

There are two types of systems in organisations; closed systems and open systems.

An **open system** interacts with its environment through giving and receiving of information.

In an open system there is a realisation that interacting with the main facets of the environment is vital to the success and prosperity of the organisation. For example, the E1 material produced by Kaplan must reflect communication from CIMA with regards to current syllabus requirements and exam format and should also reflect student feedback on style and contents.

A **closed system** is closed off from the outside environment and all interaction and knowledge is transmitted within the closed system only. Managerial attention is focused on the refinement of existing structure, the wider context is taken as given.

It is important for modern organisations to consider the external as well as the internal environment. Closed systems can hamper growth since the flow of information stays within the system and has no chance to interact with or build on knowledge from the outer environment. A 'machine bureaucracy' is an example of a closed system, holding efficiency and control as the highest goals.

5.2 Boundaryless structures

Boundaryless organisations are, essentially, an unstructured design that is not constrained by having a chain of command or formal departments, with the focus instead being on flexibility.

This is a contemporary model of organisational design, which adopts a more flexible approach to structure.

There are a number of different types of boundaryless organisations that you need to be aware of – hollow, virtual and modular.

Hollow organisations

Hollow organisations split their functions into core (i.e. strategically important) and non-core activities. Anything which is classified as non-core is outsourced to other organisations.

Outsourcing refers to the contracting out of aspects of the organisation's work to specialist providers. We will look at outsourcing in more detail in section 5.3.

For example, an accountancy training organisation might outsource less important functions (such as payroll) to a third party organisation specialising in payroll processing. Core functions, such as training students, would be kept in house and undertaken by employees of the company.

Virtual (network) organisations

This occurs where an organisation outsources many of its functions to other organisations and simply exists as a network of contracts, with very few, if any, functions being kept in-house.

For example, many internet retailers could be seen as virtual companies. Their products are bought in from manufacturers, sales are delivered to customers by third-party couriers and even their websites may be maintained and hosted by external IT specialists.

There is typically only a small central staff within a virtual business, who co-ordinate all of these different third parties and ensure that their customers' needs are therefore met.

Modular organisations

These are examples of boundaryless manufacturing companies. Rather than simply making their own product, they break the manufacturing process down into modules or components. Each component can then be made by the company or outsourced to an external supplier.

For example, a mobile phone manufacturer may pay external manufacturers to make some key components for its handsets – such as processors and screens. These are then assembled by the manufacturer along with other components it has manufactured itself.

In extreme cases, the manufacturing of all components can be outsourced, meaning that the company simply assembles them to create its final product.

5.3 Outsourcing and offshoring

Outsourcing

Outsourcing means contracting-out aspects of the work of the organisation, previously done in-house, to specialist providers.

Business process outsourcing (BPO) is a subset of outsourcing and involves the contracting-out of specific business functions such as IT or HR.

Before making a decision to outsource a company must consider what competencies exist within their business. There are two types of competencies:

Threshold competencies – actions or processes that you must be good at just to be considered as a potential supplier to a customer. They are the same as competitors' competencies and easy to imitate.

For example, in clothes retail it may be the case that most firms have outsourced production to Asian manufacturers in order to gain low costs. Outsourcing may be essential just to be a feasible player in the market.

 Core competencies – something that you are able to do that drives competitive advantage and is very difficult for your competitors to emulate. You must possess these if you want to compete effectively in the market concerned.

For our clothing retailer the core competences may relate to design and brand management.

It may be unwise to outsource aspects of the work in which you have a core competence as this could erode your competitive advantage.

Quinn and Hilmer

According to Quinn and Hilmer (1994), a major strategic factor in sourcing decisions is core competence. There are three basic tests that can be employed to identify the core competences of an organisation.

- First, a core competence should provide potential access to a wide variety of markets.

- Secondly, a core competence should also make a significant contribution to the perceived benefits as experienced by the customer of the product.

- Finally, a core competence should be difficult to imitate by competitors.

Based on these ideas, Quinn and Hilmer developed a decision matrix incorporating three factors:

(1) The potential for competitive edge derived from the activity,

(2) Any strategic vulnerability introduced by outsourcing and the need for flexibility, and

(3) The transaction costs incurred due to outsourcing.

The output from the decision matrix identifies the level of control the organisation needs to exercise on the particular activity. For example:

- If the potential for competitive edge derived from a given activity and the degree of strategic vulnerability are both "high," then a "high" level of control is in order. Coupled with a "low" need for flexibility required (due to demand variability, say), this suggests full ownership of the activity in question by the organisation.

- On the other hand, when the flexibility requirement is "high," then the authors propose outsourcing of the activity based on a short-term contract.

Naturally, there are other possible actions between these two extremes, such as partial ownership and long-term contracts, depending on the level of control and flexibility needs.

Outsourcing has become increasingly common in organisations. The advantages and disadvantages include:

Advantages of outsourcing

The main reason for outsourcing is that it is cheaper. **Cost advantages** can come from a number of sources:

- A large supplier may benefit from economies of scale in production.
- The firm concerned will benefit from reduced capital expenditure on machinery to make the items now outsourced.
- Reduced headcount in terms of workers no longer being needed to make the items.
- Research and development expenditure on the components, say, concerned will also be saved.

There can also be **quality advantages**:

- The supplier may have skills and expertise that allow them to make better products
- Outsourcing may solve the problem of the company having a skills shortage in certain areas.

Other advantages include the following:

- The supplier may have greater production expertise and efficiencies, leading to faster and more flexible supply of components.

- The management of the customer are no longer distracted by fringe areas and so can focus on core business activities.

- The organisation can exercise buyer power over suppliers ensuring favourable terms and conditions.

- The organisation has greater flexibility to switch suppliers based on changing cost/quality considerations.

Disadvantages

- Cost issues – the supplier will want to make a profit margin, suggesting it may be cheaper to do the work in house. In addition, if dealing with a major supplier the organisation may be vulnerable to future price rises.

- Loss of core competence – the service may represent (or contribute to) a core competence for the organisation and therefore outsourcing may lead to a loss of competitive advantage.

- Transaction costs – arise from the effort put into specifying what is required, co-ordinating delivery and monitoring quality. (Note: transaction costs are discussed in more detail later on in the chapter).

- Finality of decision – once a service has been contracted out it may be difficult to take back in-house at a later date, e.g. due to a loss of in-house expertise.

- Risk of loss of confidential information.

- Risk of continuity of supply if the supplier has problems.

- Difficulty agreeing/enforcing contract terms.

- Damage to employee morale if redundancies occur or if organisational culture is eroded.

Service level agreements

At least some of the potential disadvantages can be controlled though the use of effective service level agreements.

 A **service level agreement** (SLA) is a negotiated agreement between the supplier and the customer and is a legal agreement regarding the level of service to be provided.

Service level agreements

Service level agreements should include the following factors:

- A detailed explanation of exactly what service the supplier is offering to provide.

- The targets/benchmarks to be used and the consequences of failing to meet them.

- Expected response time to technical queries.

- The expected time to recover the operations in the event of a disaster such as a systems crash, terrorist attack, etc.

- The procedure for dealing with complaints.

- The information and reporting procedures to be adopted.

- The procedures for cancelling the contract.

Test your understanding 6

Could accountancy services be outsourced? Are there problems in so doing?

Transaction cost theory

Transaction costs are the indirect costs (i.e. non-production costs) incurred in performing a particular activity, for example the expenses incurred through outsourcing.

When outsourcing, transaction costs arise from the effort that must be put into specifying what is required and subsequently co-ordinating delivery and monitoring quality.

A number of kinds of transaction cost have come to be known by particular names:

- **Search and information costs** – for example, the cost of determining which supplier is cheapest.

- **Bargaining costs** – the cost of agreeing on an acceptable SLA.

- **Policing and enforcement costs** – are the costs of making sure the other party sticks to the terms of the contract, and taking appropriate action (often through the legal system) if this turns out not to be the case.

High transaction costs for outsourcing may suggest an in-house solution whereas low transaction costs for outsourcing would support the argument to outsource.

Transaction cost theory

Transaction cost theory (Wiliamson and Coase)

Organisations choose between two methods of obtaining control over resources:

- the ownership of assets (hierarchy solutions – decisions over production, supply, and the purchases of inputs are made by managers and imposed through hierarchies) and

- buying-in the use of assets (the market solution – individuals and firms make independent decisions that are guided and co-ordinated by market prices).

The decision is based on a comparison of the transaction costs of the two approaches.

Transactions have three dimensions that determine the costs associated with them:

- uncertainty – the more uncertain the environment the harder it is to write effective long-term contracts and the more likely the acquisition of a supplier is

- the frequency with which the transactions recur; and

- asset specificity – the extent to which the transacting firms invest in assets whose value depends on the business relationships remaining intact. The greater the specificity of the assets involved, the greater the likelihood that a transaction will take place within the firm.

These factors translate into 'make-or-buy' decisions: whether it is better to provide a service from within the organisation, with hierarchical co-ordination, or from outside the organisation, with market co-ordination.

Williamson and Coase argue that it is the third dimension, the degree of asset specificity, which is the most important determinant of transaction. The more specific the assets are to a transaction then, all other things being equal, the greater will be the associated transaction costs and the more likely that the transaction will be internalised into a hierarchy. Conversely, when the productive assets are non-specific the process of market contracting is the more efficient because transaction costs will be low.

Asset specificity

An asset is said to be transaction-specific if its value to a given transaction is greater than its value in its best alternative use. The greater the gap between these two values, the greater the degree of specificity of the asset. Williamson and Coase suggested six main types of asset specificity:

- Site specificity – suggests that once sited the assets may be very immobile.

  For example, a car components manufacturer locating a components factory near to a large customer's manufacturing plant.

- Physical asset specificity – when parties make investments in machinery or equipment that are specific to a certain task these will have lower values in alternative uses.

  For example, a supplier of wet cement to building sites may invest in wet cement delivery trucks (a 'hierarchy' solution) since these trucks are so specific to this task that they cannot be sourced via a network.

- Human asset specificity – occurs when workers may have to acquire relationship-specific skills, know-how and information that is more valuable inside a particular transaction than outside it.

  For example, a consultant may have to acquire detailed knowledge of a client's in-house developed systems but this knowledge may not be useful on other clients.

- Brand name capital specificity refers to becoming affiliated with a well-known 'brand name' and thus becoming less free to pursue other opportunities.

  For example, an actor may become 'typecast' in a particular role or show.

- Dedicated asset specificity entails investments in general-purpose plant that are made at the behest of a particular customer.

  For example, the car components manufacturer above invests in dedicated machinery to make bespoke components for just one manufacturer. Should the contract be lost, these components may have to be adapted for sale elsewhere.

- Temporal specificity – arises when the timing of performance is critical, such as with perishable agricultural commodities where a farmer may struggle to find alternative processors at short notice.

Offshoring

Offshoring is the relocating of corporate activities to a foreign country.

The bulk of offshored activities include call centres, IT enabled services (e.g. software development) and business process operations (e.g. human resource management and payroll processing).

Illustration 2

Reuters, the world's biggest news agency, employs dozens of journalists in Bangalore, India. They work overnight so that they can report US financial news live as it happens on the New York Stock Exchange.

These Indian financial journalists can be employed by Reuters for a fraction of the cost of employing a journalist in the New York office.

This system became feasible as a result of IT developments:

- **Obtaining information** – most US companies now put out their press releases on the internet, just as the stock market opens. Therefore, the journalists in Bangalore can access the same basic information as their colleagues in the US.
- **Sending information** – the reduced cost of telecommunications links means that the news written in Bangalore can be sent around the world as quickly as the news written in New York.

Benefits of offshoring for the home country

Test your understanding 7

Over the last decade, India has emerged as an attractive destination for offshoring. Explain why many UK companies have taken the decision to offshore their services to India.

Disadvantages of offshoring for the home country

The disadvantages for the home country, for example the UK, include:

- **Differences** – cultural, language and time differences between the home country and the recipient country may make offshoring difficult.

Illustration 3

A team of retired teachers from the UK have set up a company in India where they conduct general knowledge classes for the Indian call centre workers to teach them how to handle calls from UK customers. The call centre agents not only learn about regional accents around the UK, but also the cultural variations and political make-up of the UK.

- **Stability of the offshore countries** – economic and political instability exists in many of the countries providing the services.

- **Cost savings** – the promises of cost savings and improved productivity are not always realised.

- **Job losses** – it is argued that when jobs are lost people are freed up to do higher skilled and higher paid work. But in reality, whilst the economy as a whole may evolve in time to a higher level, the individuals who lose their jobs are not necessarily the ones gaining the new jobs.

- **Safety of information** – there is an increased risk that confidential information, e.g. customer's details, may be lost.

- **Exchange rate effects** – make offshoring risky

Impact of offshoring on the recipient countries

The benefits of offshoring for the recipient countries, such as India, include:

- The creation of much needed jobs
- Improvement in skills
- Advances in infrastructure and technology

In addition to the disadvantages for the home country, concerns to do with decent working conditions, e.g. wages, working hours, and other aspects of good practice (such as technology transfer), exist in the recipient country.

Illustration 4

Employees in Indian call centres are exposed to a host of health problems because of the time difference between India and the US. Working from late evening until early dawn can result in digestive problems, hair loss, back pain and stress.

These factors contribute to the high turnover in Indian call centres; approximately 30 – 40% of employees resign each year.

5.4 Tall and flat organisations

Scalar chain

This is the line of authority which can be traced up or down the chain of command, from the most senior member of staff to the most junior. It therefore relates to the number of levels of management within an organisation.

Span of control

A manager's span of control is the number of people for whom he or she is directly responsible.

The factors that influence the span of control include:

- **the nature of the work** – the more repetitive or simple the work, the wider the span of control can be.
- **the type of personnel** – the more skilled and motivated the managers and other staff members are, the wider the span of control can be.
- **the location of personnel** – if personnel are all located locally, it takes relatively little time and effort to supervise them. This allows the span of control to become wider.

Test you understanding 8 – OTQ

Consider the following statements:

(i)   The scalar chain relates to the number of people over whom a manager has authority.

(ii) A business with highly skilled, motivated members of staff will tend to have a wider span of control than a business with demotivated employees.

Which of these statements is/are correct?

A   (i) only

B   (ii) only

C   Both

D   Neither

Tall and flat organisations

A 'tall' organisation has many levels of management (a long scalar chain) and a narrow span of control. For example, the British Armed Forces has a very traditional hierarchical structure with a long scalar chain.

A 'flat' organisation has few levels of management (a short scalar chain) and a wide span of control.

Illustration 5 – A move by organisations to a flatter structure

Many organisations are adopting (and seeing the benefits of) a flatter structure. For example, Google's core values from the beginning were to have a flat organisation, a lack of hierarchy and a collaborative environment. This flatter organisation encourages employees to take initiative without needing approval from multiple managers. They empower employees to take charge, help make decisions and feel responsible for the company's success.

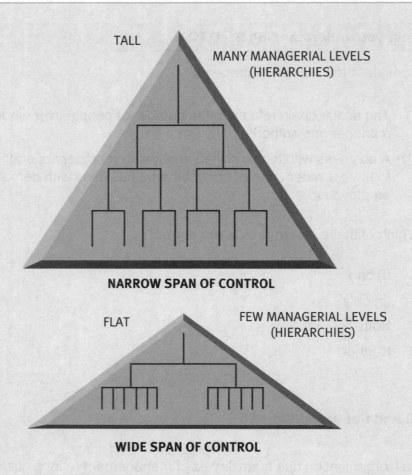

It is worth noting that tall organisations tend to be more bureaucratic and take longer to make decisions, due to the large number of levels of management that need to be involved.

However, flat organisations are not without their problems. These organisations tend to have weaker control and fewer chances for employees to progress or be promoted within the organisation.

Test your understanding 9

If a managerial structure has many levels of management, is it likely to have a narrow or wide span of control at each level of management?

5.5 Shared service approach

This approach involves restructuring the provision of certain services within the organisation so that instead of the service being found in several different parts of the organisation it is centralised into one specific part of the organisation.

For example, a medium-sized business may have a couple of staff in each department (i.e. sales, production) that deal with IT for that part of the organisation.

A shared services approach would be to form a distinct IT department that all the IT staff were transferred into. This IT department would then offer IT services to the entire organisation.

This approach has several advantages, including:

* improved quality of service provision
* improved consistency of service
* cost savings through greater efficiency and reduced duplication of roles

Note that a shared services approach is more than simply centralising the function into one place. Shared services often involves running the service, for example IT, like a separate business within the organisation and charging the rest of the organisation for the use of the service.

5.6 Strategic alliance

A strategic alliance can be defined as a co-operative business activity , formed by two or more separate organisations for strategic purposes, that allocates ownership, operational responsibilities, financial risks and rewards, to each member, while preserving their separate identity/ autonomy.

Characteristics of a strategic alliance
Seven characteristics of a well-structured alliance have been identified.   • **Strategic synergy** – more strength when combined than they have independently.   • **Positioning opportunity** – at least one of the companies should be able to gain a leadership position (i.e. to sell a new product or service; to secure access to raw materials or technology).   • **Limited resource availability** – a potentially good partner will have strengths that complement weaknesses of the other partner. One of the partners could not do this alone.

- **Less risk** – forming the alliance reduces the risk of the venture.

- **Co-operative spirit** – both companies must want to do this and be willing to co-operate fully.

- **Clarity of purpose** – results, milestones, methods and resource commitments must be clearly understood.

- **Win-win** – the structure, risks, operations and rewards must be fairly apportioned among members.

Some organisations are trying to retain some of the innovation and flexibility that is characteristic of small companies by forming strategic alliances (closer working relationships) with other organisations. They also play an important role in global strategies, where the organisation lacks a key success factor for some markets.

An example of a strategic alliance is that pursued by Starbucks in 2012, in an attempt to break into the Indian coffee shop market. It formed an alliance with Tata Global Beverages - a large Indian drinks company - with both parties investing $80m in order to open a number of Starbucks stores across India. Starbucks had significant experience of running coffee shops, while Tata had strong local knowledge of the growing Indian drinks market.

Franchising and licensing

Franchising

The purchase of the right to exploit a business brand in return for a capital sum and a share of profits or turnover.

- The franchisee pays the franchisor an initial capital sum and thereafter the franchisee pays the franchisor a share of profits or royalties.

- The franchisor provides marketing, research and development, advice and support.

- The franchisor normally provides the goods for resale.

- The franchisor imposes strict rules and control to protect its brand and reputation.

- The franchisee buys into a successful formula, so risk is much lower.

- The franchisor gains capital as the number of franchisees grows.

- The franchisor's head office can stay small as there is considerable delegation/decentralisation to the franchisees.

A classic example of franchising is McDonalds. Within the UK, for example, around half of all McDonalds restaurants are franchises.

Licensing

The right to exploit an invention or resource in return for a share of proceeds. Licensing differs from a franchise because there will be little central support.

In the UK, many beers such as Heineken and Fosters were 'brewed under licence' in the UK for many years, with the original companies that developed the beers simply taking a share of the proceeds from the local brewers.

6 Chapter summary

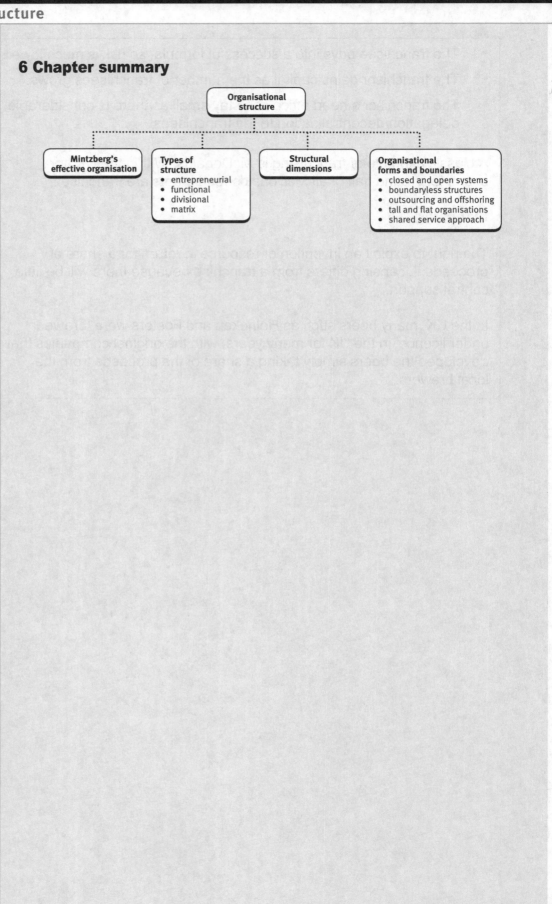

7 Practice Questions

Question 1 – OTQ

Which one of the following statements regarding the entrepreneurial structure is correct?

A   It usually allows for defined career paths for employees

B   It often enjoys strong goal congruence throughout the organisation

C   It can normally cope with significant diversification and growth

D   Control within the organisation tends to be weak

Question 2 – OTQ

Which one of the following is a disadvantage of a functional structure?

A   Lack of economies of scale

B   Absence of standardisation

C   Specialists feel isolated

D   Empire building

Question 3 – OTQ

Consider the following statements:

(i)   Tall organisations typically have narrow spans of control.

(ii)   A 'flat' organisation is one that has a short scalar chain.

Which of these statements is/are correct?

(a) (i) only

(b) (ii) only

(c) Both

(d) Neither

Question 4 – OTQ

Which one of the following is the correct definition of the term 'span of control'?

A   The number of employees reporting to one manager

B   The number of managers to whom one employee reports

C   The number of levels in the hierarchy

D   The number of employees at each level of the organisation

Question 5 – WV8 (Case style)

Background

WV8 is a large not for profit (NFP) public sector organisation responsible for organising the operation of publicly financed schools within its region. WV8 receives its income solely from government grants but, because of funding cuts, is under pressure to maintain existing services whilst operating more cost effectively. Recently, a government spokesperson publicly criticised public sector organisations claiming that they are expensive, lack skills found in the private sector, such as marketing and business acumen, and have a lack of understanding of the customers they are meant to serve.

Review of central support services

In order to meet these challenges, WV8's Chief Executive has created a policy review team comprising experts from all areas of WV8's operations. Phase 1 of the review involves looking at central support services which includes Corporate Information Systems (CIS) services. In the past there have been difficulties in recruiting specialist staff in Information Systems (the Head of CIS services claims that this is because of WV8's relatively unattractive rates of pay). In addition, service users have complained that CIS is expensive and unresponsive to their needs. Various options are currently being discussed including total outsourcing of the service to a single specialist supplier.

Task:

Discuss the issues associated with a total outsourcing of CIS for WV8.

(20 minutes)

Test your understanding answers

Test your understanding 1

A clearer focus on the core activity and hence further importance attached to operations management.

Test your understanding 2 – OTQ

The correct answer is C

By definition

Test your understanding 3 – OTQ

The correct answer is D

The separate parts of the organisation operate as SBUs in a divisional structure – not a functional structure.

The matrix structure tends to require time-consuming meetings and has significant overlap of authority between managers. This tends to slow the decision-making process down.

Test your understanding 4 – OTQ

The correct answer is B

As M has several complex products, a structure that creates a separate division to look after each one seems the most logical. Functional and geographical structures would struggle to cope with the differing needs of the products. The level of work needed to run a large, complex organisation would also probably be beyond the capabilities of an entrepreneurial structure.

Test your understanding 5

The advantages and disadvantages of decentralisation are:

Advantages	Disadvantages
• Senior management free to concentrate on strategy.	• Loss of control by senior management.
• Better local decisions due to local expertise.	• Dysfunctional decisions due to a lack of goal congruence.
• Better motivation due to increased training and career path.	• Poor decisions made by inexperienced managers.
• Quicker responses/flexibility, due to smaller chain of command.	• Training costs.
	• Duplication of roles within the organisation.
	• Extra costs in obtaining information.

Test your understanding 6

Accountancy services are often outsourced in smaller companies, but it could be argued that they are critical to the performance of the organisation and may well drive the future of the company. Also there should be some managerial control in this area.

Test your understanding 7

Cost savings – one of the biggest advantages is cost savings. Companies have been able to reduce the cost of services by 30 – 40% by offshoring to India. These cost savings are due to:

- Lower wages – Indian workers are paid much lower wages than those in the UK.

- Lower capital expenditure – infrastructure costs are lower in India.

- Improved labour management – labour is only employed as and when it is needed for a project, rather than on a permanent basis, as in the UK.

Large talent pool – India has a large pool of talented and motivated professionals. There are 2.1 million graduates each year and this number is set to grow. As a result, UK companies are able to choose between a number of suitable candidates.

Technology – advances in technology and the falling price of technology has enabled UK companies to carry out activities overseas that would have previously been done in the UK.

Common language – India has the largest English speaking population in the world. This will ease communication between the UK and India.

Fast turnaround time – the time taken to carry out a task can be reduced by between 30 – 50% when offshoring to India. This is partly due to the efficiency of the Indian professionals but is also due to the zonal time differences, e.g. many IT projects have an onsite and offsite team. The offsite team can work on the project during the day in India. When the Indian team leaves work for the evening the onsite team can take over the project in the UK.

Test you understanding 8 – OTQ

The correct answer is B

The scalar chain relates to the number of levels of management within the organisation.

Test your understanding 9

Narrow

Question 1 – OTQ

The correct answer is B

Because the entrepreneurial structure is run by one person who makes all the decisions, this powerful individual will have strong control over the organisation and its strategic direction, leading to better goal congruence.

Question 2 – OTQ

The correct answer is D

Function managers may make decisions to increase their own power, or in the interests of their own function, rather than in the interests of the company overall. Economies of scale, standardisation and specialists feeling comfortable are advantages of a functional structure.

Question 3 – OTQ

The correct answer is C

Both statements are correct.

Question 4 – OTQ

The correct answer is A

By definition. C is the definition of the scalar chain, which is the line of authority that can be traced up or down the chain of command, and thus relates to the number of management levels in an organisation.

Question 5 – WV8 (Case style)

Several issues should be taken into account when deciding whether or not to totally outsource the CIS function as a means of overcoming some of the problems facing WV8.

Relative attractiveness of alternative means of provision

Currently CIS services are provided centrally and the policy review team is obviously looking to both improve the service and overcome the difficulties that WV8 faces. A wholly outsourced CIS function is one of the various options being discussed. Such a move would involve a total outsourcing of all aspects of IT including system development, maintenance, training, etc., to a single supplier. Before WV8 decides to outsource the function other alternatives should be carefully considered including an improved central service or decentralisation. If the decision is to totally outsource the CIS function to a single provider, there will be finality to the decision. The contract would normally be for 3 to 5 years and after this it would be very difficult for WV8 to bring provision back in-house.

Outsourcing alternatives

Total outsourcing may be seen as a radical and potentially high risk solution which may not necessarily alleviate the problems WV8 is facing. Alternatives to total sourcing that might be considered might include:

- Multiple sourcing whereby WV8 would negotiate with a range of suppliers and retain a core of central or main IS/IT staff.

- Developing a strategic joint venture with an external partner to use its particular expertise to help remedy the specific difficulties and deficiencies in areas of existing provision.

Much depends upon how WV8 views the function. If CIS is seen strategically as a complementary competence, outsourcing should only be to trusted key suppliers with the necessary expertise and a strong relationship should be fostered between both parties. Alternatively if CIS is viewed as a residual competence, WV8 could outsource adopting a simple 'arms-length' relationship with the supplier; a simple 'buy' decision.

Cost implications

WV8 is wholly funded by government grants, but with funding cuts is under pressure to maintain existing services whilst operating more cost effectively. Outsourced alternatives tend to be highly competitive in terms of pay, terms and conditions of service and, after total outsourcing, WV8 may initially reduce central costs. One clear advantage of outsourcing for WV8 would be a more accurate prediction of costs and, hopefully, improved budgetary control; something crucial in the current environment.

Gaining expertise and IS specialism

In the past, there have been difficulties in recruiting IS specialists and the service quality may have deteriorated as a result. Outsourcing would, of course, represent an easy means of overcoming IS staff resourcing difficulties. Often the contracting out of non-core services to a specialist provider not only improves service quality but also leaves the service in the hands of genuine experts.

Strategic fit and flexibility

Outsourcing involves contracting out non-core services to specialist providers rather than attempting to provide them in-house. WV8 would, in effect, be relieved of the burden of managing specialist staff in an area that the organisation does not understand well. Rather than attempting to provide services in-house, outsourcing would help WV8 achieve strategic focus (being consistent with the so-called 'stick-to-your-knitting' concept). It also supports the concept of the 'flexible firm' championed by writers such as Atkinson and Handy.

Risk involved

Consistent with Quinn and Hilmer's tests for whether non-core activity should be outsourced or not, WV8 should carefully consider the level of risk associated with total outsourcing. The potential vulnerability of WV8 to market failure is higher if the whole service is outsourced. WV8 should consider what can be done to reduce these risks and should structure arrangements with suppliers in such a way as to protect itself best.

Impact on existing IS staff

WV8 may conclude that outsourcing is counterproductive and an unwelcome problem if there is likely to be strong staff and union resistance. Presently, there are centrally employed IS staff whose jobs will be threatened by total outsourcing. This could possibly lead to resistance from unions and staff groups representing these workers. Also the impact on other groups and fellow trade unionists within WV8 might be negative in terms of morale and motivation.

Contractual complications

Outsourcing will involve WV8 in contractual issues and certainly additional (transaction) costs associated with determining service specifications and then monitoring performance will be incurred. There will be a requirement to retain intelligence user expertise in-house in order to monitor outsourced provision. There may be difficulties in agreeing and managing a 'service level agreement' (SLA) particularly if WV8 has little experience in this area.

Service quality and understanding

It might be argued that the quality of CIS service under an outsourced option could be of a higher standard due to the specialist nature of the external provider. However, the provider concerned may have little empathy and understanding of a public service ethos and needs of schools if the service is outsourced. As such, the service provided might not meet user needs.

3

Governance, Regulation, Ethics and Corporate Social Responsibility

Chapter learning objectives

Lead	Component
A2. Discuss relationships between internal and external sources of governance, regulation and professional behaviour.	(a) Discuss the purpose and principles of good corporate governance, the ethical responsibilities of the organisation and individuals, and ways of achieving corporate social responsibility.

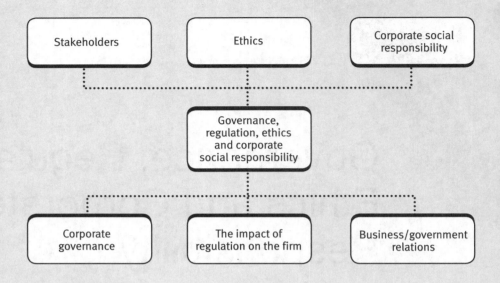

1 Stakeholders

1.1 Introduction

A **stakeholder** is a group or individual, who has an interest in what the organisation does, or an expectation of the organisation.

Managers should consider the stakeholders when setting the mission and objectives of the firms, for two key reasons:

- Stakeholder power – stakeholders can affect the success of a strategy, depending on whether they support or oppose it, e.g. a staff strike would disrupt a strategy.

- Organisational legitimacy – this view suggests that firms should be good corporate citizens and its decisions must consider the interests of stakeholders.

1.2 Types of stakeholder

Stakeholders can be broadly categorised into three categories; internal, connected and external.

Internal stakeholders

Internal stakeholders are intimately connected to the organisation, and their objectives are likely to have a strong influence on how it is run. Internal stakeholders include:

Stakeholder	Need/expectation
employees	pay, working conditions and job security
managers/directors	status, pay, bonus, job security

Connected stakeholders

Connected stakeholders either invest in or have dealings with the firm. They include:

Stakeholder	Need/expectation
shareholders	dividends and capital growth and the continuation of the business
customers	value-for-money products and services
suppliers	paid promptly
finance providers	repayment of finance

External stakeholders

These stakeholders tend to not have a direct link to the organisation but can influence or be influenced by its activities.

Stakeholder	Need/expectation
community at large	will not want their lives to be negatively impacted by business decisions
environmental pressure groups	the organisation does not harm the external environment
government	provision of taxes and jobs and compliance with legislation
trade unions	to take an active part in the decision-making process

Example of stakeholder management

R is a high-class hotel situated in a thriving city. It is part of a worldwide hotel group owned by a large number of shareholders. Individuals hold the majority of shares, each holding a small number, and financial institutions hold the rest. The hotel provides full amenities, including a heated swimming pool, as well as the normal facilities of bars, restaurants and good quality accommodation. There are many other hotels in the city, all of which compete with R. The city in which R is situated is old and attracts many foreign visitors, especially in the summer season.

The main stakeholders with whom relationships need to be established and maintained by management and the importance of maintaining these relationships is as follows.

Internal stakeholders

The employees and the managers of the hotel are the main link with the guests and the service they provide is vital to the quality of the hotel as guests' experience at the hotel will be determined by their attitude and approach.

Managers should ensure that employees deliver the highest level of service and are well trained and committed.

Connected stakeholders

The shareholders of the hotel will be concerned with a steady flow of income, possible capital growth and continuation of the business. Relationships should be developed and maintained with the shareholders, especially those operating on behalf of institutions. Management must try to achieve improvements in their returns by ensuring that customers are satisfied and are willing to return.

Each guest will seek good service and satisfaction. Different types of guests, e.g. business versus tourist, will have different needs and managers should regularly analyse the customer database to ensure that these needs are met.

Suppliers should be selected very carefully to ensure that services and goods provided (e.g. food and laundry) continue to add to the quality of the hotel and to customer satisfaction. Suppliers will be concerned with being paid promptly for goods. Maintaining a good relationship with suppliers will ensure their continued support of the hotel.

External stakeholders

The management of the hotel must maintain close relationships with the authorities to ensure they comply with legislation. Examples of external stakeholders include fire and safety authorities and food hygiene authorities. Failure to do so, could result in the hotel being closed down.

1.3 Stakeholder conflict

An organisation can have many different stakeholders, all with different needs. Inevitably, the needs of some stakeholders will come into conflict with the needs of others.

Stakeholder conflict

Stakeholder conflict

The needs/expectations of the different stakeholder groups may conflict. Some of the typical conflicts are shown below:

Stakeholders	Conflict
Employees versus managers	Jobs/wages versus bonus
Customers versus shareholders	Product quality/service levels versus profits/dividends
General public versus shareholders	Effect on the environment versus profit/dividends
Managers versus shareholders	Independence versus growth by merger/takeover

It is important that an organisation meets the needs of the most dominant stakeholders, but the needs of the other stakeholders should also be considered – nearly every decision becomes a compromise. For example, the firm will have to earn a satisfactory return for its shareholders whilst paying reasonable wages.

In the event of conflict, an organisation will need to decide which stakeholders' needs are more important. This will commonly be the most dominant stakeholder, i.e. the one with the most power.

If an organisation is having difficulty deciding who the dominant stakeholder is, they can use Mendelow's power-interest matrix.

		Level of interest	
		Low	**High**
Level of power	**Low**	Minimal effort	Keep informed
	High	Keep satisfied	Key players

By plotting each stakeholder according to the power that they have over an organisation and the interest they have in a particular decision, the dominant stakeholder(s), i.e. the key player(s) can be identified. The needs of the key players must be considered during the formulation and evaluation of new strategies.

Test your understanding 1 – (Case style)

Background

Chop Ltd is a forestry business which leases several large woodlands from the central government of country Z. It currently employs 2,000 members of staff across the country.

Chop supplies over three hundred small businesses with wood across country Z. However, recently its profitability has been poor and it has been struggling to pay any dividends.

Stakeholders

This has angered the company's three shareholders, who each own around twenty percent of Chop's share capital. The remainder is owned by the public, with no one investor owning more than one percent of the total share capital.

The three main shareholders have asked the Board of Directors to consider making 200 employees redundant. The employees are not heavily unionised.

Task

State and explain the appropriate strategy from Mendelow's matrix for each of the following stakeholders:

A   Chop's customers

B   Major shareholders

C   Employees

D   Government of country Z

(10 minutes)

2 Ethics

2.1 Introduction

Ethics is the system of moral principles that examines the concept of right and wrong.

Business ethics is the application of ethical values to business behaviour.

Whether an action is considered to be right or wrong normally depends on a number of different factors, including:

- the consequences – does the end justify the means?

- the motivation behind the action

- guiding principles – e.g. 'treat others as you would be treated'

- key values – such as the importance of human rights.

Illustration 1 – Definition of business ethics

You discover that a colleague at work has been stealing from the company. What do you do? Do you report them to management which might lead to their dismissal and the loss of a friend? Do you keep quiet and risk being punished yourself if your knowledge of the situation later becomes clear? Do you urge the colleague to confess what they've done? Does it depend on the size of the theft, e.g. a $1 pad of paper, or a $1,000 piece of machinery? Does it depend on how friendly you are with the colleague?

You can see that ethical problems require moral judgements that can be extremely difficult and depend on many different factors.

Test your understanding 2

The study of business ethics is purely concerned with legal requirements.

Is this statement:

A   True

B   False

Ethical dilemmas

An ethical dilemma involves a situation where a decision-maker has to decide what is the 'right' or 'wrong' thing to do. Examples of ethical dilemmas can be found throughout all aspects of business operations.

Accounting issues:

- Creative accounting to boost or suppress reported profits.

- Directors' pay arrangements – should directors continue to receive large pay packets even if the company is performing poorly?

- Should bribes be paid to facilitate contracts, especially in countries where such payments are commonplace?

- Insider trading, where for example directors may be tempted to buy shares in their company knowing that a favourable announcement about to be made should boost the share price.

Production issues:

- Should the company produce certain products at all, e.g. guns, pornography, tobacco, alcoholic drinks aimed at teenagers?

- Should the company be concerned about the effects on the environment of its production processes?

- Should the company test its products on animals?

Sales and marketing issues:

- Price fixing and anti-competitive behaviour may be overt and illegal or may be more subtle.

- Is it ethical to target advertising at children, e.g. for fast food or for expensive toys at Christmas?

- Should products be advertised by junk mail or spam email?

Personnel (HRM) issues:

- Employees should not be favoured or discriminated against on the basis of gender, race, religion, age, disability, etc.

- The contract of employment must offer a fair balance of power between employee and employer.

- The workplace must be a safe and healthy place to operate in.

2.2 Approaches to ethics

Imagine you are a company that runs a large chain of supermarkets. You have identified an opportunity to expand into country G. This expansion will create large numbers of local jobs and is expected to earn you significant profits.

Local officials in country G have made it clear that, in order to gain the appropriate planning permissions, you will need to pay them money as inducements (bribes). This is common practice for officials in country G, though it is illegal in your home country. What should you do?

The answer depends on your approach to ethics.

Consequentialists would argue that your decision depends on the consequences of paying the bribes.

If you were **egoist** (looking at your own needs), you would probably pay the bribes as you would still stand to earn a significant profit from the venture.

If you are a **utilitarian** company, you may also consider paying the bribe as doing so will not only mean that you can earn large profits, but will provide jobs for many locals. Paying the bribe will therefore be for the greater good. (However, it is worth noting that whatever the organisation may think about bribery, under UK law it is an illegal act.)

Pluralists would look at ensuring that the needs of none of the stakeholders are seriously compromised by paying the bribe. In this case, while the payment will involve some loss to our shareholders, paying the bribe will still allow us to expand into country G, benefiting everyone.

Relativists would look at the context of the decision to pay the bribe. In this case, bribery is a commonly accepted part of doing business in country G. Therefore, we can be flexible with our approach and may consider paying the bribe.

Absolutists would look at whether paying the bribe was fundamentally incorrect. In this case, bribery is illegal in our home country. An absolutist would therefore be likely to conclude that paying bribes to officials in country G would also be inappropriate, as doing so is always wrong.

2.3 Why business ethics are important

Businesses are part of society. Society expects its individuals to behave properly, and similarly expects companies to operate to certain standards.

Business ethics is important to both the organisation and the individual.

For the organisation	For the individual
• Good ethics should be seen as a driver of profitability rather than a burden on business. • An ethical framework is part of good corporate governance and suggests a well-run business. • Investors are reassured about the company's approach to risk management. • Employees will be motivated in the knowledge that they operate in an environment of good ethical corporate behaviour.	• Consumer and employee expectations have evolved over recent years. • Consumers may choose to purchase ethical items (e.g. Fairtrade coffee and bananas), even if they are not the cheapest. • Employees will not blindly accept orders to act in a manner that they personally believe to be unethical.

Illustration 2 – Why business ethics are important

The Fairtrade mark is a label on consumer products that guarantees that disadvantaged producers in the developing world are getting a fair deal. For example, the majority of coffee around the world is grown by small farmers who sell their produce through a local co-operative. Fairtrade coffee guarantees to pay a price to producers that covers the cost of sustainable production and also an extra premium that is invested in local development projects.

Consumers in the developed world may be willing to pay a premium price for Fairtrade products, knowing that the products are grown in an ethical and sustainable fashion.

Test your understanding 3

Adhering to ethical practice is always a cost to business.

Is this statement:

A   True

B   False

2.4 The role of the accountant in promoting ethical behaviour

At many business meetings, or on many Boards of Directors, it is only the professional accountant who belongs to a profession and therefore has a duty to act in the public interest.

Public interest refers to the common well-being or general welfare of society. Professional accountants must consider this, as they have a wider duty to act in the best interests of the public at large, as well as to the business and its owners.

The professional accountant therefore has a special role in promoting ethical behaviour throughout the business.

2.5 Corporate codes of ethics

Most companies (especially if they are large) have approached the concept of business ethics by creating a set of internal policies and instructing employees to follow them. These policies can either be broad generalisations (a corporate ethics statement) or can contain specific rules (a corporate ethics code).

There is no standard list of content – it will vary between different organisations. Typically, however, it may contain guidelines on issues such as honesty, integrity and customer focus.

Many organisations appoint Ethics Officers (also known as Compliance Officers) to monitor the application of the policies and to be available to discuss ethical dilemmas with employees where needed.

2.6 CIMA's ethical guidelines

Management accountants have a duty to observe the highest standards of conduct and integrity, and to uphold the good standing and reputation of their profession.

CIMA's Code of Ethics, based on IFAC's ethical principles, seeks to help management accountants in their day to day role. It helps management accountants to identify areas where ethical pressures may exist and provides a recommended course of action for their resolution.

In order to achieve the objectives of the accounting profession, professional accountants have to observe five fundamental principles:

Fundamental Principle	Interpretation
Integrity	Integrity means being straightforward, honest and truthful in all professional and business relationships.
Objectivity	Objectivity means not allowing bias, conflict of interest, or the influence of other people to override your professional judgement.
Professional competence and due care	This is an ongoing commitment to maintain your level of professional knowledge and skill so that your client or employer receives a competent professional service. Work should be completed carefully, thoroughly and diligently, in accordance with relevant technical and professional standards.
Confidentiality	This means respecting the confidential nature of information you acquire through professional relationships such as past or current employment. You should not disclose such information unless you have specific permission or a legal or professional duty to do so. You should also never use confidential information for your or another person's advantage.
Professional behaviour	This requires you to comply with relevant laws and regulations. You must also avoid any action that could negatively affect the reputation of the profession.

3 Corporate Social Responsibility

3.1 Introduction

Corporate social responsibility (CSR) refers to the idea that a company should be sensitive to the needs and wants of all the stakeholders in its business operations, not just the shareholders.

A socially responsible company may consider:

- the environmental impact of production or consumption, e.g. due to the use of non-renewable resources or non-recyclable inputs.

- the health impact for consumers of certain products, e.g. tobacco and alcohol

- the fair treatment of employees

- whether it is right to experiment on animals

- the safety of products and production processes.

CSR encompasses four dimensions:

- **Economic** – does the company contribute to the development of the local economy in which it operates?

- **Legal** – does the company restrict its operations to comply with the law?

- **Ethical** – does society approve of the company's operations?

- **Philanthropic** – the extent to which the company makes voluntary contributions to society.

A closely linked idea is that of **sustainable development.** Companies should make decisions based not only on financial factors, but also on the social and environmental consequences of their actions. This area is explored further in Chapter 8.

What is CSR?

A formal definition of CSR has been proposed by the World Business Council for Sustainable Development (WBCSD):

'CSR is the continuous commitment by business to behave ethically and contribute to economic development while improving the quality of life of the workforce and their families as well as the local community and society at large'.

WBSCD meeting in the Netherlands, 1998

From the same source, perceptions of CSR from different societies and cultures were given as:

- 'CSR is about capacity building for sustainable livelihoods. It respects cultural differences and finds the business opportunities in building the skills of employees, the community and the government' (Ghana).

- 'CSR is about business giving back to society' (Philippines).

We can see that there is no one definition, or theory, of corporate social responsibility. However, it is certain that there will be increasing pressure on organisations to play an increasing role in the solution to social issues. This will be particularly true of those that have a global presence. This means that multinationals and non governmental organisations (NGOs) will increasingly be expected to take a lead in addressing those issues where a national government or local firm has not been able, or willing, to arrive at a solution. With increasing globalisation, which we discussed earlier, the power of the institutions attached to the nation state (national governments, judiciary and police, for example) is declining.

Illustration 3 – The meaning of CSR

Marks and Spencer

Marks and Spencer promotes itself as a responsible business that takes the challenge of CSR seriously. It aims to listen and respond to the needs of its shareholders and build up good relationships with its employees, suppliers and society at large.

Marks and Spencer approach CSR by following three basic principles:

- products – throughout the three stages of each product's life (production, selling and usage), the aim is to encourage ethically and environmentally responsible behaviour

- people – everyone who works at the company is entitled to a mix of benefits. This approach is also encouraged amongst the company's suppliers, franchisees and other business partners

- places – the company recognises its obligations to the communities in which it trades. Successful retailing requires economically healthy and sustainable communities.

3.2 Stakeholder needs analysis

Stakeholder needs analysis involves an organisation undertaking research to determine:

- Who its key stakeholders are, and;
- What their needs are.

Typical stakeholders (internal, external and connected) and their needs have already been identified in section 1. However, a typical list is not what should be created here. Each company must sit down with a blank sheet of paper and identify the stakeholders of **their** business.

For example, if a company has $1m in the bank earning modest interest, then the bank is probably not a key stakeholder. In another company with a $100m debt to the bank and large interest payments, the bank is clearly an extremely important stakeholder.

Once the organisation has identified its stakeholders, it needs to understand what their needs and wants are. There is no better way of accomplishing this than asking them directly. Possible methods include:

- questionnaires
- focus groups
- direct interviews or interviews with representatives.

Illustration 4 – Stakeholder needs analysis

Car manufacturers

As well as being sensitive to the requirements of customers with respect to factors such as price and performance, a car manufacturer should also consider the following:

- public attitudes to pollution
- government policies on road tax and fuel tax

As a result it may choose to develop more environmentally-friendly vehicles as part of its long term strategy even if current demand is for larger cars, say.

Test your understanding 4

Supplier to a supermarket

A supermarket buys its goods on credit and sells them for cash, therefore it has strong cash flows at all times. What are the business needs of a supplier to such a supermarket in its relationship with the supermarket?

To some stakeholders, the company owes obligations arising from the law (e.g. to pay employees their salary each month, or to compensate them if they are made redundant). However, other obligations arise voluntarily due to the company's commitment to CSR (e.g. to discuss their plans with interested pressure groups before a particular plan is adopted).

Illustration 5 – Responsibilities of businesses to stakeholders

888.com

888.com is an internet gambling site that is listed on the London Stock Exchange. It is headquartered in Gibraltar and operates under a licence granted by the Government of Gibraltar. It has responsibilities to the following stakeholders:

- **Shareholders** – since it is listed on the London Stock Exchange it must comply with the rules of that exchange, including adopting the Corporate Governance Code.

- **Employees** – to be a good employer to all its members of staff.

- **Customers** – to offer a fair, regulated and secure environment in which to gamble.

- **Government** – to comply with the terms of its licence granted in Gibraltar.

- **The public** – the company chooses to sponsor several sports teams as part of strengthening its brand. The company also tries to address public concerns about the negative aspects of gambling, e.g. by identifying compulsive gamblers on their site and taking appropriate action.

Test your understanding 5

Voluntarily turning away business

Why should a gambling company like 888.com voluntarily choose to turn away certain business, e.g. known compulsive gamblers, gamblers who may be under-age, gamblers in certain countries, etc?

3.3 The importance of CSR to an organisation's success

Traditionalists argue that companies should operate solely to make money for shareholders and that it is not a company's role to worry about social responsibilities.

The modern view is that a coherent CSR strategy can offer business **benefits** in the following ways:

- Differentiation – the firm's CSR strategy (e.g. with regards to the environment, experimentation on animals or to product safety) can act as a method of differentiation.

- High calibre staff will be attracted and retained due to the firm's CSR policies.

- Brand strengthening – due to the firm's honest approach

- Lower costs – can be achieved in a number of ways, e.g. due to the use of less packaging or energy.

- The identification of new market opportunities and of changing social expectations.

- An overall increase in profitability as a result of the above – good CSR should hopefully contribute to an increase in profits and a reduction in costs in the long-term.

By aligning the company's core values with the values of society, the company can improve its reputation and ensure it has a long-term future.

The single-minded pursuit of short-term profitability will paradoxically most likely end in reduced profits in the longer-term, as customers drift away from the company if they no longer feel any attachment to it.

There is considerable evidence that the cost of CSR initiatives should be thought of as an investment in an intangible strategic asset rather than as an expense.

Illustration 6 – The importance of CSR

Heathrow Airport Holdings Ltd (formerly BAA) owns and operates four airports in the UK (including Heathrow airport). The company recognises that they are responsible, both directly and indirectly, for a variety of environmental, social and economic impacts from their operations.

Positive impacts: employing over 10,000 people; allowing business people to travel to meetings, thus supporting the global economy; allowing tourists to enrich their cultural experiences; allowing dispersed families to visit each other.

Negative impacts: large consumption of fossil fuels; emission of greenhouse gases; noise affecting people living close to airports.

The company sees its CSR programme as managing these operational impacts in order to earn the trust of their stakeholders.

For example, local people living near airports are sensitive to the noise of aircraft approaching and taking off. If the company did nothing about this issue, local people could complain to politicians who could pass laws to curb the number of flights which would damage the company. As part of its CSR programme, the company will therefore offer to buy the properties of local people concerned about aircraft noise, or will offer to pay for sound-proofing of the properties.

You should consider whether such expenditure is an expense against the company's profits, or an investment in building up a strategic asset of goodwill among the local community.

3.4 The development of CSR over time

The development of CSR over time

Pressures from various stakeholders are likely to increase CSR over time.

The norms of corporate behaviour in Victorian Britain would seem totally unacceptable in Britain today. The long hours, child labour, appalling working conditions, lack of redress for grievances, the filthy conditions of the workplace, the smoke and other pollution pouring from the factories, are not only illegal nowadays, but are totally alien to the norms of society.

Developed countries tend to have a strong sense of CSR although there are differences in approaches. For example:

- **America** has a more **philanthropic** approach to CSR, i.e. companies focus on charitable donations to address a variety of social, economic and other issues. For example, Walmart donates 4–5% of its pre-tax profit to approximately 50,000 charities making it one of America's most generous companies. The problem with this approach is that donations tend to be one of the first items of expenditure to be cut when the company is facing more challenging times.

- The **European** approach tends to focus on a combination of **responsible business practices** and **investment in communities**. For example, every year IBM UK runs the Smarter Cities Initiative. Cities apply for a grant and in return they get the services of a dedicated team of IBM consultants for three weeks to focus on the challenges the city faces. It may be argued that this is a more sustainable approach to CSR.

Many developing countries are still to embrace the practices of CSR, the ruthless forces of globalisation and non-representative governments conniving in the process of preventing the implementation of CSR practices.

Another factor contributing to the development of CSR is that activities that start as desirable but unprofitable, tend to become profitable as consumers come to expect firms to behave in socially responsible ways and punish firms that do not, by boycotting their products. Thus companies such as McDonalds, Nestle and Nike have been very concerned to 'clean up' their corporate image because of adverse publicity.

4 Corporate Governance

4.1 Why corporate governance?

Until the 1970s, the government was treated by most organisations as a regulator and tax levying body.

However, public 'scandals' of the 1980s and 1990s (such as Maxwell and Polly Peck) led to governments recognising a new role – one of protecting other stakeholders from over-aggressive, negligent or even fraudulent directors and managers. This led to the development of corporate governance.

The separation of ownership and control

The need for corporate governance arises because, in all but the smallest of organisations, there is a separation of ownership and control.

The separation of ownership and control refers to the situation in a company where the people who own the company (the shareholders) may not be the same people as those who run the company (the board of directors).

Illustration 7 – The separation of ownership and control

The agency problem in a company

The directors of a large quoted company may hold a board meeting and vote themselves huge bonuses and salaries even if only modest profit targets are achieved and may also put contractual terms in place granting them huge compensation payments if they are sacked. Those votes are in the selfish best interests of the directors, and not in the best interests of the shareholders who own the company and whose interests the directors are meant to be looking after.

4.2 The meaning of corporate governance

Corporate governance is the set of processes and policies by which a company is directed, administered and controlled. It includes the appropriate role of the board of directors and the auditors of the company.

Corporate governance is concerned with the overall control and direction of a business so that the business's objectives are achieved in an acceptable manner by **ALL** stakeholders.

4.3 Systems of corporate governance

One of the main debates surrounding corporate governance regulation is whether it should be:

- A set of **best practice** guidelines – as in the UK with its principles based approach requiring companies to adhere to the spirit rather than the letter of the law.

- A **legal** requirement – as in the US with appropriate penalties for transgression.

4.4 Features of UK corporate governance codes

The Financial Reporting Council (FRC) is the body responsible for promoting high standards of corporate governance in the UK. All companies listed on the London Stock Exchange are required to apply the principles of the UK Corporate Governance Code and must produce a disclosure statement confirming compliance with the code and explaining any departures from it.

Smaller listed companies, i.e. those not in the FTSE 350 can take a more flexible approach to applying the code. Note: the FTSE 350 is an index of the top 350 companies by capitalisation (where as the more commonly used FTSE 100 index contains the top 100 companies).

The following guidance exists:

Use of the AGM

The board should use the annual general meeting (AGM) to construct a dialogue with shareholders.

Board

The company should have an effective board that meets regularly. The annual report should identify the Chairman, Deputy Chairman, Chief Executive Officer (CEO), senior independent directors and the members and chairs of the board committees. It should also disclose the number of meetings held and the directors' attendance.

Chairman and Chief Executive Officer (CEO)

The positions of the Chairman (person responsible for leadership and board effectiveness) and the CEO (the person in charge of running the company) should be separated. This is to ensure that no one individual has too much power within the company. The Chairman should be independent on appointment.

Non-executive directors (NEDs)

Directors who are involved in the execution of day-to-day management decisions are called **executive directors (EDs)**. Those who primarily only attend board meetings (and the meetings of board committees) are known as **NEDs**.

Current guidance is that NEDs should as far as possible be 'independent' so that their oversight role can be effectively and responsibly carried out.

NEDs must not:

- have been an employee of the company in the last five years
- have had a material business interest in the company for the last three years
- participate in the company's share options or pension schemes
- have close ties with company directors or senior employees
- serve as a NED for more than nine years with the same company
- hold cross directorship (i.e. two or more directors sit on the board of the same third party company).

If any of these apply to a NED, their independence will be seriously compromised.

Typical recommendations include:

- At least half of the board (excluding the chairman) should comprise independent NEDs. A smaller company should have at least two independent NEDs.
- One of the NEDs should be appointed the 'senior independent director'. Shareholders can contact them if they wish to raise matters outside the normal executive channels of communication.

Illustration 8 – Appointing a well known NED

In 2011, the double Olympic gold medallist, Dame Kelly Holmes was appointed as a NED of TUI Education. She is a well known and well liked public figure and the public at large may have seen her as their representative on the board and would have trusted her to put their point of view forward. Despite almost a decade in the Army, and her achievements in elite sport, Dame Kelly had little experience of big business. However, the company understood that it could benefit from having someone with experience outside of traditional business.

Test your understanding 6

Independent NED

Mr X retires from the post of finance director at AB plc. The company is keen to retain his experience, so invite him to become a NED of the company. Can he qualify as an independent non-executive?

Nomination committees

Appointments to the board should be made via a nominations committee. Over 50% of this committee should be made up of NEDs. This is to provide some independence from the current board members and to ensure that all appointments are based on merit and suitability and that the composition of the board is balanced.

Remuneration committees

It is an important principle of corporate governance that no director should be involved in setting the level of their own remuneration.

A remuneration committee is a committee made up of NEDs which is responsible for deciding on the pay and incentives offered to executive directors (including pension rights and compensation payments). The Chairman can be a member but cannot chair the committee.

Remuneration should be sufficient to attract, retain and motivate quality directors but shouldn't be more than necessary. A significant proportion of director's pay should be performance related.

Remuneration committee

Advantages of having a remuneration committee:

- It avoids the agency problem of directors determining their own levels of remuneration.

- It leaves the board free to make strategic decision about the future.

Disadvantages of having a remuneration committee:

- There is a danger that NEDs may recommend high remuneration for the executive directors in the hope that the executives will recommend high remuneration for the NEDs.

- There will be a cost involved in preparing for and holding the meetings.

Test your understanding 7

Remuneration of NEDs

On what basis should NEDs be remunerated for their service to the company?

Test your understanding 8 – OTQ

Which one of the following can non executive directors accept as remuneration from the company?

A   A fixed daily rate for their time

B   Shares

C   Pension payments

D   Equity options

Audit committees

Auditors (both internal and external) have long had a problem – the people they report to and liaise with (the board) are often those people whose activities they report on.

An audit committee consists of independent NEDs (at least three for FTSE 350 companies and at least two for smaller listed companies) who are responsible for monitoring and reviewing the company's financial controls and the integrity of the financial statements.

The board should review the effectiveness of risk management and internal controls at least annually and report to shareholders covering all material controls.

The audit committee acts as an interface between the board of directors on one side and the internal and external auditors on the other side.

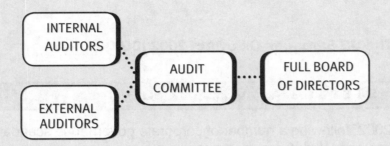

An audit committee should be the first point of contact for auditors, improving the independence and the overall quality of the audit functions.

The role of the audit committee

Responsibilities include the following:

- Reviewing accounting policies and financial statements as a whole to ensure that they are appropriate and balanced.

- Review systems of internal controls and risk management within the organisation. (Note that risk management may be dealt with by a separate committee – the risk committee.)

- Agreement of the work agenda for the internal audit department, as well as reviewing the results of internal audit work.

- Liaising with the external auditors, including dealing with problems in the audit as they arise as well as the appointment and removal of external auditors.

Test your understanding 9

Composition of audit committee

Why are the members of an audit committee required to be NEDs rather than executive directors?

4.5 Benefits of corporate governance to the organisation

Corporate governance will increase costs and will also increase the complexity of the organisation's decision making process. So why do company's adopt good corporate governance?

Test your understanding 10

Discuss the benefits of good corporate governance.

4.6 The US Sarbanes-Oxley Act 2002 (SOX)

The US Sarbanes-Oxley Act 2002 (SOX)

In 2002, following a number of corporate governance scandals such as Enron and WorldCom, tough new corporate governance regulations were introduced in the US by SOX.

SOX is only applicable in the US and for subsidiaries of US-based companies.

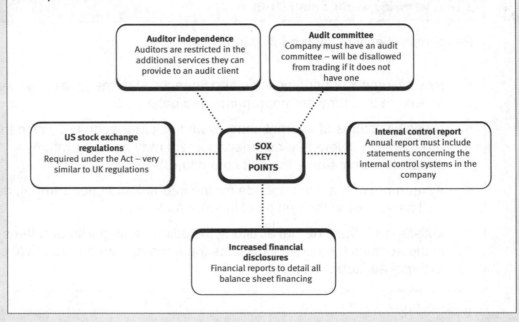

5 The Impact of Regulation on the Firm

5.1 Introduction

One of the roles of government is to act as a regulator.

Regulation is any form of government interference and is required to ensure that the needs of stakeholders can be met and that businesses act in the public interest.

Test your understanding 11

Identify some common examples of government regulation.

5.2 Efficient and effective regulation

Effective regulation will ensure that a safe and effective product or service is delivered, whilst not inhibiting the effective function of the business.

Efficient regulation is said to exist if the total benefit to the nation is greater than the total cost.

There are also schemes of **voluntary regulation**, e.g. corporate governance in the UK.

5.3 Impact of inappropriate regulation

Test your understanding 12

Briefly discuss the impact of inappropriate regulation.

Illustration 9 – Negative impact of regulation

A 2013 survey by the Institute of Chartered Accountants in England and Wales concluded that despite government efforts, 9 out of 10 businesses thought that the UK regulatory environment had not improved in the last 12 months. A number of regulations are causing particular business challenges. For example, half of businesses see pensions regulation as a challenge to the operation and development of their business. Small businesses had to deal with a number of changes in 2011, including the introduction of flexible working for employees who request it and the abolishment of the default State retirement age.

5.4 UK and international regulation

UK and international regulation

Regulation in the **UK** includes:

(1) Regulation of the level of competition in the market

- The government wants to encourage competition in the market.
- Competition drives down prices, encourages firms to be efficient with the use of their resources and improves quality.
- Therefore, competition is in the best interests of the consumer.
- Sources of regulation include:
  - The Competition Act
  - The Office of Fair Trading
  - The Competition and Markets Authority (CMA).

(2) Regulation of externalities

Externalities are costs or benefits of production experienced by society but not by producers or consumers themselves.

For example:

- an external cost may be cigarette smoke. The government may regulate this by taxing cigarettes to reduce consumption.
- an external benefit may be the health impact of vaccinations. The government may regulate this by offering free vaccinations.

(3) Regulation of people in business

The government will regulate the people managing a company to:

- prevent insider trading – it is a criminal offence to use privately held knowledge to make a profit or avoid a loss when buying or selling shares.
- to prevent trading if a company is insolvent.

(4) Other regulations

- money laundering – very extensive regulations on money laundering exist under the Proceeds of Crime Act 2002 and the Money Laundering Regulations 2007. Organisations must implement and comply with these.

Examples of **international regulation** include:

(1) **The US Sarbanes-Oxley Act 2002**

– The aim of the Act is to stop creative accounting.

– As mentioned in section 4 of this chapter, it was implemented as a result of huge corporate scandals, e.g. Enron and WorldCom.

– It has no impact on a UK company unless they are registered on the US stock exchange as well as the UK stock exchange.

– The main provisions of the Act were reviewed in Section 4 of this chapter.

(2) **International regulation of trade**

– International trade can bring about a number of benefits including increased efficiency, access to economies of scale and closer political links.

– Free trade is supported by the World Trade Organisation (WTO).

– Regional trading organisations, such as the EU and NAFTA, allow free trade between specific countries.

6 Business/Government Relations

6.1 Corporate political activity (CPA)

Corporate political activity refers to the involvement of firms in the political process, with the aim of securing particular policy preferences.

Corporate political activity can be an important element in any firm's effort to gain competitive advantage.

Illustration 10 – Corporate political activity

In the US the protection of domestic trade is among the most popular policies demanded by producers with US politicians being easily influenced by the generous donations made by US firms.

There are two types of corporate political activity:

- **Buffering** – attempts are made to influence the external environment and prevent it from interfering in internal operations, for example:
  - by employing lobbyists, who will put their case to the government to influence legislative or regulative processes.
  - by making donations to party funds. Obviously this is open to question; it could be seen as a form of bribery.

Illustration 11 – Donations to party funds

The problem of corruption continues to be strong in many developing countries. A cash-for-votes scandal overshadowed the presidential elections in Brazil in 2006.

- **Bridging** – a more reactive form of behaviour. For example, firms may track the development of laws and regulation, so to have compliance in place when the legislation is passed, or exceeding compliance levels for regulation.

Illustration 12 – President Obama's changes

In January 2009, President Obama implemented some of the toughest lobbying restrictions in US history, seeking to eliminate undue influence in American politics. New rules prohibit presidential appointees from accepting gifts from lobbying organisations and restricts appointees' ability to work on issues on which they recently lobbied while in the private sector.

However, five years into his presidency, Obama's lobby reform is broken. The rules once seen as revolutionary are now seen as counterproductive and meaningless. For example, Steve Ricchetti (a well known lobbyist) was recently appointed as a counsellor to the Vice President. He got round the lobbying ban by taking advantage of a loophole and deregistering as a lobbyist.

It is usually in the interest of a government to consult with the business sector when it is forming new policies:

- to widen its perspective
- and so that it can defend its actions politically.

6.2 Business/government relations in developed and developing countries

In most **developed** countries there is a strong business lobby consisting of individual companies and business-related organisations. They spend considerable amounts of money and are among the most prominent political players.

Very large companies are likely to be in frequent contact with government departments and parliament on an individual basis and many have distinct departments for government liaison.

Such departments will monitor and advise on political and governmental developments, make regular contacts with politicians and senior civil servants, organise representation and undertake lobbying operations in London, Brussels, Washington, Geneva etc, often assisted by non-executive directors and consultants.

Illustration 13 – Responsible business lobbying

Companies with statements on CSR must align their business activities with social responsibility. For example, mining companies making statements about responsible stewardship to the environment should not be found lobbying to dumb-down environmental legislation.

Business lobbying in the UK

In the UK, the business lobby consists of organisations such as the following:

- The Confederation of British Industry (CBI), representing the entire private business sector.

- The Federation of Small Businesses (FSB) and local Chambers of Commerce.

- The Institute of Directors (IOD).

- Several thousand trade associations and employers' organisations, representing particular industries and sectors.

In some **developing countries**, CPA is far more overt. Politicians, or even whole governments, can be persuaded to introduce, modify or remove legislation fairly cheaply. Policy-making bodies are open to threats and bribery.

Influence of business on international organisations

It may be particularly important to try to influence the drafting process of organisations such as the European Commission and the WTO. Their regulations take priority over national law or more local arrangements and their decisions may be very difficult to change because they are only arrived at after long periods of international negotiation.

- There should be no delay. Firms should monitor the issues that are being dealt with by the governing body and make their views known as early as possible in the process. The governing body will probably publish a 'green paper' discussing proposed changes and inviting comment before issuing a 'white paper' and passing a statute, a treaty or a set of standards.

- Firms should collaborate with others in the same industry and encourage firms in other countries to lobby their own governments. An organisation's opinions will carry more weight if it can show that it is not just self-seeking but that those opinions are shared by others in the industry.

Government impact on business

Required:

List the possible ways that government can impact on business both as an aid and as an impediment.

Solution:

An aid to business:

- as large buyer
- as sponsor for research and development
- as the champion of free trade (or as protector against unfair trade in certain circumstances)
- as a controller of inflation, and inflationary influences
- by providing help for wealth creation, including skill training
- by providing assistance for the start up of businesses.

An impediment to business:

- as defender of the interest of the consumer
- as the guarantor of health and safety at work
- as the protector of the environment
- as regulator of business practices
- as the protector of minority groupings.

7 Chapter summary

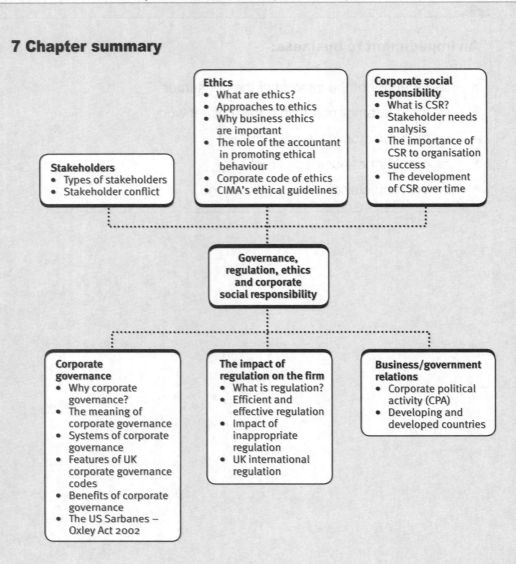

Stakeholders
- Types of stakeholders
- Stakeholder conflict

Ethics
- What are ethics?
- Approaches to ethics
- Why business ethics are important
- The role of the accountant in promoting ethical behaviour
- Corporate code of ethics
- CIMA's ethical guidelines

Corporate social responsibility
- What is CSR?
- Stakeholder needs analysis
- The importance of CSR to organisation success
- The development of CSR over time

Governance, regulation, ethics and corporate social responsibility

Corporate governance
- Why corporate governance?
- The meaning of corporate governance
- Systems of corporate governance
- Features of UK corporate governance codes
- Benefits of corporate governance
- The US Sarbanes – Oxley Act 2002

The impact of regulation on the firm
- What is regulation?
- Efficient and effective regulation
- Impact of inappropriate regulation
- UK international regulation

Business/government relations
- Corporate political activity (CPA)
- Developing and developed countries

8 Practice questions

Question 1 – OTQ

Anti-monopoly laws are based on the idea that the best way to achieve efficiency and to avoid excessive prices is through:

A   corporate governance

B   increased public ownership

C   regulation

D   an increase in corporate social responsibility

(2 marks)

Question 2 – OTQ

What is the definition of corporate governance?

A   The system by which companies are directed and controlled

B   The definition in the Sarbanes-Oxley Act 2002

C   A set of rules that a company must follow to continue being listed on the London Stock Exchange

D   A set of rules introduced as a result of several high-profile corporate collapses

(2 marks)

Question 3 – OTQ

Which one of the following is NOT the job of a NED (non executive director)?

A   Contribution to the development of strategy

B   Scrutiny of management performance

C   Decisions on which suppliers to use for the company's raw materials purchases

D   Determination of executives' remuneration packages

(2 marks)

Question 4 – Case style

An increasing number of companies have expressed their willingness to consider their wider social responsibilities. This often involves them voluntarily undertaking extra responsibilities and costs, for example:

- In order to reduce pollution, they may decide to treat waste products to a higher standard than required by legislation.

- They may decline to trade with countries whose governments they find objectionable.

- They may pay wages above minimum levels.

Task:

(a) Explain:
   (i) whether the pursuit of a policy of social responsibility necessarily involves a conflict with the objective of shareholder wealth-maximisation

   (ii) the extent to which the existence of a conflict between a company's objectives is acceptable.

(15 minutes)

(b) Explain how it is possible to encourage staff, particularly managers, to pursue and implement socially responsible policies.

(7 minutes)

(c) Explain to what extent it is possible to include the requirements of all stakeholders when creating a plan for corporate social responsibility.

(8 minutes)

(Total: 30 minutes)

Question 5 – Case style

Background

Eastborough is a large region with a rugged, beautiful coastline where rare birds have recently settled on undisturbed cliffs. Since mining ceased 150 years ago, its main industries have been agriculture and fishing. However, today, many communities in Eastborough suffer high unemployment. Government initiatives for regeneration through tourism have met with little success as the area has poor road networks, unsightly derelict buildings and dirty beaches.

Potential mining by Digwell Explorations

Digwell Explorations, a listed company, has a reputation for maximising shareholder returns and has discovered substantial tin reserves in Eastborough. With new technology, mining could be profitable, provide jobs and boost the economy. A number of interest and pressure groups have, however, been vocal in opposing the scheme.

Digwell Explorations, after much lobbying, has just received government permission to undertake mining. It could face difficulties in proceeding because of the likely activity of a group called the Eastborough Protection Alliance. This group includes wildlife protection representatives, villagers worried about the potential increase in traffic congestion and noise, environmentalists, and anti-capitalism groups.

Task:

Discuss the ethical issues that should have been considered by the government when granting permission for mining to go ahead. Explain the conflicts between the main stakeholder groups.

(25 minutes)

Test your understanding answers

Test your understanding 1 – (Case style)

A **Minimal effort**. Chop's customers are likely to have little interest in the staffing of their suppliers as long as it does not affect the service or products they receive. They will individually have little power as they do not form a significant part of Chop's revenue.

B **Key players**. The board will see the three major shareholders as having high power due to their high proportion of voting rights in the business. They are clearly highly interested in their investment in Chop.

C **Keep informed**. Employees are not heavily unionised, so have little collective power. They will be highly interested, however, as many of their jobs are at risk.

D **Keep satisfied**. The government of country Z would have significant power over Chop, if it chooses to exercise it, as it owns the forests that Chop leases. However, as long as Chop obeys the law, it is unlikely to take an active interest in the reduction of its workforce.

Test your understanding 2

The correct answer is B – False

Business ethics is partly concerned with legal requirements, but also with areas that are not covered by the law.

Test your understanding 3

The correct answer is B – False

The traditional view was always that ethical behaviour was a burden on business. If competitors were behaving unethically, then managers thought they had no choice other than to act unethically themselves. Initiatives such as Fairtrade have proved this traditional view to be false. Adherence to ethical practice can be shown to be a driver of new profit streams rather than as a cost burden.

Test your understanding 4

The needs of a supplier to a supermarket are:

- a long-term business relationship so the supplier can plan for the future
- a large value of goods sold on regular orders
- agreed quality standards that both parties can work with
- fair prices
- prompt payments on the agreed dates.

Test your understanding 5

Either you could argue that such action was ethically correct (with the company wanting to 'do the right thing'), or you could argue that a concentration on short-term profits is likely to store up problems in the longer term. If under-age gamblers are seen to be gambling on a particular website, then the public reputation of that site will be damaged and its long term profitability could be in jeopardy if governments or customers turn against it.

Test your understanding 6

It is very unlikely that Mr X can be independent since he has been an employee of the company within the last five years. If the board believes that Mr X is independent despite his recent employment then they must state the reasons for this determination.

Test your understanding 7

NEDs should be paid fees that reflect the time commitment and the responsibilities of the role, e.g. a fixed daily rate for when they work for the company. Share options should not be granted to the NEDs since this could detract from their independent judgement.

Test your understanding 8 – OTQ

The correct answer is A

NEDs should be paid fees that reflect the time commitment and the responsibilities of the role, e.g. a fixed daily rate for when they work for the company. Share options should not be granted to NEDs since this would detract from the detached judgement that they should bring, and it would also prevent them from being identified as 'independent' NEDs.

Test your understanding 9

NEDs have no day-to-day operating responsibilities, so they are able to view the company's affairs in a detached and independent way and liaise effectively between the main board and both sets of auditors.

Test your understanding 10

Good corporate governance:

- **Reduces risk** – corporate governance can help reduce the risk of fraud. It can provide a mechanism for reviewing and assessing projects.

- **Stimulates performance** – it institutes clear accountability and effective links between performance and rewards which can encourage organisations to improve performance.

- **Improves access to capital markets** – due to a reduction in the level of risk perceived by outsiders, including investors.

- **Enhances the marketability of goods and services** – due to an enhancement in reputation and public confidence.

- **Improves leadership** – the wider pool of knowledge and experience available to the board, through the inclusion of external members, helps the board to identify opportunities more readily.

- **Listing requirements** – following corporate governance guidelines is required by many stock exchanges (including the London Stock Exchange) in order to obtain a listing.

Test your understanding 11

The government may regulate:

- prices
- wages
- pollution
- product quality standards
- employment conditions.

Test your understanding 12

Inappropriate regulation:

- Makes firms less likely to innovate and adapt the quality and mix of goods and services to changing customer needs.
- Can have an adverse effect on markets, making firms uncompetitive due to bureaucracy.

Question 1 – OTQ

The correct answer is C

Regulation should help to improve efficiency and avoid excessive prices.

Question 2 – OTQ

The correct answer is A

By definition

Question 3 – OTQ

The correct answer is C

The NEDs would not be involved in deciding what supplier to use.

Question 4 – Case style

(a) (i) About 20 or so years ago, the idea that profitability was overwhelmingly the principal objective of a business would have been uncontroversial. Today's climate is different: increased public awareness of the social impact of large organisations has broadened the range of objectives which businesses must aim to achieve. New factors to be considered include pollution control, conservation of natural resources and avoidance of environmental damage.

In the short term, the measures described in the question would reduce profits; all of them involve increased profits or revenue foregone. And reduced profits imply reduced shareholders' wealth in the form of dividends and capital growth.

However, this analysis, though relatively straightforward in the short term, may not be so clear-cut in the long term. Many commentators argue that the reputation and image of corporations will suffer if they do not respond to heightened awareness of social responsibility amongst consumers. Given that many companies are already taking steps along this path, and making good public relations out of their efforts, there is pressure on other companies to follow suit. Failure to do so may lead to long-term decline.

(ii) A conflict between company objectives implies a picture of managers pulling in opposite directions, some trying to meet criteria of social responsibility, others hell-bent on maximising profit. Given that all of the managers in a company are drawing on the same pool of resources this is a recipe for disaster.

However, this does not mean that companies are doomed to fail if they pursue more than one objective. The idea is to agree on a balance between conflicting objectives, and to settle on a strategy which satisfies both sets of objectives, to the extent that they can be reconciled.

(b) Part of the difficulty in pursuing aspirations towards social responsibility lies in the relative novelty of the concept. Managers brought up in a culture of profit maximisation may find it hard to appreciate the importance of other objectives, and to adapt their behaviour accordingly. To encourage managers to pursue and implement social responsibility involves, as a first step, making managers aware of the need for it. This may be achieved by:

– appropriate training

– dissemination of targets and measures related to social objectives

- formal incorporation of social objectives into the decision-making process

- collaboration with other organisations to launch a common approach

- appointment of external consultants to assess existing performance in this area and to recommend improvements

- monitoring achievement by logging and publishing of performance indicators

- appointment of a committee to review and implement social and ethical policies.

(c) An organisation's stakeholders include:

- owners/shareholders

- employees

- business contacts, such as customers and suppliers

- the general public

- the government.

Owners/shareholders will be interested primarily in profitability, but the analysis in Part(a) above suggests that long-term profitability may depend at least in part on the adoption of social objectives.

Employees obviously have a very direct interest in at least some social objectives: for example, the question mentions a policy of paying wages above national minimum levels.

Business contacts have a less direct interest in this issue. However, as a minimum, creditors will be impressed with an ethical policy of paying debts on time, and customers who themselves have social and ethical interests, may exert pressure on their suppliers to conform as well.

The general public, as already mentioned, have shown themselves increasingly aware of these issues, and are prepared to back their principles with direct action (such as refusing to invest in companies whose objectives they disapprove of).

The government must meet international obligations as well as satisfying the demands of their own electorate. Both factors mean that they will take an interest in the social and ethical policies of organisations.

Question 5 – Case style

Ethics

Ethics are a code of moral principles that people follow with respect to what is right or wrong. General examples might include staying within the law, not engaging in bribery or theft or endangering other people.

Also a part of ethics is social responsibility; the duty towards the wider community or society in general which includes environmental issues, public safety, employment and exploitation of third world workers.

In this case, ethical issues which the government should have considered when granting permission for mining include:

- **Employment in the local area** – the government has a duty toward people to provide them with jobs. In Eastborough there is significant unemployment so it is particularly important to the government to generate jobs in the area. The effect of the mining on employment levels should therefore be considered.

- **The local economy** – the government has an obligation to the people of Eastborough to improve the wealth of the people there. This largely depends on a successful economy. The local economy of Eastborough has been performing badly despite various initiatives based around tourism. The effect of mining on the local economy generally must be considered (i.e. jobs create income which is then spent in local shops, demand for property increases and prices rise for all in the area).

- **Environmental concerns** – Eastborough has a beautiful coastline with rare birds nesting there. The government has a debt towards society generally to preserve areas of natural beauty for all to appreciate and enjoy, and a moral obligation towards other species on the planet to protect them from extinction. The effects of the mining operations on the rare birds, the beauty of the coastline and any pollution caused in the locality should therefore have been considered by the government.

- **Rights of local individuals** – Individuals have the right for their quality of life to remain high. While employment and an improved economy may enrich the quality of life of many, there may also be negative effects for some local people such as increased noise and traffic congestion. These broader effects on villagers are likely to have been considered.

- **Right to free operation of business** – Many capitalist countries believe in free trade and removing barriers to trade. This may be seen as a right of the business, and it may be considered as part of the decision to allow Digwell to open the mining operation.

Conflicts between stakeholder groups

Stakeholders are people who are affected or interested in some way by the mining operations.

In this case stakeholders include:

- national government
- local government
- local people
- wildlife protection groups
- environmental groups
- directors of Digwell
- employees of Digwell
- shareholders of Digwell.

The conflicts which may exist include the following:

- **National vs local government** – local government will be interested in Eastborough and its interests. National government have to balance those needs with the needs of all people of the country. There may be a conflict over the amount of funding available to support local initiatives such as help with starting up the mining operations.

- **Unemployed vs people based near mining operations/ working people** – unemployed people in the area will notice a direct benefit from the mining operations through increased jobs and are likely to support it. Other local residents may simply view the operations as disrupting their existing life (noise/congestion) and oppose the idea.

- **Shareholders/directors of Digwell vs environmental/wildlife protection groups** – both shareholders and Directors of Digwell wish to make profits from Digwell's operations. The mining operations will enable them to make full use of an asset they own (tin reserves) and hence increase profit. They will wish it to go ahead, and may have very little interest in the broader impact. Environmental groups aim to protect the environment and are likely to oppose any part of the mining operation which will affect the environment irrespective of profitability.

4

The Purpose of the Finance Function

Chapter learning objectives

Lead	Component
B1. Discuss the purpose of the finance function and its relationship with other parts of the organisation.	(a) Demonstrate the contribution that the finance function makes to the sustainable delivery of the organisation's strategies in a range of contexts.
	(b) Analyse the components of the finance function (financial and management accounting, treasury, company secretarial, internal audit etc.)
	(c) Discuss the potential for conflict within the role of the finance function.
B2. Explain how the finance function supports the organisation's strategies and operations.	(a) Explain the activities fundamental to the role of the finance function (accounting operations, analysis, planning, decision making and control).

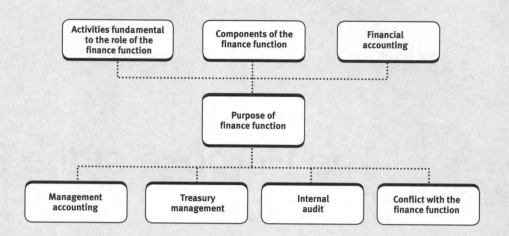

1 Activities Fundamental to the Role of the Finance Function

The finance function supports the organisation's operations and achievement of its strategy in a number of ways:

- The effective implementation of strategies requires **sufficient financial resource**.

- A **key measure of organisational success is financial performance**.

- Financial information provides a uniform measure of performance across the organisation and is a key means of making the organisation's **activities visible**.

There are five key activities that are fundamental to the role of the finance function:

- **Accounting operations** – for example, the preparation of statutory reports or working capital reporting.

- **Analysis** – provision of analysis to support decisions. For example, a pricing decision or an investment appraisal decision.

- **Planning** – the preparation of plans, forecasts and budgets to assist the organisation in achieving its objectives and formulating relevant strategies.

- **Decision making** – using the information that has been prepared and provided to help make decisions. For example, choosing the optimum source of finance to fund a particular investment decision.

- **Control** – information relating to the actual results is used to take control measures and to re-assess and amend original budgets and plans. The systems in place should provide timely and accurate control information.

2 Components of the Finance Function

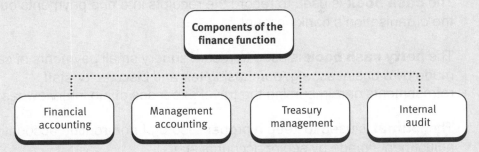

The finance function is responsible for the stewardship and control of physical and financial resources within the organisation.

In larger organisations, the range of tasks that the finance function performs is very wide. This often means that the finance department is split into different components, each of which deals with a separate set of responsibilities. The finance director will take overall charge of the finance function.

Each of these components will be explored in turn below.

3 Financial Accounting

3.1 What is financial accounting?

Financial accounting is concerned with the production of financial statements in accordance with the relevant accounting standards and legislation.

Whenever a business transaction takes place (such as a sale, purchase or payment of an expense), there is a need to record the transaction in the organisation's accounting records. The transaction is first entered into the **books of prime entry**.

Books of prime entry

There are five main books of prime entry:

The **purchases day book** is used to record the purchases made by a business, listing the invoices received from suppliers.

The **sales day book** is used to record the sales made by a business, listing the invoices issued to customers.

> The **cash book** is used to record the receipts into and payments out of the organisation's bank account.
>
> The **petty cash book** is used to record sundry small payments of cash made by a business, e.g. purchasing tea and biscuits for staff refreshments or reimbursing the travel expenses of job interviewees.
>
> The **journal** is used to keep a proper record of non-routine accounting adjustments made by senior accounts staff.

On a regular basis (often daily or weekly, depending on the volume of transactions), the day books are totalled and these totals are entered into the ledger accounts.

At the end of the accounting year of the business, the balance is calculated on each ledger account and these balances are used to create the financial statements of the organisation for the period.

There are three main financial statements produced by most businesses each year. These are:

- the **statement of profit or loss (SOPL)** for the year, which details the income as well as the costs incurred in the period. This allows the business to calculate whether it has made a profit (if income exceeds costs) or a loss (if costs exceed income)

- the **statement of financial position (SOFP)** as at the year end, which shows the assets (business resources such as motor vehicles, buildings and cash) and liabilities (money owed to third parties such as banks and suppliers) of the business. This statement also shows the stake that the owners of the business have in the organisation (or their 'capital'). In a company, this is often referred to as 'shareholder's equity'.

- the **statement of cash flows** for the year, which summarises the cash receipts and payments for the year. This helps to show whether the company is solvent (has sufficient cash) and where the cash has been spent in the year.

In summary, the normal sequence of steps in the accounting function is:

TRANSACTIONS ···· DAY BOOKS ···· LEDGER ACCOUNTS ···· FINANCIAL STATEMENTS

Test your understanding 1 – OTQ

J has been asked to find four pieces of information about FGH Ltd for his manager from the company's statement of profit or loss (SOPL) and statement of financial position (SOFP). He has been asked to find:

(1) The ratio of current assets to current liabilities

(2) Total shareholders equity

(3) Gross profit as a percentage of turnover

(4) Total rent paid for the year

Which of the following (A, B, C or D) correctly match the information needed with the financial statement each would be found in?

	(1)	(2)	(3)	(4)
A	SOFP	SOFP	SOPL	SOPL
B	SOPL	SOPL	SOFP	SOFP
C	SOFP	SOPL	SOFP	SOPL
D	SOPL	SOFP	SOPL	SOFP

3.2 Why do businesses need to prepare financial statements?

The preparation of financial statements is a time-consuming and expensive process. So why do most organisations have a financial accounting component?

The main reason is to satisfy groups of people who have an interest in the financial performance of the business. These could include:

- **Owners** – interested in how profitable the business is and how well it is being run.

Illustration 1 – Investor ratios

A number of ratios will be of interest to the investor. These include:

Earnings per share (EPS)

EPS is a measure of the profit attributable to each ordinary shareholder.

$$EPS = \frac{\text{Profit after tax (less preference dividends)}}{\text{Weighted average number of ordinary shares in issue}}$$

Price/ earnings (P/E) ratio

$$P/E\ ratio\ =\ \frac{Share\ price}{EPS}$$

A high P/E ratio means that investors are paying more for today's earnings in anticipation of future growth.

Dividend yield

$$Dividend\ yield\ =\ \frac{Dividend\ per\ share}{Current\ share\ price}\ \times\ 100$$

- **Managers** – interested in the company's financial situation so that they can plan effectively for the future.

- **Banks** – may wish to see whether the business can afford the repayments on loans and overdrafts.

- **Employees** – interested in the financial position of the company and the impact this will have on their jobs and wages.

- **Suppliers and customers** – may wish to check the financial stability of the business to ensure it will be able to make payments/supply goods as needed.

- **Government** – may wish to check that the business is obeying relevant laws on reporting and taxation.

Companies must send a copy of their financial statements to each of their shareholders at the end of the year. Large and publicly-quoted companies are also required to appoint external auditors each year to give an independent opinion on whether the financial statements have been drawn up properly and whether they give a true and fair view.

3.3 Integrated reporting

Many organisation, adopt an integrated reporting approach which means that their financial statements cover the organisation's financial performance and position (using the three primary financial statements mentioned earlier), but also report on any other relevant information that would be of interest to the users.

Other relevant information might include (but is not limited to):

- major risks the organisation faces and any actions they have taken to deal with these risks

- the organisation's performance regarding ethics and corporate social responsibility (as discussed in chapter 3)

- the organisation's performance with regard to sustainable development (discussed further in chapter 8).

4 Management Accounting

4.1 What is management accounting?

Management accounting is carried out to assist management in discharging their duties to plan, direct and control the operations of the business. It is concerned with the process of measuring, analysing, interpreting and communicating information to management in a form which is easy for them to understand.

Management accountants will use the financial accounting records as a source of data for their work, but they may choose to use any other sources of data (both internal and external) that they feel will be useful for managers.

While there are no legally required formats for management accounts, there are several key management reports that are common to many businesses. Three of the most common are **cost schedules**, **budgets** and **variance reports**.

4.2 Cost schedules

A **cost schedule** lists the various expenses involved in manufacturing units of a product. This is often shown as a list of the costs incurred when making a unit of each type of product we make. This may be called a **standard cost card**.

Illustration 2 – Standard cost cards

ABC Ltd manufactures toys. One of its products is a wooden train set, which has the following standard costs per unit:

	$
Direct materials (wood and paint)	5.50
Direct labour (time spent cutting and painting)	6.50
Prime cost	12.00
Variable overheads (heat and light)	4.00
Marginal cost	16.00
Fixed overheads (factory rent)	5.00
Total (absorption) cost	21.00

There are several key business decisions that this report can help a business to make:

- **Pricing decisions** – How much should we sell our products for in order to ensure we make a profit?

- **Break-even analysis** – Which products are profitable or loss-making? Is a new product worth producing? Can we sell enough units to cover the costs of making the product?

- **Key factor analysis** – should products be made in-house or should their manufacture be outsourced to somewhere cheaper?

- **Investment appraisal** – should a new machine be bought to replace an old machine? Should we begin a new project, such as launching a new product?

4.3 Budgets

In addition, once the costs per unit have been identified, it should be possible to produce a **budget**. This shows the total planned revenues and costs for our business for the coming period. It is based on the cost schedules mentioned earlier.

Budgets are useful for several reasons. A useful memory aid is the acronym **CRUMPET**.

- **C**o-ordination – the budget provides guidance for managers and ensures they are all working together for the good of the company.

- **R**esponsibility – the budget authorises managers to make expenditure, hire staff and generally follow the plans laid out in the budget.

- **U**tilisation – budgets (especially cash budgets) help managers to get the best out of their business resources in the coming period.

- **M**otivation – the budget can be a useful device for influencing the behaviour of managers and motivating them to perform in line with business objectives.

- **P**lanning – budgets force managers to look ahead. This may help them to identify opportunities for, or threats to, the business and take effective action in advance.

- **E**valuation – budgets are often used as the basis for management appraisal. The manager has performed well if he has met his budgets in the period.

- **T**elling – also called 'communication', budgets ensure that all members of the business understand what is expected from them during the coming period.

One major drawback of budgets is that they are only estimates of what will happen in the coming period. In reality, most businesses will not perfectly achieve the targets set out for them in their budgets.

This means that they will have to prepare a **variance report** at the end of each period.

4.4 Variance reports

A **variance report** compares the budget to the actual results achieved for the budget period and identifies any significant differences, or variances, between the two.

For control purposes, management may need to establish why a particular variance has occurred. Once the reason has been established, a decision can be taken as to what, if any, control measures might be appropriate to:

- prevent adverse variances from occurring again in the future, or

- repeat a favourable variance in the future, or

- bring actual results back on course to achieve the budgeted targets.

The management accountant will assist and interact with other functions in providing solutions to variances.

4.5 Feedforward control

A **feedforward** control system operates by comparing budgeted results against a forecast. Control action is triggered by differences between budgeted and forecasted results.

This is a much superior method of control than a **feedback** system, which would simply compare the actual historical results to the budgeted results.

4.6 Management accounting and business policy and performance

In addition, the management accounting function has a particularly important role in formulating, implementing and controlling business policy and performance.

For example, a business may have an objective to grow its revenue and profits. It will then need to examine possible ways of achieving this – such as by the launch of new products, or acquisition of a competitor. Finally it will have to assess which of these approaches will achieve its goals and select the best one(s).

The accounting function can clearly contribute to this process. Since the achievement of an organisation's plans is usually measured in monetary terms, accountants are needed to help establish objectives and then evaluate the various possible strategies to identify which are the most financially attractive.

Once a strategy has been selected, such as the launch of a new product, the business must carefully monitor and control it to ensure that it is being implemented properly and performing as desired.

This is usually done by undertaking variance analysis, which was outlined earlier.

4.7 The differences between financial and management accounting

	Management accounting	Financial accounting
Why information is mainly produced	For internal use, e.g. managers and employees.	For external use, e.g. shareholders, creditors, banks, government.
Purpose of information	To aid planning, controlling and decision making.	To record the financial performance in a period and the financial position at the end of the period.
Legal requirements	None.	Limited companies must produce financial accounts.
Formats	Management decide on the information that they require and the most useful way of presenting it.	Format and content of financial accounts must follow accounting standards and company law.
Nature of information	Financial and non-financial.	Mostly financial.
Time period	Historical and forward-looking.	Mainly a historical record.

Test your understanding 2 – OTQ

Consider the following two statements regarding the management accounting function.

(i) Variance analysis enables a business to identify why the actual financial results were different to those predicted by the budget.

(ii) Management accounts follow a set, pre-determined format as laid out in relevant accounting standards.

Which of these statements is/are correct?

A (i) only

B (ii) only

C Both

D Neither

5 Treasury Management

5.1 What is treasury management?

Treasury management is the corporate handling of all financial matters, the generation of external and internal funds for business, the management of currencies and cash flows, and the complex strategies, policies and procedures of corporate finance.

The key roles of the treasury function include:

Working capital management	The treasury section will monitor the organisation's cash balance and working capital to ensure that it never runs out of money.
Cash management	Preparation of cash budgets and arrangement of overdrafts where necessary.
Financing	The treasury section will monitor the organisation's investments and borrowings to ensure the gain as much investment income as possible and incur as little interest expense as possible.
Foreign currency	The treasury section will monitor foreign exchange rates and try to manage the organisation's affairs so that it minimises losses due to changes in foreign exchange rates.
Tax	The treasury section will try to manage the organisation's affairs to legally avoid as much tax as possible.

5.2 Management of working capital

Working capital is the capital available for conducting the day-to-day operations of an organisation, calculated as the excess of current assets over current liabilities. Thus:

Inventory	X
Trade receivables	X
Cash	X
	___
Total current assets	X
Less: Trade payables	(X)
	___
Working capital balance	X
	___

The treasury function is responsible for deciding on an appropriate level of investment in working capital for the business.

There are advantages in holding either large or small balances of each component of working capital, as shown below.

	Advantage of large balance	Advantage of small balance
Inventory	Customers are happy since they can be immediately provided with goods.	Low holding costs. Less risk of obsolescence costs.
Trade receivables	Customers are happy since they like credit.	Less risk of irrecoverable debts. Good for cash flow.
Cash	Creditors are happy since bills can be paid promptly.	More can be invested elsewhere to earn profits.
Trade payables	Preserves your own cash.	Suppliers are happy and may offer discounts.

Management must decide on the appropriate balance to be struck for each component.

Test your understanding 3 – OTQ

Conservative managers will have a policy of holding a large working capital balance, while aggressive management will hold a low working capital balance. Which one of the following is a consequence of an aggressive management policy?

A   Increased bad and doubtful debts

B   Increased credit periods attract more customers

C   Increased inventory obsolescence

D   Increased risk of inventory outages

5.3 Evaluating and obtaining finance

The organisation may need additional funding to allow it to grow and invest in new projects. It may therefore need to raise finance from external sources. There are two main types of external finance.

Debt

This involves borrowing cash from a third party and promising to repay them at a later date. Normally, the company will also have to pay interest on the amount borrowed.

There are various sources of debt that an organisation can raise funds from, including bank loans and overdrafts, venture capitalists and through selling bonds or debentures.

The main advantages of raising cash through debt finance are:

- Interest payments are allowable against tax. Note that dividend payments made to shareholders, by contrast, are **not** an allowable deduction.

- Raising debt finance does not change the ownership of the organisation.

- Debt tends to be cheaper to service than equity, as it is often secured against the assets of the company and takes priority over equity in the event of the business being liquidated.

Equity

This involves selling a stake in the business in order to raise cash. For companies, this involves selling shares to either new or existing shareholders.

Raising equity finance has the following advantages:

- There is no minimum level of dividend that must be paid to shareholders. This means that dividends can be suspended if profits are low and the company cannot afford them. Interest payments on debt finance **must** be paid each year.

- A bank will normally require security on the company's assets before it will offer a loan. Some companies may lack quality assets to offer, making equity more attractive as it does not require security.

Financial gearing

$$\text{Financial gearing} = \frac{\text{Long-term debt}}{\text{Shareholders' funds}} \times 100$$

A high gearing ratio indicates a high level of risk since debt obligations (such as interest payments) must be met, whereas returns to shareholders (such as dividends) are voluntary.

Generally

The treasury and finance function will weigh up which source of finance best suits the circumstances of the business.

Test your understanding 4 – OTQ

AHG plc needs to raise $50m to launch a new product. AHG hopes the new product will be a success, but the returns are highly uncertain, with a 30% chance that the launch will be a failure. The product is expected to sell for around 5 years.

AHG is currently trying to decide whether the launch should be financed using a 5 year bank loan, or through raising equity.

Which one of the following statements is correct?

A   Equity will be cheaper, as dividends are allowable against tax

B   AHG should choose equity due to the risky nature of the project

C   Equity should be chosen as AHG needs a permanent increase in its finance

D   Debt usually does not require security, meaning it may be easier for AHG to raise

5.4 Foreign currency

Companies may have borrowings in foreign currencies, or may have customers/suppliers who will pay/expect payment in a foreign currency. The treasury department will try to manage affairs to minimise the company's exposure to foreign exchange losses, i.e. minimise losses.

Illustration 3 – Managing foreign currency risk

Background

Assume a UK company buys goods costing US$1m from a US company on 1 January 20X1.

The goods are due to be paid for on 31 March 20X1.

The exchange rate at 1 January is £1:US$1.5, so the goods will cost £666,667 ($1m/1.5).

However if the exchange rate changes to, say, £1:US$1.3, then the payment to be made will be £769,231 ($1m/1.3).

Managing the risk

The company can manage this risk by entering into a 'forward exchange contract' at 1 January to fix the rate of exchange at which it can buy $1m at 31 March.

The rate in the forward exchange contract will depend on what the market thinks will happen to exchange rates.

Let us say, for example, that the company can enter into a contract to purchase $1m at the rate of £1:S1.48. The company's cost, in sterling, is then fixed at £675,676 ($1m/1.48).

5.5 Determining business tax liabilities

One of the roles of the finance and treasury function is to calculate the business tax liability for the organisation and mitigate, or reduce, that liability as far as possible within the law.

 Tax avoidance is the legal use of the rules of the tax regime to one's own advantage, in order to reduce the amount of tax payable by means that are within the law.

 Tax evasion is the use of illegal means to reduce one's tax liability, for example by deliberately misrepresenting the true state of your affairs to the tax authorities.

The directors of a company have a duty to their shareholders to maximise the post-tax profits that are available for distribution as dividends to the shareholders, thus they have a duty to arrange the company's affairs to avoid taxes as far as possible. However, dishonest reporting to the tax authorities (e.g. declaring less income than actually earned) would be tax evasion and a criminal offence.

While the traditional distinction between tax avoidance and tax evasion is fairly clear, recently authorities have introduced the idea of **tax mitigation** to mean conduct that reduces tax liabilities without frustrating the intentions of Parliament, while **tax avoidance** is used to describe schemes which, while they are legal, are designed to defeat the intentions of Parliament. Thus, once a tax avoidance scheme becomes public knowledge, Parliament will nearly always step in to change the law in order to stop the scheme from working.

Tax avoidance

The traditional view of neutrality towards tax avoidance can be shown by judges' comments in the past, for example Lord Clyde in 1929:

'No man in this country is under the smallest obligation, moral or other, so to arrange his legal relations to his business or to his property as to enable the Inland Revenue to put the largest possible shovel into his stores.'

More recently, even tax avoidance can be regarded with hostility. Some countries such as Australia have a General Anti-Avoidance Rule. Other countries such as the UK have used retrospective legislation to counteract the purpose of some tax avoidance schemes. In general it is safer now to stick with tax mitigation measures.

6 Internal Audit

6.1 What is internal audit?

Internal audit is an independent activity, established by management to examine and evaluate the organisation's risk management processes and systems of control, and to make recommendations for the achievement of company objectives.

6.2 The purpose of internal audit

Company directors have a legal requirement to produce true and fair annual financial statements. To help ensure this is done, companies are required to have their published financial statements audited by an external team of experts (**external auditors**).

Directors also need assurance on other financial matters. This assurance is primarily for their own internal use, although in recent years pressure has grown for increasingly more of such work to be made publicly available.

This additional work is carried out by internal auditors, who may be company employees or outside experts from a firm of accountants.

Internal audit is part of the organisational control of a business; it is one of the methods used by management to ensure the efficient and orderly running of the business as a whole, and is part of the overall control environment.

Internal auditors' work has expanded in recent years, and the role of internal audit often now includes:

- helping to set corporate objectives

- helping to design and monitor performance measures for these objectives.

Corporate governance

A properly functioning internal audit department is part of good corporate governance, as recognised by all national and international corporate governance codes.

Internal audit enables management to perform proper risk assessments (another central theme of corporate governance codes) by means of properly understanding the strengths and weaknesses of all parts of the control systems in the business.

The function of internal audit in the context of corporate risk management

Internal audit has a particular interest in evaluating the company's risk management structures. Internal audit can:

- manage the basic data used by management to identify risks

- identify techniques for prioritising and managing risks

- report on the effectiveness of risk management solutions (e.g. internal controls).

The structure and operation of an internal audit function

The Corporate Governance Code states that companies without an internal audit function should **annually review the need for one.**

Where there is an internal audit function, the board should **annually review its scope of work**, authority and resources.

Ideally, the internal audit function should be staffed with **qualified, experienced staff**, whose work is closely monitored by an audit committee.

Scope of internal audit

Internal audit staff are typically expected to carry out a variety of tasks:

- reviewing internal controls and financial reports
- reviewing risk management systems
- carrying out special assignments (e.g. fraud investigations)
- conducting operational reviews (e.g. into efficiency of parts of the business).

The purpose of internal audit can be summarised in the table below:

Role	To advise management on whether the organisation has sound systems of internal controls to protect the organisation against loss.
Legal basis	Generally not a legal requirement. However the Combined Code on Corporate Governance recommends that if a listed company does not have an internal audit department, it should annually assess the need for one.
Scope of work	Determined by management. Covers all areas of the organisation, operational as well as financial.
Approach	Increasingly risk-based. Assess risks. Evaluate systems of controls. Test operations of systems. Make recommendations for improvements.
Responsibility	To advise and make recommendations on internal control and corporate governance.

Test your understanding 5

'The internal audit is simply a necessary cost that must be incurred by a company and offers few tangible benefits for the organisation.'

Is this statement:

A   True

B   False

Test your understanding 6

'Internal audit may be carried out by employees of the company being audited, or may be carried out by external accountants who are paid for delivering this service.'

Is this statement:

A   True

B   False

Test your understanding 7 – OTQ

In a large company, to whom do internal auditors normally report their conclusions?

A   Executive directors

B   Board of directors

C   Shareholders

D   Non-executive directors

6.3 The role of internal audit in preventing and detecting fraud

Fraud is an intentional act involving the use of deception to obtain an unjust or illegal advantage – essentially 'theft by deception'. Fraud is a criminal offence, punishable by a fine or imprisonment.

As far as the financial statements are concerned, fraud comprises both the use of deception to obtain an unjust or illegal financial advantage and intentional misrepresentations affecting the financial statements. It is ultimately up to the courts to decide in each instance whether fraud has occurred, for example:

- deliberate falsification of documents/records

- deliberate ignoring of errors requiring correction

- deliberate suppression of relevant information.

The prerequisites of fraud

There are three prerequisites that are required for fraud to occur:

- **dishonesty** – relates to a lack of integrity or honesty. An honest employee will be unlikely to commit a fraud.

- **opportunity** – the individual must have the opportunity or opening for a fraud to be committed. These opportunities will often be created due to weak internal controls.

- **motivation** – the individual must feel that the rewards that can be earned by the fraud will outweigh the potential costs if they are caught.

All three are usually required – for example an honest employee is unlikely to commit fraud even if given the opportunity and motive.

Factors that might indicate an increased risk of fraud and error include (amongst others):

- **management domination by one person, or a small group of people** – dominant individuals often find it easy to circumvent controls and procedures.

- **unnecessarily complex corporate structure** – this makes it harder to trace transactions, meaning it is easier for employees to hide fraud.

- **poor staff morale** – if staff dislike the company they work for, it may give them additional motivation to perpetrate frauds.

- **personnel who do not take leave/holidays** – this may indicate that staff members are unwilling to pass their duties over to other members of staff in case they identify fraudulent activities.

- **lavish lifestyles of employees** – if an employee is clearly living beyond their means, it may indicate they are committing fraud in order to fund it.

- **inadequate segregation of duties** – if tasks are not shared between employees, the risk of fraud rises

- **lack of monitoring of control systems** – for controls to be effective, they need to be monitored on a regular basis

- **unusual transactions** – in cash, or direct to numbered bank accounts

- **payments for services disproportionate to effort** may also be an indication of fraudulent activity.

If management has established a strong system of internal control then the potential for fraud is greatly reduced.

It is up to the directors to decide what internal audit should do, but normally, where there is an effective internal audit department, the internal auditors will be given the responsibility to test the internal control system and to recommend improvements. The better the control system, the less likely it is that fraud will be attempted, or will succeed if it is attempted.

The directors may also ask the internal auditors to carry out a specific investigation into situations where fraud has been discovered, to learn lessons for the future and ensure that such a fraud cannot be repeated.

The possible implications of fraud to the company

There is a spectrum of implications of fraud, from the immaterial to the critical. Including

- Loss of shareholder confidence
- Loss of assets
- Financial difficulties
- Collapse of the company
- Fines by tax and other authorities.

Once a fraud has been identified, internal audit should be sent to the department to investigate the circumstances and to make recommendations to improve the controls in the area to deter future fraud. Internal audit should report their findings to the audit committee who can monitor whether the recommendations are swiftly implemented by management.

6.4 Limitations of internal audit

Limitations of internal audit

- Internal auditors have an unavoidable independence problem. They are employed by the management of the company and yet are expected to give an objective opinion on matters for which management are responsible.

- Internal audit will only succeed if it is properly staffed and resourced.

- If internal auditors identify fraud, they may be unwilling to disclose it for fear of the repercussions (which could involve the collapse of the company and the loss of their jobs).

These limitations can be reduced if an **audit committee:**

- sets the work agenda for internal audit
- receives internal audit reports
- is able to ensure the internal audit is properly resourced
- has a 'voice' at main board level.

7 Conflict within the finance function

Three key factors can result in conflict within the role of the finance function:

- interdependence versus independence
- short-term versus long-term and
- capital versus revenue expenditure.

Each of these will be explored in turn.

7.1 Interdependence versus independence

Between different components of the finance function

Interdependence	Independence
The different components of the finance function will rely on each other for a variety of reasons: • The variance reports prepared by the management accountants will rely on actual financial information prepared by the financial accountants. • The tax liability calculated by treasury will be used for financial accounting purposes.	• Financial activities serve different and sometimes conflicting purposes. For example, management accountants produce information for **internal** use (e.g. by employees and managers) where as financial accountants produce information for **external** use (e.g. by shareholders and banks). • The different components of the finance function use different information which may or may not be reconcilable. For example, management accountants decide on the information that they require and the most useful way of presenting it where as the format and contents of financial accounts must follow accounting standards and company law.

Between the finance function and the other areas of the organisation

Interdependence	Independence
The organisation will be impacted by how well the finance function works with other areas of the organisation. The interaction between the finance function and other operating functions is not purely based on the use of management accounting information. Rather there are multiple interrelated interactions which include discussions spanning management information, financial controls, tax, statutory accounts, investor relations and so on.	The finance function needs to also remain independent from the other operating functions. For example, to ensure that the financial accounts represent a true and fair view of the organisation's activities to allow internal audit to give an objective opinion on matters for which management are responsible.

7.2 Short-term versus long-term

Many of the tasks carried out by the finance function have a short-term focus. For example:

- variance reports may be complied monthly

- financial accounts will be prepared on an annual basis.

However, this short-term focus may be to the detriment of long-term success, for example:

- The development and training budget may be cut to boost short-term profitability. However, employees are now a key resource for many organisations and a lack of investment in this area could lead to a loss of competitive advantage and a resultant fall in profit.

- An adverse material price variance may result in a decision to change to an alternative and cheaper supplier but without fully considering the quality implications and impact on long-term profitability of such a decision.

7.3 Capital versus revenue expenditure

As mentioned above, the finance function may be inclined to make decisions which maximise short-term gains to the detriment of long-term performance.

For example, investment in new assets may be cut. This may result in a short-term boost in profits but long-term profitability may suffer as a result of old, potentially inefficient assets being used that may require high levels of maintenance expenditure.

8 Chapter summary

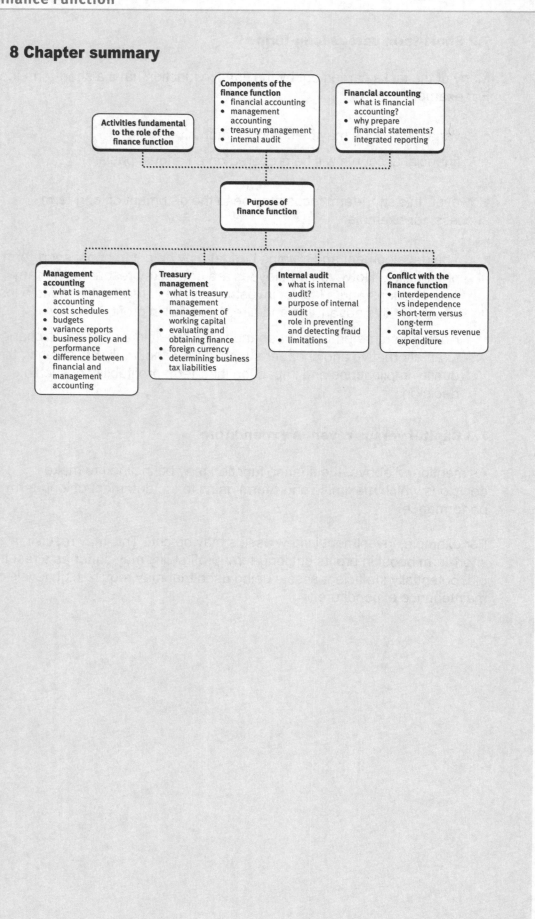

Components of the finance function
- financial accounting
- management accounting
- treasury management
- internal audit

Financial accounting
- what is financial accounting?
- why prepare financial statements?
- integrated reporting

Activities fundamental to the role of the finance function

Purpose of finance function

Management accounting
- what is management accounting
- cost schedules
- budgets
- variance reports
- business policy and performance
- difference between financial and management accounting

Treasury management
- what is treasury management
- management of working capital
- evaluating and obtaining finance
- foreign currency
- determining business tax liabilities

Internal audit
- what is internal audit?
- purpose of internal audit
- role in preventing and detecting fraud
- limitations

Conflict with the finance function
- interdependence vs independence
- short-term versus long-term
- capital versus revenue expenditure

9 Practice Questions

Question 1 – OTQ

The key purpose of internal auditing is to:

A   detect errors and fraud

B   evaluate the organisation's risk management processes and systems of control

C   give confidence as to the truth and fairness of the financial statements

D   express an internal opinion on the truth and fairness of the financial statements

Question 2 – OTQ

In a very large company managing the total level of working capital would probably be the responsibility of the:

A   Finance director

B   Chief accountant

C   Treasurer

D   Management accountant

Question 3 – OTQ

Consider the following two statements regarding management and financial accounting.

(i)   Financial accountants usually produce information for the organisation's external stakeholders.

(ii) There is no legal requirement for companies to have a management accounting function.

Which of these statements is/are correct?

A   (i) only

B   (ii) only

C   Both

D   Neither

Question 4 – OTQ

S is considering creating a financial accounting department within her business, but is unsure of what such a department would actually do. Which of the following would usually be prepared by a financial accounting department?

A   Cost schedules

B   Statement of cash flows

C   Variance analysis

D   Tax calculations

Question 5 – OTQ

An important advantage of using loans to finance investment is:

A   loan interest payments can usually be suspended if profits are low

B   the timing of loan payments is often at the company's discretion

C   loan interest is tax deductible

D   banks will often not require security for loan advances

Test your understanding answers

Test your understanding 1 – OTQ

The correct answer is A

Test your understanding 2 – OTQ

The correct answer is A

Statement (i) is correct. However, statement (ii) describes a feature of financial accounting, rather than management accounting.

Test your understanding 3 – OTQ

The correct answer is D

Keeping a low level of receivables means that money is collected promptly, decreasing the chance of bad debts. Low receivables would also mean we are offering less credit to customers, which they may find unattractive. Low levels of inventory mean that the company is less exposed to inventory obsolescence, but it does mean the company may run out of inventory if demand is unexpectedly high.

Test your understanding 4 – OTQ

The correct answer is B

A is incorrect, as dividends are not tax allowable - interest is.

B is correct as, in the event of the product being a failure, AHG would not need to make unaffordable repayments to investors if it raises finance from equity.

C is incorrect as AHG only needs the money for 5 years. It could be argued that a 5 year loan would match the term of the project and therefore be more appropriate than equity finance, on which the company will have to pay dividends forever.

D is also incorrect as debt does normally require security from the company. Equity does not.

Test your understanding 5

The correct answer is B – False

The benefits of internal audit should exceed the costs. The IIA definition stresses that internal audit is a value-adding activity by helping an organisation to manage its risks and achieve its objectives. If an organisation believes that the costs of internal audit would exceed the benefits, then it shouldn't operate that internal audit function. This is a choice to be made by the directors of a company; there is no requirement to operate an internal audit department.

Test your understanding 6

The correct answer is A – True

Internal auditors can either be employees of the company being audited, or may be external experts brought in. Compare this with external auditors who have to be external to the company; employees of the company are not allowed to carry out an external audit of that company.

Test your understanding 7 – OTQ

The correct answer is D

Internal audit reports to the management of the company. In a smaller company, internal audit is likely to report directly to the board of directors of the company being audited. In a larger company where there is an audit committee, internal audit is likely to report to the audit committee, which will be made up of non-executive directors.

Question 1 – OTQ

The correct answer is B

The internal audit also makes recommendations for the achievement of company objectives. C is the role of the external auditors.

Question 2 – OTQ

The correct answer is B

The treasurer would also be responsible for debt strategy, currency management, banking forecasting and risk management.

Question 3 – OTQ

The correct answer is C

Both statements are correct.

Question 4 – OTQ

The correct answer is B

Financial accountants would usually prepare the external financial statements, including the statement of cash flows, the income statement and the statement of financial position. A and C would normally be the responsibility of management accountants, while D would usually be undertaken by the treasury function.

Question 5 – OTQ

The correct answer is C

A, B and D are not true. They describe advantages of using the issue of share capital to finance investment.

5

The Contemporary Transformation of the Finance Function

Chapter learning objectives

Lead	Component
B2. Explain how the finance function supports the organisation's strategies and operations.	(b) Explain the contemporary transformation of the finance function.

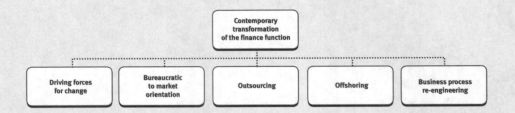

1 Introduction

The continuous and ever increasing pace of change in the business environment has resulted in significant changes to the finance function.

- The role has changed focus from financial control and reporting to **business support**. Accountants may now spend much of their time as internal consultants and although they still produce standardised reports, more time is spent analysing and interpreting information rather than preparing reports.

- This new role has been called a **hybrid accountant** since the accountant has a valuable combination of both accounting and operational/ commercial knowledge.

- Traditionally, it was thought that accountants had to be independent from operational managers in order to allow them to objectively judge and report their accounting information to senior managers. However, today accountants **do not necessarily work in a separate accounting department** but may be fully integrated into other departments, thus playing a key part in the operation and decision making process of the department.

2 Driving Forces for Change

The three main forces for change are:

- **Management structure** – head office has delegated much responsibility to the strategic business units thus reducing the involvement of accountants in areas such as detailed budgeting. The accountant may now provide a link between operational reports, the financial consequences and the strategic outcomes desired by the board.

- **Technology** – management information systems (MIS) allow users access across the organisation to input data and run reports giving the type of analysis once only provided by the management accountant.

- **Competition** – the competitive environment has driven organisations to take a more strategic focus. Accountants no longer focus on the final profit figure (this is seen as short-termism) but focus on a range of measures which try to capture long-term performance.

3 Bureaucratic to Market Orientation

Unprecedented developments in computer hardware and software capabilities, and international communications have meant that the 'traditional' bureaucratic functions of the finance staff – **transaction processing** and 'number crunching' – can be performed almost instantly.

The primary implication of this for finance staff is that their expertise will be called upon to add value and to contribute to strategy and business management decisions to a far greater extent than ever before. Rather than just crunching the numbers, finance professionals will be an integral part of business decision-making and in the **transformation** of the business.

The emphasis of the finance function has changed from one that was largely **bureaucratic** in nature to one that is **market orientated**, i.e. the work of the finance function is focused on meeting the needs of the organisation's customers both now and in the future. The finance function has focused on a number of value-adding transformational activities. These include:

- outsourcing
- offshoring and
- Business Process Re-engineering (BPR).

Each of these will be explored in turn.

4 Outsourcing

4.1 Introduction

The outsourcing of many aspects of business activity is one of the strategies that has been suggested as a source of adding value and streamlining activities to maintain competitive advantage.

4.2 Definition

As mentioned in Chapter 2, outsourcing means contracting-out aspects of the work of the organisation, previously done in-house, to specialist providers.

4.3 Which activities can be outsourced?

In theory, any of the operations that a business performs which are not either in direct or strategic support of its business activity could justifiably be outsourced. Such operations and often termed **non-core activities** and may include:

- facilities management
- personnel management

- cleaning services
- printing services
- catering services
- property maintenance/management and
- legal services.

What about the finance function – isn't this a core activity?

The question of outsourcing is less clear cut in relation to the finance function than it might be for other support services, because the activities and outputs of the finance function serve multiple purposes for multiple uses.

The best indication of a core activity is whether it adds direct value to an organisation's products or services. For businesses that sell financial services (such as the administration of payroll services), it could be argued that the finance function is a core activity.

However, for the large majority of organisations, their financial services operations are largely 'non-core' and consequentially there remain potential benefits of some degree of outsourcing.

4.4 Benefits of outsourcing the finance function

Cost reduction

In a fiercely competitive business environment, businesses strive to deliver greater value at reduced cost. The cost of the finance function is one such cost. Outsourcing aspects of the finance function may, therefore, secure cost savings – since suppliers with a large customer base will be able to benefit from economies of scale.

Focus on core competencies to add value

In assigning responsibility for the provision of non-core services to a third party, businesses are afforded more opportunity to focus on the core competencies integral to the creating/addition of value.

Furthermore, by careful selection of an experienced supplier, it is possible that the non-core services supplied will be provided not only at a reduced cost, but also at a higher quality than could be provided in-house.

Illustration 1 – Outsourcing success at Microsoft

In 2006, Microsoft was achieving extraordinary growth by allowing a high degree of autonomy for its subsidiaries. However, autonomy also resulted in high fragmentation of the company's finance and accounting function. In 2007, Microsoft partnered with Accenture to standardise the processes globally with the aim of reducing costs, improving service and compliance and focusing on more strategic activities.

The Microsoft-Accenture relationship has since been lauded within the outsourcing community and has won a number of awards. Huge benefits have been enjoyed by Microsoft since the inception of this agreement, including:

- a 20% reduction in costs by streamlining, simplifying or automating processes

- increased transparency allowing Microsoft to see every $ spent and timely measures on performance.

4.5 What will the outsourced finance function look like?

Outsourcing the finance function will require different skills on the part of the remaining staff who have to manage the service provider.

There will be a shift in emphasis from providing those services to managing the relationship with the organisation that does. A robust service level agreement (SLA) regarding the level of service to be provided will be required.

However, outsourcing will free up time for the finance function to concentrate on value-adding activities. It should be seen as an opportunity.

4.6 What does internal outsourcing mean?

The term 'internal outsourcing' describes a situation whereby a (usually large, multinational) organisation, with processing centres in all or several of the countries in which it operates, chooses to consolidate these activities at one site, or **shared service centre** (SSC).

Internal outsourcing is sometimes viewed, and entered into, as a first step towards 'full' outsourcing. It allows the organisation to explore the potential benefits of consolidation of its activities, while maintaining full internal control thus minimising the risks associated with the assignment of control to an external party.

Test your understanding 1

What are the benefits and risks of establishing a shared service centre?

Tips on establishing a successful SSC

- A clear vision of how the shared service centre fits into the overall business model.

- Senior management commitment – senior management need a clear vision and strategy and to support the process.

- Integration with other change initiatives.

- Clear scope with delineation of responsibilities.

- Buy-in of operating units impacted by the change.

- Ensuring that the organisation that remains after service transfer is robust.

- Support from those who have implementation experience to help navigate through the challenges faced.

- A strong customer-focused culture.

- A commitment to continuous improvement.

5 Offshoring

The transformation of the finance function may see value being added through offshoring. High volume, low complexity tasks will be processed in a country with a significantly lower cost base. Cost reductions should arise and the organisation may gain access to new markets.

Illustration 2 – Offshoring success at GE Capital

GE Capital viewed offshoring as the cornerstone of a sweeping effort to transform the company's finance function. By thinking big they have offshored between 35 and 40% of their finance activities. These activities include not only typical accounts payable but also a full range of accounting and control functions, decision support and regulatory activities.

These changes have enabled GE Capital to cut labour costs in this area by 70%, increase productivity by 5% and improve their control and risk management.

Alternatives to offshoring

The risks associated with offshoring (as discussed in chapter 2, such as cultural differences, or failure to realise promised cost savings) have resulted in some organisations choosing to **retain the function in-house**. The business is kept closer to its customers, reducing supply chain complexity and risk and potentially allowing greater flexibility to changes in demand.

A middle ground between offshoring and retention is **near-shoring**. The organisation still moves its tasks overseas but to a neighbouring country. For example, for Western Europe this would be Eastern Europe and for the United States this would be Canada or Mexico. The cost base will be lower but geographical proximity and cultural similarities can create an easier working relationship.

6 Business Process Re-engineering

6.1 Introduction

Business process re-engineering (BPR) is the fundamental rethinking and radical redesign of business processes:

- to achieve dramatic improvements in performance

- to increase the ability of the organisation to meet the needs of its customers

- to challenge existing ways of doing business and eradicate inefficient processes

- to use technology innovatively to carry out business in totally new ways.

6.2 The main stages of BPR

(1) **Process identification**

Each task performed within the organisation or department being re-engineered is broken down into a series of processes. Each process is recorded and analysed to find out whether it is:

– Necessary

– Adding value

– Supporting another value adding process.

(2) **Process rationalisation**

Those processes which are not adding value, or which are not essential to supporting a value-adding process are discarded.

(3) Process redesign

The remaining processes are redesigned so that they work in the most efficient way possible. At this stage detailed operating procedures need to be produced for all processes that are to be performed manually.

(4) Process reassembly

The re-engineered processes are implemented, resulting in tasks, departments and an organisation that work in the most efficient manner.

Illustration 3 – BPR mortgage processing

BPR Example – Mortgage processing

- Prior to BPR: In one organisation it was found that the processing of a mortgage application involved eight different application form with 217 questions, 750 steps, four IT systems, five functional areas of business, and four interviews with the customer. The whole process culminated in a mortgage offer being offered, on average, some 30 days from form completion.

- Post BPR: The process involved one interview, completion of one application form, and resulted in an offer being made within 24 hours.

Advantages and disadvantages of BPR

Advantages of BPR

- It is useful in providing an organisation with cost advantages over competitors, and with improved customer service. Because significant, rather than incremental, changes in working practices are sought, an approach is encouraged which is more strategic than operational.

- It helps to reduce organisational complexity by focusing on core processes and driving out unnecessary or uneconomic activities.

- It offers an alternative perspective on formulating strategy based upon operating processes, rather than on products and markets.

- It helps to link together the functional areas of an organisation.

Disadvantages OF BPR

- It is often used as the pretext for staff reductions;

- It is viewed as a 'quick fix' to organisational problems – one-off cost savings;

- It delegates decision making to lower levels of management – may affect employee attitudes and behaviour;

- Senior management may lose commitment, once the programme has been implemented;

- It may destroy existing controls within the organisation – reduced internal controls, quality of staff and accounting procedures, combining procedures, reduced segregation of duties;

- It overlooks the impact on human resources – BPR is a very time-consuming exercise. Introduction of new processes will involve new patterns of work, break-up of traditional workgroups, redundancies, loss of staff goodwill;

- It increases stress on staff – reduction in staff numbers at middle and line management levels – overload the remaining staff, resulting in reduced effectiveness;

- BPR focuses too much on improving existing business rather than developing new and better lines of business.

7 Chapter summary

8 Practice Questions

Question 1 – OTQ

Which one of the following normally presents the biggest challenge in providing business support services, such as finance, in-house?

A   Ensuring contract compliance

B   Ensuring adherence to predetermined standards

C   Assembly and maintenance of suitably skilled staff

D   Cost of additional monitoring

Question 2 – OTQ

Which of the following are disadvantages of BPR? Select TWO only.

A   It may destroy existing controls within the organisation

B   It tends to result in only incremental improvements in performance

C   It increases organisational complexity

D   It is often viewed as a pretext for staff reductions

E   It does not make full use of technology

Question 3 – POOL Publishing (Case style)

Background

POOL Publishing is a publisher of books with a listing on the stock exchange of the country in which it is based. POOL has a large number of customers. Almost five years ago, it outsourced its accounting to an external service provider, ITW. The accounting system is fully computerised, and is a bespoke system developed several years ago for POOL, and updated occasionally since that time.

The service from ITW has operated fairly well until recently, but ITW now appears to have difficulty in dealing with the rapidly-growing accounting requirements of POOL, as its business has expanded.

A decision has therefore been taken that the contract with ITW will not be renewed when it expires in six months' time. The accounting work will be given to a different outsourcing firm.

Changeover to new outsourcing firm

As management accountant and internal auditor for POOL, you have been asked to plan the changeover from ITW to the new outsourcing firm. In addition, in accordance with the contractual agreement with ITW, you will be required to carry out an audit of the accounts system before the changeover occurs.

Task:

Describe the potential risks that need to be considered in the changeover from ITW to the new outsourcing firm, and recommend measures to limit those risks.

(20 minutes)

Test your understanding answers

Benefits of shared service centres

- Headcount reductions – the more routine/number crunching functions would benefit from economies of scale resulting in a reduction in the number of employees required.

- Reduction in premises and associated costs.

- Systems consolidation.

- Potential tax savings.

- Potentially favourable labour rates.

- Quality of service provision – almost all organisations operating a shared service centre for the provision of financial services report marked improvements in the quality of service delivered. The quality improvements arise from the change in the relationship between finance and other staff. In establishing a dedicated shared financial centre, the relationship adopts a more professional supplier/customer nature.

Risks of establishing a shared service centre

- Staff morale may reduce leading to staff turnover.

- How much will it cost to make staff redundant if necessary?

- Lack of systems integration across and organisation – what resources will be required to migrate diverse systems?

- Has the organisation got the resources to spread the major set up costs?

- Is outsourcing to a third party, which specialises in providing such services, a better option?

Question 1 – OTQ

The correct answer is C

The assembly and maintenance of suitably skilled staff is a challenge when providing business support services in house. Answers A, B and D are all challenges of outsourcing services.

Question 2 – OTQ

The correct answers are A and D

A and D are disadvantages of BPR. Answer B is false since BPR should result in dramatic improvements in performance. Answer C is incorrect since BPR should reduce organisational complexity. Answer E is also incorrect; technology will be used innovatively to carry out business processes.

Question 3 – POOL Publishing (Case style)

A significant risk in switching from one service provider for accounting services to another is the risk of loss or corruption to data during the change. ITW will be required to supply up-to-date and accurate files at the end of its contract, either to POOL or to the new service provider. During this handover process, records might be lost from files, or entire files might be corrupted. For example, ITW might hand over out-of-date files, missing some recent transactions. POOL needs to be able to check that all the information has been properly transferred.

One way of dealing with this problem might be to arrange for a short period during which both ITW and the new service provider are maintaining accounting records for POOL. An internal (or external) audit can then carry out a check on the files in the two systems, to ensure that they appear identical (e.g. with the same total number of records and same control totals).

There might be technological or software difficulties if the accounts are moved from ITW's computer system to the system of another provider, and there might be difficulties in getting the system to operate properly on the system of the new service provider. The solution to this problem is also to have a period of time during which the two systems are running in parallel, so that any technical problems can be identified and resolved.

There is also a risk of unauthorised retention of files. An individual within the ITW organisation might retain copies of the accounts files of POOL. This would create a risk of file data about customers getting into the possession of another organisation. Alternatively, the individual retaining the file copies might subsequently use the information they contain for fraudulent purposes. POOL needs to check, if possible, that there are no duplicate copies of files that have been retained within ITW without authorisation.

This risk is difficult to deal with. However, ITW should be asked to demonstrate that after the handover of the files, copies have not been retained in ITW's computer system. If ITW is an ethical organisation, it should be willing to comply with this request, and demonstrate that it no longer holds files for POOL.

There could be operational difficulties in changing from ITW to a new service provider, particularly if ITW is unwilling to be helpful. ITW might have no incentive to give assistance to another company that has taken their contract with POOL. Inevitably, operational problems will arise, and the new service provider might need to ask questions. Unless ITW is willing to provide assistance, operating difficulties might arise.

The efficiency and success of the change to the new service provider depends on the goodwill of ITW for a number of reasons, and POOL might wish to consider offering a bonus payment to ITW after the change has taken place, provided this has happened in a satisfactory way, and with the full co-operation and assistance of ITW's staff.

It has been assumed that the same system operated on behalf of POOL by ITW will be used by the new service provider. This is not necessarily the case, and it might be the intention of POOL to switch its accounting system to a different accounting system that is better able to handle the growing volume of transactions and data. If a new system is required, all the risks associated with new system design, development and implementation will arise.

The Purpose and Management of the Technology and Information Function

Chapter learning objectives

Lead	Component
C1. Demonstrate the purpose of the technology and information function and its relationship with other parts of the organisation.	(a) Demonstrate the value of information systems within organisations. (b) Demonstrate ways of organising and managing information systems in the context of the wider organisation.
C2. Explain how information systems support the organisation's strategies and operations.	(a) Explain the technical components and options for information technology system design. (b) Explain the role of emerging technologies, e.g. Big Data, digitisation and their uses.

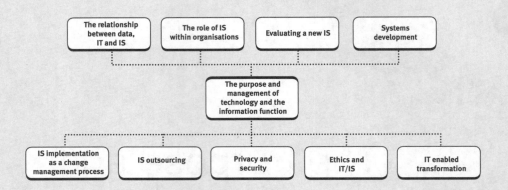

1 Introduction

The hunger for information has never been greater than for today's organisations, likewise the value of information systems that deliver this information has never been so keenly felt. It follows that information technology (IT) and information systems (IS) assume increasing managerial importance within the modern organisation.

2 The Relationship Between Data, Information Technology and Information Systems

Data are facts or figures in a raw, unprocessed format.

To become useful to a decision maker data must be transformed into information.

Information is data that has been processed in such a way that it has a meaning to the person who receives it, who may then use it to improve the quality of decision-making.

Converting data into information

The process of turning data into information may include the following stages:

(1) Data **collection**: raw data is collected from both the internal (within the organisation) and the external environment (outside of the organisation).

(2) Data **evaluation**: collected data is filtered for relevance.

(3) Data **analysis**: different dimensions of the data are analysed, e.g. comparison with budget, with the historical record, with industry best.

(4) Data **interpretation**: meaning added to the data.

(5) Data **reporting**: information is disseminated to users.

Characteristics of good information

The information produced by a system should have the following characteristics (identified by the acronym ACCURATE):

Accurate – sufficiently accurate to be relied upon.

Complete – managers should be given all the information they need, but information should not be excessive.

Cost effective – the value of information should exceed the cost of producing it.

Understandable – information needs to be clearly presented and displayed in an understandable form.

Relevant – the information should be relevant to its purpose.

Accessible – information should be accessible in an appropriate way, e.g. by email, verbally or by written report.

Timely – information should be provided in sufficient time for decisions to be made based upon that information.

Easy to use – the information should be clear and easy to use.

The value of information

- Collecting and processing information for use by managers has a cost.
- The value of the information to the business must be greater than the cost.

Value of information	Cost of information
Information may: • reduce unnecessary costs • eliminate losses • result in better marketing strategies • assist in attaining competitive advantage.	• Design and development costs, e.g. system design, testing, capital cost of equipment. • Running costs, e.g. staff salaries, security. • Storage costs, e.g. for hardware.

Levels of information

Decision making is an important aspect of any organisation.

Three levels of decision making are normally identified; strategic, tactical and operational. Each results in different information requirements.

Strategic decisions are long-term, complex decisions made by senior management. For example, a UK based supermarket chain may put a strategic plan in place outlining its aim to be the market leader. This plan is a long-term plan and the achievement of this aim will have far reaching implications for the whole organisation.

Tactical decisions are medium term, less complex decisions made by middle management. They follow on from strategic decisions. For example, in order to become the market leader the supermarket chain may have to launch new products/ services or open new branches.

Operational decisions are day-to-day decisions made by junior managers, e.g. the ordering of supplies to ensure the new product lines are stocked.

Within an organisation, management information requirements can be classified into three different levels:

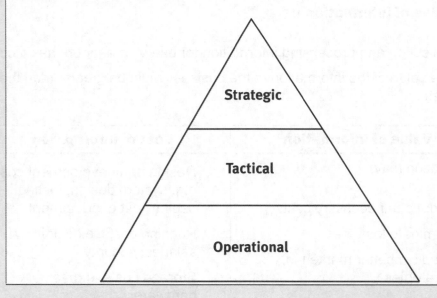

Strategic information is mainly used by directors and senior managers to choose between alternative courses of action, to plan the organisation's overall objectives and strategy and to measure whether these are being achieved. For example:

- profitability of main business segments
- prospects for present and potential markets.

Tactical information is used by managers at all levels, but mainly at the middle level for tactical planning and management control activities, such as pricing, purchasing, distribution and stocking. For example:

- sales analysis
- stock levels
- productivity measures.

Operational information is used mainly by managers on the operational level such as foremen and section heads who have to ensure that routine tasks are properly planned and controlled. For example:

- listings of debtors and creditors
- payroll details
- raw materials requirements and usage.

Information systems (IS) refer to the provision and management of information to support the running of the organisation.

Information technology (IT) is the supporting equipment (hardware) that provides the infrastructure to run the information systems.

Within a **factory** setting complex problems have been solved through the use of IS, for example:

- Computer aided design (CAD)
- Computer aided manufacturing (CAM).

CAD and CAM have resulted in innovative solutions to product design and can lead to the use of robots and computerised inventory management.

In the **office**, automation has been brought about by technology such as:

- Electronic data interchange (EDI) – replacing traditional paper based documents; it allows the computer-to-computer transmission of data contained in standard business documents such as customer invoices and purchase orders.
- The Internet
- Email
- Video and teleconferencing.

3 The Role of Information Systems within Organisations

An organisation's information systems serve two important purposes:

- processing, storing and reporting **day to day transactions**.
- supporting **managerial activities**, such as decision making, planning and control.

Test your understanding 1

Active First has grown rapidly over the past three years by acquiring a number of smaller gyms and health clubs. This strategy resulted in the organisation inheriting many different systems and it is now considering replacing these systems with a fully integrated, state of the art, organisation wide system.

Required:

Briefly describe the benefits to Active First of the implementation of the new system.

Role of IS within modern organisations

Information systems play a vital role in modern day organisations at a number of levels, for example:

- improving operations and manufacturing
- contributing to enhanced products and services
- offering the opportunity for cost reduction
- improving communication
- allowing managers to make better informed decisions.

4 Evaluating a New Information System

4.1 Introduction

When an organisation sees a possibility for introducing a new IS, an evaluation of the new system should be made to decide whether the potential benefits are sufficient to justify the costs.

 Cost-benefit analysis (CBA) can be used to assess the expected costs and benefits of the IS.

The benefits of the new IS should be greater than its cost. If this is the case, the new IS is worth implementing.

4.2 Costs of a new system

Initial costs	Running costs
• Costs to design and develop system if software is bespoke.	• Cost of labour time to run the system.
• Purchase price of software if it is not bespoke.	• Cost of materials, e.g. replacement parts.
• Purchase cost of new hardware.	• Cost of service support, e.g. IT helpdesk.
• Cost of testing and implementation of the new system.	
• Training costs.	

4.3 Benefits and drawbacks of a new IS

These may be more difficult to quantify in monetary terms but could include:

- Enhanced efficiency and capacity – e.g. resulting in labour savings.
- Better quality of information – information may be more 'ACCURATE'.
- Better access to information – e.g. by means of an Intranet.
- Improved sharing of information – e.g. through the creation of a database.
- Improved communication – e.g. through the introduction of an email system.
- Better decision making and customer service.

The IS could be a source of competitive advantage but it is not without its drawbacks.

Test your understanding 2

Discuss the potential disadvantages of a new IS.

Cost-benefit analysis

A sales director is deciding whether to implement a new computer-based sales system. His department has only a few computers, and his sales people are not computer literate. He is aware that computerised sales forces are able to contact more customers and give a higher quality of service to those customers. They are more able to meet commitments, and can work more efficiently with production and delivery staff.

His financial cost/benefit analysis is shown below:

Costs

New computer equipment:

- 10 network-ready PCs with supporting software @ $2,000 each
- 1 server @ $3,000
- 3 printers @ $1,000 each
- Cabling & Installation @ $4,000
- Sales Support Software @ $10,000

Training costs:

- Computer introduction – 8 people @ $300 each
- Keyboard skills – 8 people @ $300 each
- Sales Support System – 12 people @ $500 each

Other costs:

- Lost time: 40 man days @ $150/day
- Lost sales through disruption: estimate: $10,000
- Lost sales through inefficiency during first months: estimate: $10,000

Total cost: $76,800

Benefits

- Tripling of mail shot capacity: estimate: $30,000/year

- Ability to sustain telesales campaigns: estimate: $15,000/year

- Improved efficiency and reliability of follow-up: estimate: $30,000/year

- Improved customer service and retention: estimate: $20,000/year

- Improved accuracy of customer information: estimate: $5,000/year

- More ability to manage sales effort: $20,000/year

Total Benefit: $120,000/year

5 Systems Development

5.1 The systems development life cycle

Systems development follows a cycle called the systems development life cycle (SDLC). This is characterised by a number of stages:

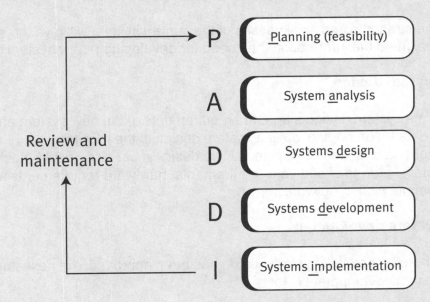

171

Planning

Planning should begin by establishing the objectives of the new system, and evaluating its expected benefits and costs. Within a formal reporting system, this stage of planning might take the form of a feasibility study and a feasibility report.

It will be necessary to prepare an outline design of the planned new system at this stage.

The planning stage ends when a decision is made to go ahead to a more detailed analysis of the new system requirements.

System analysis

System analysis is the first stage in the design or selection of the new system. It should begin with a detailed analysis of the current system in order to establish how the system operates, and:

- how the current system meets the users' needs, but
- how the current system fails to meet the users' needs.

The strengths and weaknesses of the current system will give the system designers the information they need for developing a new system design.

System design

In the system design stage, the requirements of the new system are set out in detail. The original outline system design in the feasibility study and report might be changed at this stage. The design must also go into much greater detail, in terms of software requirements, hardware requirements and communication networks.

System development

When the detailed system design has been approved, the next stage in the system development is to:

- write the software, and
- acquire the hardware and network links.

The overall software system will consist of many different programs, and during this implementation stage the programmers will test each program independently to ensure that it appears to perform the tasks required of it.

System implementation

When the system has been developed, it can be implemented. Before implementation, however, there should be testing to make sure that the system operates properly and that there are no design faults or software errors. Systems testing should reveal any errors that exist whereby the output from one program cannot be read or processed by another program. In other words, the system as a whole should be tested, not just the individual programs independently.

The users' files must be converted to the format required for the new system. The user might also wish to carry out additional user tests prior to the system 'going live'. After testing, the new system is implemented and becomes operational

Review and maintenance

Although not included in the PADDI list, review and maintenance are critical processes.

After implementation, the system should be reviewed and maintained.

- A review is required to ensure that the system has achieved the expected benefits.

- Maintenance is required because errors might be discovered in the software after the system has become operational, and the errors should be corrected by writing the amendments and producing a new version of the software. The user's requirements might also change, and new software can be written to meet them.

Implementation and system **maintenance** will be explored in more detail below.

5.2 Systems implementation

Introduction

Systems implementation involves a number of activities that take the new system and brings it into full-scale use. These activities include **testing** and **changeover**.

Testing

A critical activity prior to changeover is testing the new system to ensure that it is working correctly before going live. Ultimate users should be involved in conducting tests.

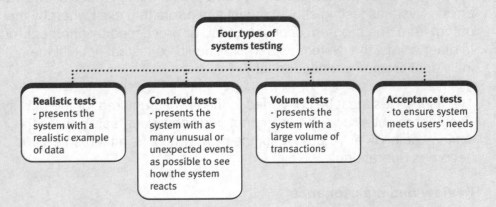

System changeover

System changeover is the change from operating the current system to introducing the new system operationally.

There are four approaches to system changeover, and the most appropriate approach will vary according to circumstances.

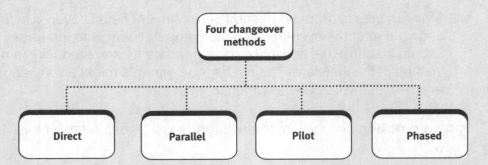

Direct

- The computer user ceases to operate the old system and switches completely to using the new system.

- Appropriate when:
  - The new system has been used elsewhere (for example, an off-the-shelf package) and there is confidence that it will function properly.
  - The problems for the computer user will be tolerable, even if the system fails to function properly.

Parallel

- The old system and the new system are both operated together for a while. If the new system performs to an acceptable level, a decision can be taken to stop operating the old system, and change entirely to the new system.

- Appropriate when:
  - The new system is critical to the business and problems can't be tolerated.
  - The new system has not been used elsewhere, thus implementation is high risk.

Pilot

This can be implemented in two ways:

- A retrospective data pilot operates the new system with old data. The results can be cross-checked to the existing system.

- A restrictive data pilot takes one whole part of the complete system and runs it as the new system. If this operates correctly then the remaining elements can be transferred gradually.

Phased

- Involves gradual implementation for example:
  - of one sub-system such as the sales system or purchasing system at a time
  - by implementing a complete system but in one geographical location at a time.

- Appropriate when the system can be implemented in distinct parts.

5.3 System maintenance

System **maintenance** is the repair, correction or further enhancement of systems once it is in operation and can take several forms:

- **Corrective maintenance** – This relates to the need to correct technical difficulties that have arisen in the operation of the system. These include virus infection, hardware failure and file corruption as well as delaying response times due to systems overload.

- **Adaptive maintenance** – This relates to the need to make changes to the system in order to reflect the changing needs of the organisation over time. Such changes are inevitable given the changing nature of the business environment. Major changes will eventually lead to the need to replace the system entirely.

- **Perfective (preventative) maintenance** – This relates to general upgrades to both hardware and software in order to maximise the overall speed and functionality of the system, e.g. installing the latest version of an application. These improvements should prevent possible failures in the future.

6 IS Implementation as a Change Management Process

6.1 Reasons for project failure

There are a number of reasons for project failure. These include:

- **Insufficient user involvement** – the risk of project failure is increased if users are not involved in the implementation. New systems will bring about change, and users reject the system simply because they don't like the change, or the changes have resulted in loss of status or control. Insufficient user involvement is the major cause for failure.

- **Lack of management support** – little commitment to implementation or poor problem solving.

- **Project is too complex** for the organisation to manage.

- **Poor planning** and scheduling.

- **Unrealistic deadlines** being set.

- **Poor monitoring and control**.

- IT staff may have the technical skills but **may not have the management skills** required.

- **Insufficient training** for users.

Test your understanding 3
Identify **three** reasons why user involvement is so important when implementing a new system.

Test your understanding 4
Identify potential problems that might arise if there is inadequate or inappropriate user training following the introduction of a new system.

The 3Cs

Three broad conditions are necessary to implement IT successfully – commitment, coordination and communication.

Commitment

- It is important to get all users that are involved or affected by a project to become committed. The resources of the users will be necessary in the planning, development, testing and implementation stages of any IS project. Gaining their dedication and joint ownership of the project ensures that they are equally responsible for its eventual success or failure.

- Commitment must exist from top management and across all management levels. Commitment from senior management is shown by the allocation of resources in terms of people, money, time, information and technology.

Coordination

- A disorganised project will take considerably longer to achieve success, and normally at a greater cost than an organised one will. This increases the likelihood that such a project will never be completed.

- A disorganised project will have constantly moving targets, which are seldom attained.

- Coordination through planning and control of all the relevant factors will help to ensure that the right people are doing the right things in the right way, using the right resources at the right time.

Communication

- Through good relationships and communication with all interested parties, obstacles within, among and between them can be avoided in the planning and implementation of an information system.

- All stakeholders need to be kept informed and be encouraged to become actively involved throughout the whole process.

- IS projects often suffer severe communication chain problems between the various people involved. The chain is only as strong as its weakest link.

6.2 Overcoming user resistance

Kotter, Schlesinger and **Sache** identified six main methods of dealing with resistance:

Method	Advantages	Disadvantages
Education and communication	• Communication about the benefits of change should result in employees accepting the change.	• Time consuming. • Employees may not agree with benefits. • Usually used to reinforce another approach.
Participation	• Employees are more likely to support the change as they 'own' the change. • Utilises employee expertise.	• Time consuming. • Requires a strong relationship between management and the workforce.
Facilitation and support	• Techniques, such as counselling, will help employees overcome their fears and anxieties about change.	• Can't always address the reason for resistance, e.g. change may threaten job security.
Negotiation	• Conflict dealt with in an orderly fashion, preventing problems such as industrial action. • Since employees agree on the outcome it should encourage commitment and preserve morale.	• Time consuming. • Not always possible to reach a compromise.

| Manipulation and co-optation (involves presentation of misleading information or buying off key individuals by giving them positions of authority). | • Quick
• Relatively inexpensive | • May lead to future problems if individuals realise that they have been manipulated.
• May raise legal/ethical problems. |
| Power/coercion (compulsory approach by management to implement the change). | • Speed
• Managers can implement required changes. | • Poor commitment.
• Results in weak motivation
• When employees enjoy a stronger position in the future, e.g. union representation, they are less likely to co-operate
• May raise legal/ethical problems. |

- The most appropriate approach will be dependent on the goals of the change programme and the likely reactions of the people involved.

- One of the problems of choosing the 'right' approach is that people will not always openly admit the real reasons for opposing change, e.g. the reason may be related to self-interest but is disguised as a 'technical objection'.

- In reality, managers may find it effective to use a **combination of the approaches**.

Test your understanding 5

If a manager discovers that there are instances of non-usage of a new system how might this be interpreted?

Lewin's Force Field Analysis

Lewin developed a technique for visualising the change process called force field analysis.

Force field analysis maps out the driving forces that are pushing towards a preferred state (i.e. the implementation of the new system) and the restraining forces, which are pushing back to the current state (i.e. continuing to use the old system).

Restraining forces

The first step of any successful change process is to identify the restraining forces and overcome them:

Potential restraining force	Potential method for removing restraining force
Fear of loss of control	Education, participation
Fear that there will not be enough time for training or to attend meetings or that the new system will be too difficult to use	Give employees the time required for training/meetings and to learn the skills required
Doubt that the initiative will be properly implemented	Participation in the change process, education about benefits
Anxiety about job security	Reassure employees about job security
Employees don't feel the change is needed	Education regarding the benefits of change

Driving forces

Once the restraining forces have been addressed, the second step of the change process is to implement the new system. There may be a number of driving forces for this change:

- Management believe that the system will improve organisational performance.
- Competitors have implemented a new system and achieved significant improvements in productivity, quality and financial returns.
- Improved information.
- Difficult to maintain the current system.
- Reduced running costs.
- Fresh challenge in job.

These forces may be enough to drive the positive change. However, action can be taken to increase the strength of the driving forces, e.g. by providing exact figures regarding the increase in financial returns that could be enjoyed, and to introduce further driving forces, e.g. small rewards may be offered to staff who participate in the implementation of the new system.

Once the new system has been implemented, the final step of the change process is to reinforce the new behaviour. This may involve praising and rewarding those employees who embrace the new system.

7 IS Outsourcing

7.1 Introduction

IS outsourcing involves purchasing from outside the organisation the IS services required to perform business functions.

The scope of IS outsourcing can range from single system development to complete outsourcing of IT capability, i.e. systems development, maintenance, operations and training.

An organisation that has decided to outsource its IS function will need to address the following issues:

- **Communication with the workforce** – staff must understand the rationale for the decision and be aware of the timescale. Appropriate support should be offered if any redundancies/redeployment is anticipated.

- **Invitation to tender** – reputable contractors should be invited to tender for the work.

- **Choice of contractor** – the most appropriate contractor should be chosen based on robust criteria. A service level agreement (SLA) should be drawn up.

- **Establishment of relationships** – a strong client-contractor relationship should be established, e.g. through the use of an in house client contract manager.

- **Handover** – this may be done in a phased or direct manner.

- **Monitoring cost** – the budget needs to be carefully controlled and any additional costs accounted for.

- **Monitoring of standards** – the terms of the contract should be adhered to and user satisfaction should be evaluated. Any necessary steps should be taken to identify problems identified.

Illustration 1

In 2008, Shell agreed a $4 billion IS outsourcing deal with three companies; AT&T, EDS and T-systems. In a bid to minimise redundancies for its 3,000 IT staff, Shell negotiated that almost 99% of their staff would be transferred to the three companies.

7.2 Advantages and disadvantages of IS outsourcing

Test your understanding 6

Many organisations are taking the decision to outsource their non-core activities, such as IT. Identify the advantages and disadvantages of IT outsourcing.

Illustration 2 – Risks of outsourcing

Suppose that a regional hospital authority agrees a contract with a software company. The software company agrees to develop a new system that the hospital will use for maintaining patient records, communicating with patients at home, scheduling operations and charging the patients for services that are not free. After the system has been implemented, the software company will operate the system itself for a contract period of five years, and the hospital staff will only be involved with the system to the extent of providing the software company with the data for input.

The risks of the outsourcing agreement for the development and operation of this system include:

- The system might be imperfectly specified when system development work begins. If the hospital authority subsequently changes the specification, the software house might be able to increase its fee substantially.

- Since the software company will operate the system, it could be difficult for the staff of the hospital authority to test it.

- The software company will wish to make a profit from the contract, and will be reluctant to agree to changes, and might even argue against maintenance, unless it is paid for as an 'extra' cost.

- Once the system becomes operational, the hospital authority might have very little control over the communications between the software company's staff and the general public (the patients or 'customers').

- If the system creates bad publicity, due to errors in the system relating to scheduling of operations or invoicing, the hospital authority will have no control over the damage to its reputation.

- What happens at the end of five years? Will the hospital authority be forced to renew the contract with the software house because no one else understands the system? Alternatively, will the authority be obliged to abandon the system and buy a new system to replace it?

7.3 Managing the relationship

The use of contracted expertise raises the issue of establishing and maintaining strong client-vendor relationships.

When choosing a vendor, careful evaluation and selection processes should be followed, for example:

- background checks of vendor financial performance
- references
- litigation history.

Vendors should be chosen in accordance with pre-determined selection criteria. Relationships should be built on trust and mutual respect and so it would be helpful to:

- set out the terms and conditions of the outsourcing arrangement in a service level agreement (SLA).

- ensure the vendor understands, and will comply with, organisational ethical practices.

- ensure easy contact with the vendor by establishing relationships at various levels, e.g. key account managers, operators, executives.

- put in place mechanisms to periodically review and evaluate customer satisfaction and agree remedial action if necessary.

8 Privacy and Security

8.1 Controls

There are two forms of IT/IS controls that exist to safeguard the privacy and security of data as well as ensuring complete and accurate processing of data:

General controls – ensure that the organisation has overall control over its information systems, e.g.:

- Personnel controls – includes segregation of duties, policy on usage, hierarchy of access.

- Access controls – such as passwords and time lock-outs.

- Computer equipment controls – to protect equipment from destruction, damage or theft.

- Business continuity planning – a risk assessment to decide which systems are critical to the business continuing its activities.

Application or program controls – performed automatically by the system and include:

- Completeness checks to ensure all data is processed.

- Validity checks to ensure only valid data is input/processed.

- Identification and authorisation checks to ensure users are identified and authorised.

- Problem management facilities to ensure problems are recorded/managed on a timely basis.

Test your understanding 7

Data integrity and security is a particular issue in a database. For data to have integrity, it must be accurate, consistent and free from accidental corruption.

Required:

What controls are required in a database to ensure that data integrity and security are maintained?

8.2 Privacy and security risks

Potential threat	Solution
Natural disasters – e.g. fire, flood.	• Fire procedures – fire alarms, extinguishers, fire doors, staff training and insurance cover. • Location, e.g. not in a basement area liable to flooding. • Physical environment – e.g. air conditioning, dust controls. • Back up procedures – data should be backed up on a regular basis to allow recovery.
Malfunction – of computer hardware or software.	• Network design – to cope with periods of high volumes. • Back up procedures (as above).
Viruses – a small program that once introduced into the system spreads extensively. Can affect the whole computer system.	• Virus software – should be run and updated regularly to prevent corruption of the system by viruses. • Formal security policy and procedures. • Regular audits to check for unauthorised software.
Hackers – deliberate access to systems by unauthorised persons.	• Firewall software – should provide protection from unauthorised access to the system from the Internet. • Passwords and user names – limit unauthorised access to the system.
Electronic eavesdropping – e.g. users accessing private information not intended for them.	• Data encryption – data is scrambled prior to transmission and is recovered in a readable format once transmission is complete. • Passwords and user names (as above),

Human errors – unintentional errors from using computers and networks.	Training – adequate staff training and operating procedures.
Human resource risk – e.g. repetitive strain injury (RSI), headaches and eye strain from computer screens, tripping over loose wires.	• Ergonomic design of workstations should reduce problems such as RSI. • Anti-glare screens reduce eye strain. • Cables should be in ducts.

9 Ethics and IT/IS

As with other areas of an organisation, there are ethical issues connected with IT/IS that need monitoring and, at time, intervention. These include the following:

Data protection

- It is a major embarrassment to firms if confidential customer information is leaked or stolen.

- The UK Data Protection Act (DPA) provides a framework to ensure that information is handled properly and gives individuals the right to know what information is held about them.

Incorrect use of systems

Most firms have "acceptable use" policies (with accompanying disciplinary procedures) concerning employees using company equipment for non-business and other undesirable uses such as :

- Downloading improper materials – i.e. fraudulent, harassing, sexually explicit, profane, obscene or illegal

- Misusing the systems – e.g. visiting chat rooms, online gambling, Internet auction sites, playing computer games, or performing any type of hacking-related activity.

- Violating copyright laws.

10 IT Enabled Transformation

10.1 Introduction

IT has enabled, and continues to enable complete organisational transformation. Organisational restructuring might accompany IT changes to take full advantage of technology.

Two significant changes include:

- An increase in remote working and hot desking.
- The emergence of virtual organisations and virtual teams.

10.2 Remote working

IT developments, such as email and the internet, have enabled employees to work away from the office (for example, at home). Remote working is sometimes called teleworking or homeworking.

Impact of remote working on the organisation

The **advantages** of remote working include:

- Increased employee motivation and productivity.
- Increased commitment to the organisation.
- Attracting individuals because of the availability of such conditions.
- Reduced absenteeism and staff turnover.

The **disadvantages** of remote working include:

- Difficulties in co-ordinating staff.
- Loss of control of staff.
- Dilution of organisational culture.
- Less commitment to the organisation.
- Extra labour costs, e.g. providing employees with equipment.

Impact of remote working on the employee

Remote working can have both benefits and drawbacks for the employee.

Test your understanding 8

Consider your own employment. Would you like or dislike working from home? Discuss the reason for your opinion on this issue.

10.3 Hot desking

A closely related concept is **hot desking**. This is the practice of not giving employees their own desk in the office. Instead, the organisation provides a pool of fully equipped desks which are occupied as required. This has been driven by:

- technology advances meaning that information can be accessed through any computer

- an increase in remote working meaning that not every member of staff will require a permanent desk.

10.4 Virtual companies and virtual teams

Virtual companies

A **virtual company** is an organisation that uses computer and telecommunications technologies to extend its capabilities by working routinely with employees or contractors located throughout the country or the world. Using e-mail, faxes, instant messaging, data and videoconferencing, it implies a high degree of working away from the office as well as using remote facilities.

Illustration 3 – Examples of virtual companies

- **Amazon** – a virtual business pioneer.

- **Wordpress** – a service that powers over 30 million blogs.

- **IBM and Apple** – although they are usually competitors, IBM and Apple teamed up with Motorola to develop a virtual company to develop an operating system and microprocessor for a new generation of computers.

- **Not on the High Street** is an internet based business selling luxury homeware, clothing and gifts. It has enjoyed rapid growth and success since it was launched in 2006. The founders work with over 900 small British businesses. These businesses design, produce and deliver the products to customers. This enables Not on the High Street to sell a unique range of products to fulfil the needs of the demanding modern customer and to keep costs low.

Characteristics of a virtual company include:

- A virtual company is a business that **operates with very little physical presence**. The most extreme type of virtual company is one with only 'virtual employees' and no central office. Everyone works from home, including top management.

- Virtual companies **use IT**, e.g. the internet, email, faxes, videoconferencing and instant messaging, to enable the company to work with employees or contractors located throughout the country or the world.

- Virtual companies enable executives, scientists, writers, researchers and other professionals to **collaborate** on new products and services without ever meeting face to face.

- The important issue is that these organisations **feel 'real' to the client**, and meet their needs at least as adequately as the more 'traditional' organisations.

- A virtual company will **outsource most or all of its functions**.

Illustration 4

A firm manufactures wedding dresses. It could outsource:

- the design to a wedding dress designer

- marketing to a specialist marketing firm

- manufacture to a sub-contractor

- delivery to a specialist logistics firm

- collection of money from customers to a specialist debt collection company

- tax returns and accounts to a specialist accountancy firm.

It is important to understand that the formation of a virtual company can bring about a number of **benefits** but is not without its **drawbacks**.

Test your understanding 9

Discuss the benefits and drawbacks of adopting a virtual company strategy.

Drawbacks of virtual companies

- It may be difficult to negotiate a revenue sharing agreement between the different partners.

- Loss of control may result in a fall in quality.

- The partners may also work for competitors thus reducing any competitive advantage.

Virtual teams

A **virtual team** is a group of people who interact through independent tasks guided by a common purpose and work across space, time and organisational boundaries with links strengthened by IT.

They are essentially teams of people who are not present in the same office or organisation.

IT/IS has enabled the formation of virtual teams:

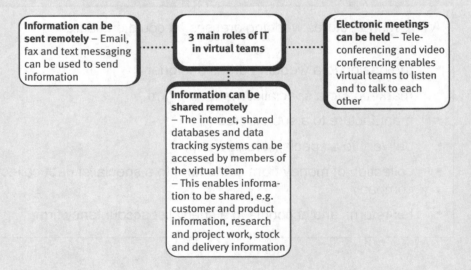

The following **challenges** face virtual teams:

- **Forming a team** – it may be difficult to establish a cohesive and trusting team.

- **Knowledge sharing** – may prove more difficult due to the absence of face to face contact.

- **Processes and goals** – it may be more difficult to establish clear decision making processes and goals.

- **Leadership** – this may be more difficult since employees will be working at different times, in different locations and in different ways.

- **Cultural differences** – team members will be from different backgrounds and cultural differences may make working together more difficult.

- **Morale** – some team members may find this way of working isolating.

Test your understanding 10

Identify the ways in which the challenges faced by virtual teams can be overcome.

Skyrme and Meall's work on virtual teams

Skyrme (1997) proposes certain principles for creating and maintaining innovative virtual teams. Some of the main principles are:

- high levels of trust

- being mutually supportive

- giving as much as you get, in terms of support, transfer of information and knowledge

- teams that are small and multi-disciplinary

- every worker should belong to at least two teams

- every team must have a sense of purpose

- frequent communication

- accept that decision-making will often be ambiguous

- use one email per topic, especially when multiple recipients are involved

- if face-to-face conversations take place summarise the meeting by email

- emails are conversations, so insert a level of informality.

The piecemeal harnessing of new IS by organisations of all shapes and sizes has, however, left many with a mixture of disparate and disconnected systems that do little to improve their efficiency or effectiveness. **Meall** (2004) reports that the accounting profession has been particularly hard hit, and the growing burden of bureaucracy threatens many.

11 Chapter Summary

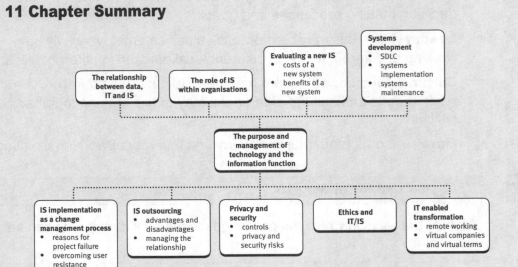

12 Practice Questions

Question 1 – OTQ

A working definition of information would be:

A   facts you can work with

B   facts

C   facts useful to the production manager

D   facts useful to the decision maker

Question 2 – OTQ

Electronic data interchange (EDI) is:

A   the provision of management information to support the running of an organisation

B   a changeover method used to electronically transfer data from the old to the new system

C   the supporting system that provides the infrastructure to run the information systems

D   the computer-to-computer transmission of data contained in standard business documents

Question 3 – OTQ

Outsourcing can lead to:

A   reliance on a third party solicitor

B   increased reliance on internal departments

C   increasing staff numbers

D   retaining managers to monitor the contract

Question 4 – OTQ

Which of the following are advantages of a parallel changeover method? Select TWO only.

A   Reduces changeover risk when the system has not been used elsewhere

B   Is the quickest changeover method

C   Reduces the risk associated with changeover when the system is a business critical system

D   Is appropriate for gradual implementation of one sub-system at a time

E   Tends to be the cheapest changeover method

F   Is useful for implementing the system in one geographical location at a time

Question 5 – OTQ

Which one of the following is an example of a program control?

A   Business continuity planning

B   Validity checks

C   Access controls

D   Personnel controls

Question 6 – Changeover methods (Case style)

Background

A manufacturing company has decided to replace its inventory control system. The current system was implemented 10 years ago but has restricted reporting facilities and a text-based interface. It is to be replaced with a Windows-based package which undertakes the same basic functions, but is easier to use, has flexible reporting facilities and interfaces easily with other Windows-based software. Both systems run on the same hardware.

Changeover methods

The manager of the project is now considering the details of implementation. He has been advised that he should consider both 'parallel running' and 'direct changeover/direct conversion'.

Tasks:

(a) Briefly explain what the terms 'parallel running' and 'direct changeover' mean.

(8 minutes)

(b) Briefly describe THREE advantages of 'direct changeover' over 'parallel running'.

(9 minutes)

(c) Identify the main risk of direct changeover and suggest how this risk might be reduced for the manufacturing company's inventory control system implementation.

(8 minutes)

(Total: 25 minutes)

Question 7 – DS (Case style)

Background

The directors of DS are not satisfied with the GDC facilities management company, which was contracted two years ago to run the IT systems of the company. At that time, the existing in-house IT development and support department was disbanded and all control of IT systems handed over to GDC. The appointment of GDC was relatively rushed and, although an outline contract was agreed, no detailed service level agreement was produced.

Outsourcing issues

Over the last few weeks, the number of complaints received from staff regarding the service has been increasing and the provision of essential management reports has not been particularly timely.

A recent exchange of correspondence with GDC failed to resolve the matter. Staff at GDC recognised the fall in standards of service, but insisted that it had met its contractual obligations. DS's lawyers have confirmed that GDC is correct.

Key features of DS's contract with GDC facilities management company

- The contract can be terminated by either party with three months' notice.
- GDC will provide IT services for DS, the service to include:
    - Purchase of all hardware and software
    - Repair and maintenance of all IT equipment
    - Help desk and other support services for users
    - Writing and maintenance of in-house software
    - Provision of management information
    - Price charged to be renegotiated each year but any increase must not exceed inflation, plus 10%

Tasks:

(a) Explain, from the point of view of DS, why it might have received poor service from GDC, even though GDC has met the requirements of the contract.

(15 minutes)

(b) Explain the courses of action now available to DS relating to the provision of IT services. Comment on the problems involved in each course of action.

(10 minutes)

(Total: 25 minutes)

Test your understanding answers

Test your understanding 1

- **Reduced duplication** of data and activities.
- **Improved system quality** of the new state of the art system.
- **Reduced costs** in the long term due to simplification of operation.
- **Improved accuracy** due to the use of just one data system.
- **Better control** because managers have all the information in one system.
- **Improved reporting and decision making** due to the speed and accuracy of the new system.
- Potential source of **competitive advantage** over rivals.
- Potential **improvement in security**.

Test your understanding 2

- Security problems, e.g. risk of unauthorised access or fraud.
- Failure of the system to meet its objectives.
- Redundant data, i.e. the system might produce a large amount of data which no one uses.
- Maintenance problems – maintenance may prove to be more difficult or more expensive than expected.

Test your understanding 3

User involvement:

- Ensures system meets requirements.
- Reduces resistance.
- Incorporates knowledge and expertise into the system.

Test your understanding 4

- Fear of the new system's effect on jobs.
- Fear of the unknown.
- Reluctance to use the new system.
- Errors in processing.
- Slower processing due to, say, lack of confidence or unfamiliarity.
- Staff turnover or absence arising from avoidance of the new system.

Test your understanding 5

Non-usage may be due to:

- An expression of resistance. In this case, appropriate influencing measures should be applied.
- A lack of confidence in the new system, in which case enhanced communication is required and system modification should be applied where appropriate.
- A lack of confidence in their own abilities to cope with the new system. In this case, training and other support mechanisms should be employed.

Test your understanding 6

Advantages

- Cost reduction: e.g. due to economies of scale since equipment is bought in bulk.
- Improved performance: management can concentrate on core competencies and suppliers used will be IT experts.
- Avoids problem of shortage of IT experts.
- Organisation can keep up with technological change.
- Cost control: creating a formal relationship tends to concentrate the focus on cost control which is sometimes lost when functions are performed internally.
- Flexibility to increase or decrease IT capacity.
- Time to market: outsourcing can accelerate the development and implementation of new IS.

Disadvantages

- Dependent on supplier – the supplier may not understand the business process and the organisation may lose control over its IS.

- Loss of confidentiality (outsourcing company may work for competitors).

- Locked into contract.

- Lose expertise.

- Loss of competitive advantage since the outsourcing company may work for competitors.

- Costs may be high, e.g. if the vendor keeps charging for updating the technology.

Test your understanding 7

- Control of access to workstations.

- User identification required for access by individual passwords.

- Users only see the icons for the functions where they have access rights.

- Restrictions on access to certain aspects of the database, e.g. using passwords.

- Users only to have access to those aspects that they need to do their job.

- Restrictions on use of functions or programs, e.g. writing off debts as bad debts.

- Transaction logs maintained automatically for checking and for back-up purposes.

Test your understanding 8

Advantages

- Reduced travel time and hence cost savings.

- Reduction is stress due to the removal of the daily commute and the removal of the distractions of a busy office.

- Better work/life balance due to the removal of the daily commute and potential opportunities to work more flexible hours than the traditional '9 to 5'.

- Control – employees may feel an improved sense of control if they have more flexibility to decide their working patterns and hours.

- Employment opportunities for disadvantaged individuals, e.g. disabled people may now find it possible to work due to the removal of travel and the office environment.

Disadvantages

- May not suit those with poor personal motivation or who are not self starters.

- May be distracted at home, e.g. by family members.

- Loss of learning/sharing of ideas from face to face contact.

- Loss of social interaction and stimulation.

- Difficultly in separating home and work life – an inability to 'switch off' from work may lead to 'burn out' or damaged personal relationships.

Test your understanding 9

Benefits

- **Can exploit opportunities** – a business may not have the time or resources to develop the manufacturing and distribution infrastructure, people competencies and information technology required to exploit new opportunities. Only by forming a virtual company, of all-star partners, can it assemble the components it needs to provide a world-class solution for customers and capture the market opportunity.

- **Look bigger than they are** – virtual companies can be made to look much bigger than they actually are, enabling them to compete with large and successful organisations and to win large and lucrative contracts.

- **Flexibility** – teams of experts can be formed to meet the specific needs of a project. This team can then be dissolved and a new team formed for the next project. The performance of each project team should be much better than those of non-virtual competitors.

- **Lower costs** – one of the main aims of virtual companies is to reduce costs. Investment in assets, e.g. land and buildings, is minimal. This should help to drive competitive advantage.

Drawbacks

- It may be difficult to negotiate a revenue sharing agreement between the different partners.

- Loss of control may result in a number of issues such as a fall in quality, use of unethical suppliers or a lack of adherence to prescribed legislation.

- The partners may also work for competitors thus reducing any competitive advantage.

Test your understanding 10

The challenges faced by virtual teams can be overcome by:

- training in technology and teamwork

- spending time getting to know each other, e.g. team identity, jokes, occasional face to face meetings, team trips out

- clear roles and responsibilities

- detailed and timely feedback between the leader and team members

- regular and predictable communication matters. The benefits should be maximised, e.g. the use of email, video conferencing, social networking sites and blogs could all assist in overcoming some of the challenges. Time zone differences may mean that managers and employees may have to accept that response times may not be immediate

- paying attention to cultural differences. This may require training in cross-cultural appreciation

- choosing dependable and self-reliant employees but managers should still be on hand to offer support

- valued staff should be made to feel wanted and a sense of loyalty to the firm instilled

- managers may need to view their role differently, the emphasis being on co-ordination rather than leadership

- clear communication from managers of information coming from higher up in the organisation to ensure that employees are fully informed and share the organisation's vision.

Question 1 – OTQ

The correct answer is D

Question 2 – OTQ

The correct answer is D

By definition

Question 3 – OTQ

The correct answer is D

Question 4 – OTQ

The correct answers are A and C

Answers B and E are advantages of direct changeover. Answers D and F are advantages of a phased changeover.

Question 5 – OTQ

The correct answer is B

The other answers are examples of general controls.

Question 6 – Changeover methods (Case style)

(a) Parallel running and direct changeover are both methods of systems implementation

With a parallel running approach, the old and the new systems are run together and the results and outputs are compared until the user has sufficient confidence in the new system to switch to it permanently and stop using the old system. Transactions are run through both systems and the outputs of one system are checked against the outputs of the other to check the accuracy and usability of the proposed new system.

With a direct changeover approach, the old system is removed on a specific date and operations switched, immediately and in full, to the new system. There is no period where the systems are operationally used together. The verification of the new system takes place during system and user acceptance testing.

(b) Possible advantages of direct changeover over parallel running include:

Cost and time savings

The direct changeover approach should be cheaper and less time-consuming than the parallel running approach. With parallel running, there is usually a significant cost in entering data twice (staff overtime, temporary staff) and checking the outputs of the two systems against each other. With the direct changeover method, data is entered into the new system only.

Increases commitment to the new system

Users of the system are usually very familiar with the operation and outputs of the current system. During parallel running there may still be a tendency to rely on the old system and not identify properly and investigate the differences between outputs from the current and the new system. As a result, significant problems may only be properly tackled when the parallel running period has ended and the old system is discarded.

Proper attention to system and user acceptance testing

Although the stages of system testing and user acceptance testing are formally recognised in an approach using parallel running, there may be a tendency to underrate their importance because users are aware that the current system will be available as a 'fail-safe' during the implementation stage. The immediate nature of direct changeover means that proper attention has to be paid to both system and user acceptance testing.

(c) The main risk of direct changeover is that the system fails and there is no other system to fall back on to. As a result, the company may not be able to process the transactions required to carry on its business. This places it at considerable business risk and could create an exposure to claims from its customers for consequential damages.

This risk may be reduced in several ways:

- Comprehensive systems and user acceptance testing prior to implementation. Strict testing requirements and acceptance criteria must be laid down and adhered to.

- Effective training of users and operations staff before the new system goes live. Users will need familiarisation with the Windows style of interface with the enhanced reporting facilities, and with interfaces to other software.

- Contingency plans that enable the business to process transactions manually while the new system is corrected and recovered.

- A temporary increase in stock levels to reduce the risk of stock-outs while any problems with the new system are corrected.

Question 7 – DS (Case style)

(a) From the point of view of DS, there are many reasons why it may have received poor service, even though the terms of the contract have been fulfilled. The terms are as follows:

(i) **Purchase of all hardware and software**. GDC may have a preference for hardware and software that they are familiar with and this may not be a suitable fit to the existing system. Unfortunately, hardware and software become obsolete very quickly and GDC may not have been replacing it fast enough to keep up with the demands of the company. It could be that they have bought software to upgrade the system and they have not trained staff sufficiently to maintain it. A similar situation could have occurred with networking and routing equipment. Problems can occur that are very difficult to sort out without available expertise.

(ii) **Repair and maintenance of all IT equipment**. This is a tall order for any company. When the equipment was purchased, DS should have arranged a maintenance service through the manufacturers themselves. There could easily be a misunderstanding over the type of maintenance required from GDC. Are they supposed to fix faults when they occur or do regular maintenance checks to ensure the smooth running of the equipment?

(iii) **Help desk and other support services for users**. Users often have an inadequate understanding of existing systems and develop unrealistic expectations. This means that they may generate unreasonable and unmanageable volumes of requests for change. GDC might suffer from high programmer turnover rates. Their employees may not have the necessary skills or motivation. Many programmers prefer development work to maintenance work and may be reluctant to get involved in help desk support.

(iv) **Writing and maintaining software**. Since the contract is vague and the scope so large, there are bound to be areas of poor service from GDC. Maintenance may be required to:

– correct faults

– adapt the system to reflect the changing needs of the organisation

– upgrade the system if product enhancements are released.

(v) **Provision of management information**. Unless the type, content and timing of the management report required is specified, then there is ample scope for poor service. A new person at GDC may be responsible for producing the reports and he or she may not know the full routine. The report may have been left in the wrong place, or delivered to the wrong person first. However, the problem may not be due to a fault at GDC. To obtain essential management reports, the information must be kept up to date by the staff at DS. If the employee responsible for maintaining the database is sick or the files containing the data get damaged or corrupted, then the production of reports is likely to be delayed.

(b) There are several options available to DS:

Re-write contract with the help of GDC

The first is to re-write the contract with the help of GDC so that there is some flexibility but no vague areas and each party knows what is expected from them. This could be done through negotiation while the existing contract is still running. The problems with this course of action is that DS are locked into the current arrangement and GDC will be aware of the problems it could cause by giving three months' notice and leaving DS. They would be in a very strong position to increase the price substantially or restrict their commitment to DS in any negotiations that might take place.

Obtain help in re-writing the contract

The second would be to obtain help in re-writing the contract and, when satisfied, give GDC three months' notice and ask them, and other facilities management companies, to tender for the new contract. The problems with this course of action is that DS might just be trading in one company that is giving poor service for another that they do not know. There is no guarantee that service standards will always be as expected.

End outsourcing agreement

The third option would be to revert to an in-house IT development and support department solution. This would require a lot of effort and expense and, if new staff have to be recruited, there will be a long period before they could understand the system and be in a position to do what GDC are already doing.

Emerging IS Trends and their Role in Supporting Organisational Strategy and Operations

Chapter learning objectives

Lead	Component
C1. Demonstrate the purpose of the technology and information function and its relationship with other parts of the organisation.	(a) Demonstrate the value of information systems within organisations. (b) Demonstrate ways of organising and managing information systems in the context of the wider organisation.
C2. Explain how information systems support the organisation's strategies and operations.	(a) Explain the technical components and options for information technology system design. (b) Explain the role of emerging technologies, e.g. Big Data, digitisation and their uses.

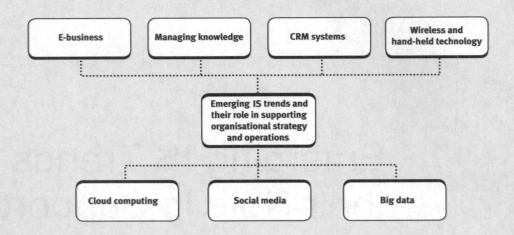

1 Introduction

Developments in IT and IS have, and continue to have, a major impact on many organisations and how they are run. A number of recent developments and emerging trends will be explained in this chapter.

2 E-business

2.1 Introduction

E-business has been defined as the transformation of key business processes through the use of internet technologies.

E-commerce is a subset of e-business. It is trading on the internet, i.e. through a digital market, buying and selling products and services online.

2.2 The categories of e-business

	Delivery by	
	Business	**Consumer**
Business **Exchange initiated by:**	B2B Business models, e.g. VerticalNet	B2C Business models, e.g. Amazon.com
Consumer	C2B Business models, e.g. Priceline.com	C2C Business models, e.g. eBay.com

2.3 Benefits of e-business

Most companies employ e-business to achieve the following:

- cost reduction – e.g. lower overheads, cheaper procurement
- increased revenue – e.g. online sales, better customer relationship management
- better information for control – e.g. monitoring website sales
- increased visibility
- enhanced customer service
- improved marketing – e.g. emailing customers with special offers
- market penetration – e.g. even small suppliers can gain a global presence via the internet
- the combination of the above should be to enhance the company's competitive advantage.

2.4 Barriers to e-business

Barriers to e-business can be seen in both the organisation itself and in its suppliers and customers. They include:

- technophobia – in managers and employees
- security concerns – for example, about hackers or electronic fraud
- set-up costs – a quality system will be expensive to set up
- running costs – for example, rental of web-server, maintenance and upgrades
- limited opportunities to exploit e-business
- limited IT resources in-house
- customers may not be interested in e-business.

2.5 Digital goods

In e-business, digital goods is a term used to describe any goods that are stored, delivered and used in an electric format. Digital goods are 'shipped' to consumers through email or downloaded from the internet.

Examples of digital goods include e-books, music downloads and software.

3 Managing Knowledge

3.1 What is knowledge management?

Knowledge management is a relatively new approach to business in which an organisation gathers, organises, shares and analyses its knowledge to further its aim.

3.2 Where does the knowledge reside?

Knowledge resides in:

- **Human capital** – the knowledge, skills and experience possessed by employees, suppliers and customers.

- **Structural capital** – includes intellectual capital (e.g. patents) and client information (e.g. address lists and client records).

3.3 What is a knowledge management system?

A knowledge management system is any system that helps the organisation in its process of knowledge management.

Types of knowledge management system include:

- **Networks** – a network is where a number of computers and other devices are linked in such a way that any one device can communicate with any other so enabling resource sharing between a number of users.

  Most organisations connect their PCs and other computers together in local area networks (**LANs**), enabling them to share data and peripherals such as printers.

  LANs can also be interconnected to create sophisticated, geographically dispersed wide area networks (**WANs**).

- **Groupware** – this software helps teams to work together and collaborate on projects. Examples include:

  - A **calendar** allowing users to, for example, plan meetings and generate reminders of deadlines or meetings.

  - An **address book** allowing contact details to be accessed.

  - A **journal** for automatically recording interactions with people involved in a project, e.g. emails.

- **Intranet** – An intranet is an internal organisational network that is based on internet technologies and can only be accessed by authorised employees. One of the main advantages of an intranet is that it allows confidential internal information sharing, e.g. corporate policies, training documents, telephone directories.

- **Extranet** – An extranet is an extended intranet. It links the organisation to business partners such as suppliers and customers and allows information to be shared. For example, an organisation could connect its purchase order system to the product catalogue database on a supplier's intranet.

Test your understanding 1

A barrier to knowledge management is that many people believe that keeping knowledge secret gives them unique power. Knowledge management, however, requires that knowledge is uncovered and shared.

Required:

What arguments could be used to encourage individuals to freely give up and share information?

Illustration 1

Modern IT systems have made sharing and distributing knowledge easier. The UK government has a massive project in progress to computerise the medical records of all UK residents. The aim is that a patient's medical history will be made available to any health professional in any hospital or clinic.

4 Customer Relationship Management (CRM) Systems

4.1 Introduction

CRM consists of the processes an organisation uses to track and organise its contacts with its current and prospective customers, with particular emphasis on software-based approaches.

CRM systems help the organisation to know their customers better and to use that knowledge to serve customers better. They enable a business to manage its relationship centrally through the storage of existing and potential customer contact information.

> **Illustration 2**
>
> Diagnostic and tracking tools, such as Google Analytics, have allowed firms to analyse the usage of their websites, whether customers revisit, what percentage repurchase an item, etc.

4.2 Benefits of CRM

Improved coordination and integration of systems

CRM technology could help transform an organisation's practices particularly if some of its systems and processes are not currently automated. The software has the potential to organise and synchronise business processes, sales, marketing, customer service and technical support electronically.

Improved customer relations

The overall goal of a CRM is to help an organisation:

- identify, attract and win new customers
- retain existing customers
- entice past customers back.

A CRM system enables efficient marketing communication with customers by holding mail and email addresses for mass distribution notifying customers of special offers and features, so building and maintaining a good customer relationship.

Improved control and management

The system will supply the organisation's marketers and managers with the information needed to control, develop and manage the organisation's marketing activities more effectively. A CRM system will maintain a record of lost sales as well as sales made, allowing further investigations to be made. CRM systems also allow progress on enquiries to be tracked which can be used to identify and eliminate inefficiencies. The reports produced by the system should strengthen decision making, planning, implementation, and control.

Improved motivation

As a by-product, CRM could lead to improved satisfaction and motivation amongst users who may feel that they are being properly equipped to do the job they are employed to do.

A source of competitive advantage

The software may offer a means of gaining a competitive advantage over rivals that do not currently have such a system.

Cost effective

CRM software is widely used, tried and tested and there should be few difficulties in the functionality and operation. Packages can be off the shelf or bespoke.

4.3 Criticisms of CRM

Software purchase

The cost of CRM will depend on what the organisation requires the system to do, what current off the shelf packages there are on the market and their associated costs.

Associated costs

The organisation will also need to consider related costs such as new hardware required as a result of CRM, and running costs associated with maintaining the new system. It is also conceivable that certain marketing, sales and invoicing systems are computerised at the moment but may need scrapping. This will have cost implications.

Cost of staff training and cost of disruption

New systems involve employees undergoing training in their use. This may involve the cost of hiring external consultants and the 'cost' of the participants' time away from activities such as dealing with customer enquiries.

Opportunity costs

Inevitably, the provision of a budget for CRM will represent an opportunity cost as there will be many other pressures and potential projects competing for budgetary provision.

Adjustment of business processes to fit software

There may be a need to adjust existing business processes, work flows and responsibilities to fit the software, including possibly production.

Cost of getting staff buy-in

The introduction of any new system will require time and effort. Communication with staff not just the 'how' of using the system but also 'why' introduce this system and 'what' the benefits are.

5 Wireless and Hand-held Technology

- There has been a huge growth in the ownership of i-pads, android tablets and other hand-held computing technologies. For example, it is estimated that almost 200 million i-pads have been sold since introduction.

  Many consumers now **use their phones and tablets to buy products** and firms have responded by **making their websites tablet-friendly** and by **developing apps** to make the purchasing process easier.

- Access to information – taken together with cheaper and faster **wireless** and broadband, many organisations now use tablets to **access key information**.

  For example, hospital consultants may do a ward-round and use tablets to access (and update) patient records as they go rather than relying on having paper files.

6 Cloud Computing

Cloud computing means storing and accessing data and programs over the internet instead of on a computer's hard drive.

It includes the following features:

- Storage – the best known aspect of cloud computing is that it gives users storage capacity to enable documents to be accessed more easily from different locations or on different machines.

- Additional service models – cloud computing also includes "software as a service" (SaaS) where users can use software without having to buy the full version for their own computers and "infrastructure as a service" (IaaS), where users can access additional computers, say to process transactions during busy periods.

  A common feature of cloud computing is that it is on-demand and self-service

7 Social Media

7.1 What is social media?

Social media itself is a catch-all term for a range of sites that may provide radically different social actions. For example:

- Twitter is designed to let people share short updates or "tweets" with others.

- Facebook, in contrast is a full-blown social networking site that allows for sharing updates, photos, joining events and a variety of other activities.

- LinkedIn is a professional business-related networking site

- Instagram is a free photo-sharing program.

7.2 Opportunities offered by social media

Social media offers a number of opportunities. These include:

- **Advertising** – for example, Starbucks is tweeting to customers and you can join their Facebook site to find out about its news and promotions.

- **Brand development** – for example, Volkswagen uses Flickr to develop its brand. Individuals are able to post pictures of their Volkswagen Beetle or their camp-a-van on the site.

- **Method of listening to customers** – sites where customers and potential customers discuss the products of the company and of its competitors can be vital, e.g. customer ratings on Amazon.com.

- **Communication** – for example, Deloitte Australia have held employee performance reviews in World of Warcraft and BDO uses Second Life as an avenue for meetings, presentations and events for staff and for clients.

- **Recruitment and selection** – firms seeking to recruit can ensure a wide range of potential candidates see their advert by using social networking sites such as Facebook and Twitter.

- **Selection** – many firms are screening candidates by researching their web presence, for example on LinkedIn or Facebook to see what interesting facts, photos and opinions can be found that might be relevant to their future careers.

8 Big Data

8.1 What is Big Data?

There are several definitions of Big Data, the most commonly used referring to **large volumes of data** beyond the normal processing, storage and analysis capacity of typical database application tools. Although Big Data does not refer to any specific quantity, the term is often used when speaking about petabytes and exabytes of data.

Illustration 3 – Size of data

The most commonly understood term used to describe disk space, data storage capacity or system memory is a Gigabyte (GB). For example, you may have an 80 GB hard drive.

Big Data refers to much larger volumes of data such as petabytes and exabytes:

    1,024 Gigabytes = 1 Terabyte

    1,024 Terabytes = 1 Petabyte

    1,024 Petabytes = 1 Exabyte

The definition can be extended to incorporate the types of data involved. Big Data will often include much **more than simply financial information** and can involve other organisational data which is operational in nature along with other **internal and external data** which is often **unstructured** in form.

One of the key challenges of dealing with Big Data is to identify repeatable business patterns in this unstructured data, significant quantities of which is in text format. However, managing such data can lead to significant business benefits.

8.2 Characteristics of Big Data

The three V's represent the defining characteristics of Big Data

Velocity

Data is now streaming from sources such as social media sites at a virtually constant rate and current processing servers are unable to cope with this flow and generate meaningful real-time analysis.

Volume

More sources of data and an increase in data generation in the digital age combine to increase the volume of data to a potentially unmanageable level.

Variety

Traditionally data was structured and in similar and consistent formats such as Excel spreadsheets and standard databases. Data can now be generated and collected in a huge range of formats including rich text, audio and GPS data amongst others.

8.3 Key Definitions

Big Data management is the storage, administration and control of vast quantities of both structured and unstructured data

The main aim of Big Data management is to ensure the data stored is high quality and accessible. Effective Big Data management can leverage large sets of data from a variety of relatively new sources such as social media sites.

New technologies combine traditional data warehouses with Big Data systems in a logical data warehousing architecture.

Big Data analytics is the process of scrutinising Big Data to identify patterns, correlations, relationships and other insights. This information can have a wide reaching effect on the organisation's competitive strategy and marketing campaigns and can therefore have a direct impact on future profitability.

Big Data sources may not fit into currently available data stores and Big Data analytics may require more advanced software tools than those commonly used in traditional data analysis.

Hadoop is an open source programming framework which enables the processing of large data sets by utilising multiple servers simultaneously.

Open source technologies such as Hadoop are increasingly utilised to manage the constantly evolving data processing requirements of Big Data.

Illustration 4 – Hadoop use at Morgan Stanley

Morgan Stanley uses Hadoop to analyse investments and claims to see better results in doing portfolio analysis compared to when using traditional databases and traditional grid computing due to the scale and complexity of data involved. This allows the company to identify and understand the most appropriate investments for clients.

8.4 Why is Big Data so important?

Several major business benefits arise from the ability to manage Big Data successfully:

- **Improved customer service** – access to rich customer data enables marketers to provide a personalised, narrowly targeted, experience for customers, with relevant advertising and recommendations, increasing loyalty and brand engagement as well as driving sales.

Illustration 5 – Improved customer service

Amazon's use of real-time, item-based, collaborative filtering (IBCF) to fuel its 'frequently bought together' and 'customers who bought this also bought' features have helped to generate 20% more revenue.

- **Driving innovation** by reducing the time taken to answer key business questions and therefore make decisions. For example, making connections between things such as purchase history and physical location means that precisely targeted real-time marketing becomes possible.

- Storage of **transactional data in a digital format** – companies can collect more accurate and more detailed performance information on everything from product inventories to sick days. The analysis of this data should help to improve decisions and boost performance.

- Big Data can be used to develop the **next generation of products and services**. For example, manufacturers are using data from sensors embedded in products from children's toys to industrial goods to determine how these products are actually used in the real world. This knowledge should improve the design of products and services.

- **Source of competitive advantage** – Big Data is becoming a crucial way for leading companies to outperform their competitors.

- **Access to external information** – an understanding of external (e.g. social and economic) factors is crucial to business success. Big Data will allow an organisation to, for example, scan and analyse newspaper reports or social media feeds so that they can permanently keep up to speed with the latest developments.

- **Can create new revenue streams** – insights gained from Big Data may not only be valuable to the organisation itself but could be sold to generate a whole new revenue stream.

Illustration 6 – Big Data use at Shazam

An impressive example of the ability to generate new revenue streams comes from Shazam, the song identification application. It helps record companies identify where music sub-cultures are arising by monitoring the use of its service, including the location data provided by mobile devices. The record companies can then make sure that the artists they sign up meet the needs of the market.

8.5 Risks associated with Big Data

- **Availability of skills to use Big Data systems** which is compounded by the fact that many of the systems are rapidly developing and support is not always easily and readily available. There is also an increasing need to combine data analysis skills with deep understanding of the industry being analysed and this need is not always recognised.

- **Security of data** is a major concern in the majority of organisations and if the organisation lacks the resource to manage data then there is likely to be a greater risk of leaks and losses.

- **Data Protection issues** as organisations collect a greater range of data from increasingly personal sources (e.g. Facebook).

- It is important to recognise that **just because something can be measured, this does not necessarily mean it should be**. There is a risk that valuable time is spent measuring relationships that have no organisational value.

- If organisations are to effectively utilise Big Data, this will require a **change in perspective** to ensure sense can be made of the information.

- There may be **technical difficulties** associated with integrating existing data stores with systems such as Hadoop.

8.6 How do we use it?

Examples of data which may input into Big Data systems

- social network traffic
- web server logs
- streamed audio content
- banking transactions
- web pages content
- GPS tracking
- financial market data

Illustration 7 – examples of how Big Data is used

- **Consumer facing organisations** monitor social media activity to gain insight into customer behaviour and preferences. This source can also be used to identify and engage brand advocates and detractors and assess responsiveness to advertising campaigns and promotions.

- **Sports teams** can use data of past fixtures to tracking tactics, player formations, injuries and results to inform future team strategies.

- **Manufacturing companies** can monitor data from their equipment to determine usage and wear. This allows them to predict the optimal replacement cycle.

- **Financial Services organisations** can use data on customer activity to carefully segment their customer base and therefore accurately target individuals with relevant offers.

- **Health organisations** can monitor patient records and admissions to identify risk of recurring problems and intervene to avoid further hospital involvement.

- **Consumers** can access real-time traffic information by using smart routing.

Illustration 8 – supply chain, logistics, and industrial engineering

UPS uses telematics to improve performance. Delivery vehicles are equipped with sensors which monitor data on speed, direction, braking performance, drive train performance and other mechanical aspects of the vehicle. This information is then used to optimise maintenance schedules and improve efficiency of delivery routes saving time, money and reducing wastage.

Data from the vehicles is combined with customer data, GPS information and data concerning the normal behaviour of delivery drivers. Using this data to optimise vehicle performance and routes has resulted in several significant improvements::

- Over 15 million minutes of idle time were eliminated in one year. This saved 103,000 gallons of fuel.

- During the same year 1.7 million miles of driving was eliminated, saving 183,000 gallons of fuel.

Test your understanding 2

Using the 3 V's, explain the problems associated with Big Data management.

9 Chapter Summary

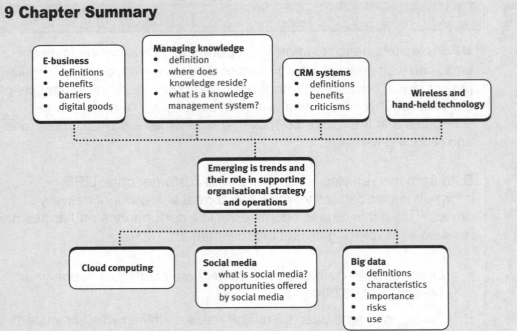

10 Practice Questions

Question 1 – OTQ

A system that enables a business to manage its relationships centrally through the storage of existing and potential customer information, accounts and leads is known as:

A   networked computing

B   an intranet

C   E-commerce

D   a customer relationship management system

Question 2 – OTQ

Which one of the following is not normally associated with Gartner's 3Vs definition of 'Big Data'?

A   High volume

B   High variety

C   High value added

D   High velocity

Question 3 – OTQ

The storage and accessing of data and programs over the internet instead of on a computer's hard drive is achieved using:

A   social media

B   an intranet

C   cloud computing

D   Big Data

Question 4 – JG (Case style)

Background

JG company is a motor vehicle manufacturer specialising in a range of passenger vehicles from high performance convertible cars to large multi-people vehicles. With the exception of the convertible cars, the majority of vehicles are manufactured for inventory rather than for specific customer orders. JG manufactures in a single country in Asia and ships the cars to worldwide destinations, in particular European countries.

Challenges facing JG

The industry is highly competitive and JG has suffered in recent years as it has failed to react quickly to market demand for certain types of vehicle. This has led to declining sales and increasing stock levels.

Task:

Describe three ways in which the effective management of Big Data can improve the speed of decision making for JG company.

(15 minutes)

Test your understanding answers

Test your understanding 1

The following arguments could be used:

- If everyone shares their knowledge, each person should gain more than they give up.

- Organisations are often so complex that it is rare that one person can achieve much alone. Teamwork and sharing knowledge is the best way of assuring a safe future.

- Knowledge is perishable. If knowledge is not used quickly then it is wasted. If knowledge cannot be shared the chances are that it will become useless before it can be used.

- Knowledge management is vital to the success of many businesses. If an organisation uses knowledge creatively, the chances are that it will gain a competitive advantage. People within the organisation should not be competing with each other at the expense of the company.

Test your understanding 2

Big Data management involves using sophisticated systems to gather, store and analyse large volumes of data in a variety of structured and unstructured formats. Such data can be difficult to manage for a variety of reasons and these can be summarised using the 3 V's of velocity, volume and variety.

Velocity

The speed at which data is now generated from sources such as social media networks makes it incredibly difficult for traditional database management systems to cope and give relevant and timely insights. If this data is not managed effectively it is, at best, wasted but could also result in significant increases in the data storage capacity required, without seeing any particular benefits.

Volume

Companies can now gather and generate data from a huge range of sources including internal systems, e-commerce sources, competitor and customer websites and social media networks. Not only has the overall volume of sources increased but the amount of data gathered from each source is now much higher than from traditional reporting. For example the data gathered from a single e-commerce sales transaction can be up to ten times higher than a standard in-store transaction.

It is important that data is only gathered (and therefore stored and analysed) from relevant sources that can actually add value to company decision making as there is a danger that companies become obsessed with gathering all data that is available rather than just that which is useful.

Variety

An increasing number of incompatible and inconsistent data formats is emerging at a fast rate. Most traditional data management systems are based around extracting data from, and storing data in, standard formats such as XML. Collecting data in a wide variety of formats including sound files and GPS data creates challenges for a system managing such big data.

Question 1 – OTQ

The correct answer is D

By definition

Question 2 – OTQ

The correct answer is C

The 3V's are velocity, volume and variety.

Question 3 – OTQ

The correct answer is C

By definition

Question 4 – JG (Case style)

Capturing Big Data and having the capability to manage and analyse such data has many business benefits, one of which is improved decision making. Not only can more appropriate and relevant decisions be made but also the speed of decision making can be improved.

JG is struggling to remain competitive and needs to improve its speed and ability to react to market demand. There are various ways that more effective Big Data management can help the company with this weakness.

- Firstly JG can analyse customer sales data as well as following customer comments and preferences through social media to try and more accurately predict which vehicle types are likely to be required in which location. This will allow the company to ship vehicles to the relevant locations in advance of orders being received which will allow the company to more effectively meet customer demand. This may mean a greater need for storage facilities in a European location but this may be a worthwhile investment if it halts the decline in sales.

- JG can also track and analyse similar sources of information, including social media sources for competitors, to determine consumer trends with respect to colours and features of various types of vehicle. The company can then incorporate this analysis into both product design and the choice of colours they manufacture for inventory to try and minimise stock levels required.

- Another way that JG can use more effective Big Data management is by using it to produce more useful and insightful competitor analysis. JG is finding it hard to remain competitive so a clear understanding of what it's competitors are doing and what their customers are commenting on will help to show JG possible areas for improvement. As most data generated through social media sites is unstructured by nature, it is essential that JG applies the principles of Big Data management to ensure all relevant data is utilised effectively.

The Purpose of the Operations Function

Chapter learning objectives

Lead	Component
D1. Demonstrate the purpose of the operations function and its relationship with other parts of the organisation.	(a) Demonstrate the contribution of operations management to the efficient production and delivery of fit-for-purpose goods and services. (b) Demonstrate how supply chains can be established and managed.
D2. Apply tools and techniques of operations management.	(a) Apply the tools and concepts of operations management to deliver sustainable performance. (b) Explain how relationships with the supply chain can be managed.

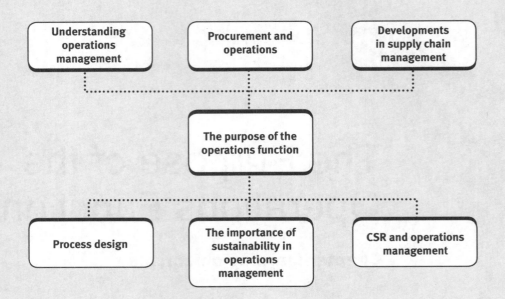

1 Introduction

During the eighteenth century the UK experienced dramatic change through what became known as the industrial revolution. It was during this period that the economy was transformed from agricultural to industrial and the population migrated to towns from the countryside.

Studies during this time clearly show that the productivity of organisations depended both on the technology available and how key resources were managed. 'Good' management constituted an application of knowledge and skills of a 'scientific' nature, rather than intuition and guesswork.

This thinking laid the foundation for the study of an area later referred to as **operations management**. At its simplest, operations management tries to ensure that organisations are run as efficiently as possible.

2 Understanding Operations Management

2.1 Definitions

All organisations have an operations function whether it is explicitly called this or not.

 Operations – those activities concerned with the acquisition of raw materials, their conversion into finished products and the supply of that finished product to the customer.

Contemporary thinking has broadened the definition to 'what the company does' to include service as well as manufacturing operations.

 Operations management – refers to the activities required to produce and deliver a product or a service. It includes purchasing, warehousing and transportation.

Illustration 1 – Examples of operations

Organisation	Operations function	Operation
McDonalds	Kitchen and serving staff	Selling fast food
Vauxhall	Production line	Making cars
Dell	Production line, internet	Making and selling computers
Real Madrid	Football coaches, training facilities	Playing football

Test your understanding 1

The O Company, founded in the early 1970s, manufactures electric pumps.

Required:

Describe the key activities in the operations function of an organisation such as O Company.

2.2 Organisational differences in operations functions

Although all of the operations of an organisation have similar transforming properties there are organisational differences according to:

- volume
- variety
- variation and
- visibility.

Four Vs of operations

Volume

Operations differ in the volume of inputs they process. High-volume operations are likely to be more capital-intensive than low-volume operations, and there is likely to be a greater specialisation of labour skills.

Variety

Some operations handle a wide range of different inputs, or produce a wide range of output products or services. Others are much more restricted in the range of inputs they handle or outputs they produce.

Variation in demand

With some operations, demand might vary significantly from one season of the year to another, or from one time of the day to another, with some periods of peak demand and some periods of low demand. Other operations might handle a fairly constant volume of demand at all times.

Visibility

Visibility refers to the extent to which an organisation is visible to its customers. When an operation is highly visible, the employees will have to show good communication skills and interpersonal skills in dealing with customers.

2.3 Contemporary thinking

It is clear from the discussion above that operations are of vital importance to an organisation. Many organisations now view operations as a strategically significant issue and a vital means of gaining competitive advantage.

2.4 Porter's value chain

Porter developed his value chain to determine whether and how a firm's activities contribute towards its competitive advantage.

Value chain analysis helps managers to decide how individual activities might be changed to reduce the costs of operations or to improve the value of the organisation's offerings. Such changes will increase 'margin' – the residual value created by what customers pay minus the costs.

Infrastructure					
Human Resource Management					
Technology					
Procurement					Margin
Inbound logistics	Operations	Outbound logistics	Marketing and sales	After Sales Service	

The approach involves breaking the firm down into five 'primary' and four 'support' activities, and then looking at each to see if they give a cost advantage or a quality advantage.

'Primary' activities – directly concerned with the creation or delivery of a product/service.

Activity	Description	Example
Inbound logistics	Receiving, storing and handling raw material inputs.	A just-in-time stock system could give a cost advantage (see chapter 9).
Operations	Transformation of raw materials into finished goods and services.	Using skilled employees could give a quality advantage.
Outbound logistics	Storing, distributing and delivering finished goods and services.	Outsourcing activities could give a cost advantage
Marketing and sales	The mechanism by which the customer is made aware of the product or service.	Sponsorship of a sports celebrity could enhance the image of a product.
After sales service	All activities that occur after the point of sale, such as customer enquiries, returns and repairs/maintenance.	Marks and Spencer's friendly approach to returns gives it a perceived quality advantage.

Operations management is concerned with all of these primary activities apart from marketing and sales.

'Support' activities – helps improve the efficiency and effectiveness of the primary activities.

Activity	Description	Example
Infrastructure	How the firm is organised.	A firm could have a very "lean" structure at head office in contrast to competitors with more staff and more bureaucracy.
Human resource management	How people contribute to competitive advantage. Includes activities such as recruitment, selection, training and development and reward policies.	Employing expert buyers could enable a supermarket to purchase better wines than competitors.
Technology	How the firm uses technology.	The latest computer-controlled machinery gives greater flexibility to tailor products to customer specifications.
Procurement	Purchasing, but not just limited to materials.	Buying a building out of town could give a cost advantage over High Street competitors.

Operations management is directly concerned with procurement and some elements of firm infrastructure and technology development.

Illustration 2 – Value chain

One particular clothes manufacturer may spend large amounts on:

- Buying good quality raw materials (inbound logistics)
- Hand-finishing garments (operations)
- Building a successful brand image (marketing)
- Running its own fleet of delivery trucks in order to deliver finished clothes quickly to customers (outbound logistics).

All of these should add value to the product, allowing the company to charge a premium for its clothes.

Another clothes manufacturer may:

- Reduce the cost of its raw materials by buying in cheaper supplies from abroad (inbound logistics)

- Making all its clothes by machinery running 24 hours a day (operations)

- Delaying distribution until delivery trucks can be filled with garments for a particular request (outbound logistics).

All of these should allow the company to be able to gain economies of scale and be able to sell clothes at a cheaper price than its rivals.

The supply chain

More recently, organisations have started to consider supply chain partnerships. The **value system** looks at linking the value chains of suppliers and customers to that of the organisation. A firm's success depends not only on its own value chain, but on its ability to manage the value system of which it is a part.

A **supply chain network** is a group of organisations which relate to each other through the linkages between the different processes involved in producing the finished product.

- Traditionally, businesses within the supply chain operated independently.

- However, organisations are recognising that there are benefits associated with establishing links between the different companies in the supply chain.

- Co-ordination of the different firms within the supply chain should lead to better planned production and distribution which may cut costs and give a more attractive final product leading to increased sales and profit for all of the businesses involved.

- Competition is no longer on a company versus company basis but rather takes on a supply chain versus supply chain form.

- A **demand network** is the evolution of a supply chain network and involves the collaboration between buyers to influence what goods are supplied.

3 Procurement and Operations

3.1 Sourcing strategies

There are four main sourcing strategies available:

Strategy	Explanation
Single sourcing	The organisation chooses one source of supply.
Multiple sourcing	The organisation chooses several sources of supply.
Delegated sourcing	The organisation chooses one supplier (1st tier). This supplier then co-ordinates and works with other suppliers (2nd tier) to ensure the supply requirements are fulfilled.
Parallel sourcing	The organisation uses a mix of the three approaches

It is important to consider the **advantages** and **disadvantages** of each of these methods.

Test your understanding 2

State the advantages and disadvantages of:

(i)   Single sourcing

(ii) Multiple sourcing

(iii) Delegated sourcing

(iv) Parallel sourcing

Kyoryoku kai

In most countries, suppliers' associations are organised and run by the suppliers themselves. In Japan, there are supplier associations known as kyoryoku kai, which are organised by a major buyer/customer in the industry. For example, an association of suppliers in the automotive industry might be set up and organised by a major car manufacturer. The first such association was set up by Toyota in 1943. Its original purpose was to provide an assurance of business to suppliers who were suffering from the consequences of the war effort in Japan. Over time, the main focus of interest in these supplier associations has been:

- Improving quality
- Reducing costs by means of efficiency improvements throughout the industry
- Health and safety standards.

The benefit of having a supplier association organised by a major buyer is that the buyer is able to exert strong influence over its suppliers, and encourage the open exchange of ideas and information between suppliers.

3.2 Purchasing versus supply

The key distinction between purchasing and supply is that supply is a strategic issue for firms. It is a vital means of gaining competitive advantage.

Purchasing:

- concentrates on the day to day buying of goods
- emphasis is on the price, quality and accurate delivery of goods
- may be viewed as an out of date approach to supply chain management.

Supply – a more modern approach dealing with important issues beyond the day to day including:

- planning and implementing a supply strategy
- managing the overall supply process

- considering the appropriateness of outsourcing arrangements
- investigating whether strategic partnerships could be developed with key stakeholders and customers
- the number of suppliers it should use.

4 Developments in Supply Chain Management

4.1 The strategic positioning tool – Reck and Long

The extent to which supply chain management is a strategic issue can be considered through **Reck and Long's** strategic positioning tool.

There are four stages of development that the purchasing function should pass through in order to attain a strategic status:

Stage 1 = The **passive** stage	• Purchasing is seen as an administrative task and attempts are made to get the best deal. • Purchasing has no strategic direction and passively reacts to requests from other departments.
Stage 2 = The **independent** stage	• Involves a more professional approach to purchasing, using the latest purchasing practices and technology. • Strategic direction is still independent from corporate strategy. • Emphasis is on price negotiations.
Stage 3 = The **supportive** stage	• Greater awareness that purchasing can affect the firm's strategic goals. The function supports the organisation's competitive strategy. • Emphasis is on better co-ordination between departments involving timely communication about changes in price and availability of materials.
Stage 4 = The **integrative** stage	• Purchasing is seen as a key part of strategic planning and is integral to the organisation's competitive strategy. • The emphasis is on developing relationships with suppliers, who are seen as vital partners.

4.2 The strategic supply wheel – Cousins

Organisations considering moving from price-based procurement and policies would do well to consider Cousin's strategic supply wheel.

Cousin's thinking is based on the notion that an organisation's supply strategy should involve a number of key areas described as 'spokes' in the wheel. As such, the model can help an organisation concentrate on key areas for attention and action.

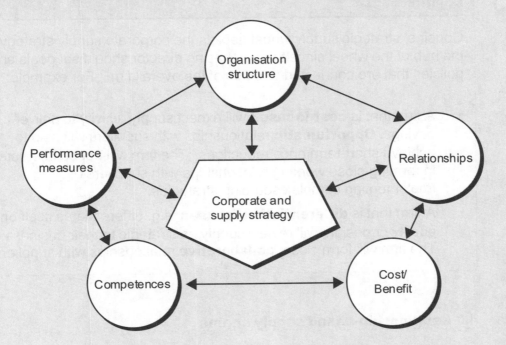

The model emphasises the importance of viewing supply as central to the organisation and its effectiveness. The wheel depicts the corporate supply strategy at the hub of the wheel and underlines the need for an integrated approach to supply strategy involving balancing all five 'spokes'.

Spoke of wheel	Explanation
Organisation structure	The choice of structure (centralised, decentralised or a mix of these) impacts control and interaction. It should enhance rather than hinder supply strategy.
Relationships with suppliers	Relationships can be: • opportunistic/competitive – based on price deals, or • collaborative – a more positive relationship based on a joint quest to reduce costs and/or improve quality.
Cost/benefit	Supply decisions should be based on benefits as well as costs. Cost/benefit analysis should be at the heart of any strategic decision.

Competences	Do the skills exist to achieve the chosen strategy? For example, the development of long term supplier relations may lead to a need to retrain key personnel.
Performance measures	Necessary for monitoring and controlling the strategy chosen. Measures should extend beyond price and should be aligned with the strategy.

Relationships

Cousins' strategic supply wheel depicts the corporate supply strategy at the hub of the wheel since the purchasing director should set goals and policies that are connected to those of the overall firm. For example:

- A firm that is **cost focused** will expect supply activity to deliver savings. **Opportunistic** relationships with suppliers will help to achieve short-term price reductions. The firm will not be interested in forming close working relationships with suppliers or implementing complex sourcing strategies.

- A firm that is **differentiation focused**, e.g. differentiates itself on quality or design, will review supply as strategic to their business. The firm will form close, **collaborative** relationships with suppliers.

4.3 Relationship-based supply chains

As mentioned above, Cousins identified two broad approaches to supplier relationships; competitive (also known as opportunistic) and collaborative.

Competitive (opportunistic)

In the past the supply chain was typically defined by competitive relationships.

- The purchasing function sought out the lowest-price suppliers, often through a process of tendering, the use of 'power' and the constant switching of supply sources to prevent getting too close to any individual source.

- Supplier **contracts** featured heavy penalty clauses and were drawn up in a spirit of general mistrust of all external providers.

- The knowledge and skills of the supplier could not be exploited effectively. Information was deliberately withheld in case the supplier used it to gain power during price negotiations.

Hence, no single supplier ever knew enough about the ultimate customer to suggest ways of improving the cost-effectiveness and quality of the trading relationship.

Collaborative

It is now recognised that successful management of suppliers is based upon collaboration and offers benefits to an organisation's suppliers as well as to the organisation itself. By working together and forming **relationships**, organisations can make a much better job of satisfying the requirements of their end market, and thus both can increase their market share.

- Organisations seek to enter into partnerships with key customers and suppliers so as to better understand how to provide value and customer service.

- Organisations' product design processes include discussions that involve both customers and suppliers. By opening up design departments and supply problems to selected suppliers, a synergy results, generating new ideas, solutions, and new innovative products.

- To enhance the nature of collaboration, the organisation may reward suppliers with long-term sole sourcing agreements in return for a greater level of support to the business and a commitment to on-going improvements of materials, deliveries and relationships.

Rationale for change

Porter's model of competitive advantage can be useful to understand why firms have switched to a more collaborative approach.

Porter argued that essentially firms have to decide between the following:

- **Differentiation**, where the advantage is based on offering a higher quality product/service to customers, and

- **Cost leadership**, where a standard quality product or service is supplied but the advantage comes from having a lower cost base, that allows the firm to cut prices if necessary to compete.

- Within either of these the firm can target the whole market of have a degree of **focus** on a narrower set of market segments.

From our discussion above it is clear that collaboration could result in a higher quality product, thus supporting differentiation. It could also be used to support a strategy of cost leadership with cost savings coming from elimination of inefficiencies, smoother production, lower inventory levels due to better forecasting and so on.

5 Process Design

5.1 Introduction

Process design is one of the latest developments in operations management. It is the method by which individual specialists seek to understand business activities and ensure that these activities are designed to be as efficient and effective as possible. The design of processes will go hand in hand with the design of new products and services.

Before any changes in processes are undertaken it is necessary to understand the organisation's mission, goals and customer needs and to carry out a detailed analysis of existing processes.

Processes may be improved through the operation of methods such as:

- the use of process maps

- Business Process Re-engineering (BPR)

- Total quality management (TQM) – this will be discussed in chapter 9

- Kaizen – this will be discussed in chapter 9

- supply chain management with the aim of improving links with suppliers and customers

- reorganisation to reflect processes and not functions.

Process maps and BPR will be explored in more detail below.

5.2 The use of process maps

The re-design of business processes requires a detailed analysis of existing processes. Process maps can assist in such an examination.

A process map provides a visual representation of the processes by which a product or transaction is processed.

The map will include workflow either within a process or within the organisation and the flows of information or products along supply chains and across networks.

Advantages of process maps

- **Management understanding** – allows a better understanding of the basic processes that are undertaken, so providing management with a convenient overview demonstrating responsibilities and key stages in the supply chain.

- **Role understanding** – allows workers to understand what their job is and how their work fits into the whole process (and therefore the importance of undertaking their role effectively). Process mapping also allows consideration of role reallocation.

- **Standardisation** – highlights where opportunities exist to standardise processes and strengthen practices through simple depiction.

- **Highlights inefficiencies** – visually highlights areas where inefficiencies are present through analysis of queues, value and location, so pinpointing areas of waste. This provides an agenda to tackle duplication of effort, the requirement to complete unnecessary paperwork, and misdirected queries that hold up production, etc.

- **Supports corporate initiatives** – mapping can be used as a tool as part of a corporate initiative such as customer satisfaction improvement programmes, lean operations, business process re-engineering, etc.

Example of a process map

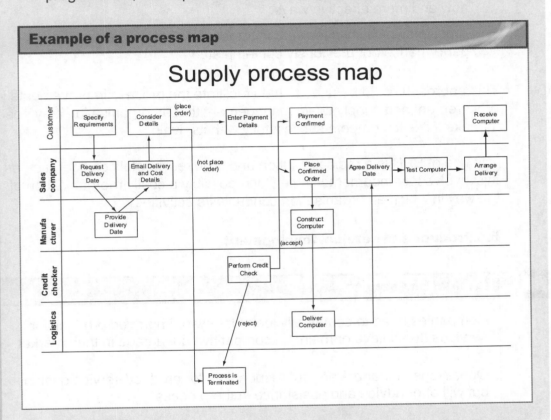

5.3 Business Process Re-engineering (BPR)

When the analysis of processes has been completed a number of tools are available for the improvement of processes. These include the use of TQM, Kaizen (continuous improvement), structural reorganisation and the most radical method of process design: Business Process Re-engineering (BPR).

BPR, an approach developed by Hammer and Champy, involves the fundamental re-thinking and redesign of existing business processes to achieve improvements in performance as measured in terms of cost, quality, service and speed.

BPR challenges managers and staff to totally rethink the way they do things in order to improve organisational effectiveness. The creators identify four major themes as follows:

- Process re-orientation which involves a focus on jobs, tasks, constraints and resources with the intention of carrying out jobs and tasks more efficiently and overcoming constraints and making better use of resources.

- Creative use of IT wherever this can enhance business processes.

- Rule breaking, which in this context means a readiness to do things in new and more effective ways.

- Ambition which involves setting targets for improvements in performance not previously contemplated.

This approach could be used to help facilitate the process improvements in procurement and supply chain management that an organisation may need to make if it is to compete successfully with its rivals.

The use of BPR is a radical solution and requires careful consideration as this involves a fundamental review and possibly a costly reorganisation of the way in which an organisation conducts its activities.

5.4 Product and service development

Product and service development

Companies need to continually look for new or improved products or services, to achieve or maintain competitive advantage in their market.

Operations managers are not responsible for product/ service design but will offer advice and assistance in the process.

The stages of product/service development are as follows:

Stage 1: Consider customers' needs

The product/service should satisfy the needs of the customer, e.g. value for money, high quality, cutting edge design.

Stage 2: Concept screening

The new product/service concept should be vetted. It will only pass through to the design and development process if it meets certain criteria. For example, does the company think that the new product/ service will be profitable?

Stage 3: The design process

This may include procedures such as:

- Building a physical prototype or a virtual prototype (using computer aided design).
- Value engineering, i.e. ensuring that all components/ features add value.

Stage 4: Time-to-market

A short time-to-market is desirable since:

- New product/service may be released ahead of competitors.
- Developments costs may be lower.

Stage 5: Product testing

The new product should be tested before it is released to the market:

- Does it work properly?
- Do customers like it?

6 The Importance of Sustainability in Operations Management

6.1 Introduction

Companies are beginning to consider how their operations affect the environment and future generations.

Sustainable development is about meeting the needs of the present without compromising the ability of future generations to meet their own needs.

It is the practice of doing business in a way that balances economic, environmental and social needs.

6.2 How sustainability impacts operations management

Operations management might contribute to achieving an organisation's sustainability targets in a number of ways:

Process design

The process should be designed to minimise waste, reduce energy use and reduce carbon emissions.

Product design

The product design should consider factors such as:

- Use of recycled inputs.
- Use of sustainable inputs.
- Ability to recycle product or dispose of it safely.
- Minimising wastage, e.g. unnecessary packaging.

Supply chain management

- **Purchasing**: Only products from a sustainable and ethical source should be purchased, e.g. a furniture manufacturer may purchase timber from sustainable forests only.
- **Supplier selection**: One of the key criteria to use when choosing between suppliers should be their adoption of sustainable development policies.
- **Location**: The distance between the supplier and the company should be minimised.

Quality management

Higher quality should help to improve efficiency and reduce waste.

Test your understanding 3
Explain the potential benefits of sustainability to a firm.

7 CSR and Operations Management

Organisations need to be aware of how effective supply chain ethics can help them to avoid costly product recalls and brand damage that results from an unethical supply chain decision.

Illustration 3 – Lush and ethics

Companies may talk about ethical supply chains, but if they don't independently monitor and audit suppliers, nothing will change.

Lush, the UK-based handmade cosmetics firm, is often cited as an example of why ethical supply chains and financial success aren't mutually exclusive. The business looks beyond the lowest price and bottom line and instead buys the best, safest and most suitable products in accordance with their ethics. It now has close to 1,000 stores worldwide with annual sales of over $500 million.

Illustration 4 – danger of poor supply chain management

Companies doing business in China have had difficulties maintaining quality throughout the supply chain, as illustrated by recent food and product recalls. For example, in 2008 there was a melamine-tainted baby milk scandal, which caused the death of at least six infants. Inherent problems in manufacturing processes and supply chains led to a breakdown of quality assurance. The scandal severely damaged China's dairy industry and shattered consumer confidence.

8 Chapter Summary

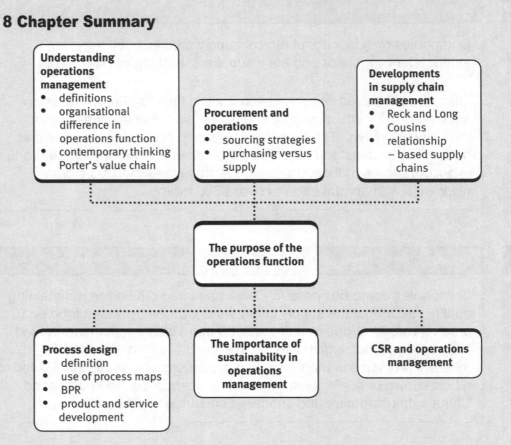

Understanding operations management
- definitions
- organisational difference in operations function
- contemporary thinking
- Porter's value chain

Procurement and operations
- sourcing strategies
- purchasing versus supply

Developments in supply chain management
- Reck and Long
- Cousins
- relationship – based supply chains

The purpose of the operations function

Process design
- definition
- use of process maps
- BPR
- product and service development

The importance of sustainability in operations management

CSR and operations management

9 Practice questions

Question 1 – OTQ

Which one of the following is a value-added activity?

A   Painting a car, if the organisation manufactures cars

B   The board of directors who decide on the financial structure and technicalities of a business

C   Storing materials

D   Repairing faulty production work

Question 2 – OTQ

What is the first stage in product development?

A   Product design

B   Investigating the product offerings of competitors

C   Considering customers' needs

D   Investigating ways to reduce the time-to-market

Question 3 – OTQ

Which one of the following is not an example of a 'support activity' as described in Porter's Value Chain?

A   Technology development

B   Human resource management

C   Procurement

D   Firm structure

Question 4 – OTQ

Reck and Long's strategic positioning tool identifies an organisation's:

A   purchasing approach

B   sales approach

C   manufacturing approach

D   warehousing approach

Question 5 – OTQ

Supply chain partnerships are developed due to:

A   recognising a supply chain and linkages in a value system

B   a requirement to meet growing demand

C   the adoption of new information systems

D   a requirement for quality accreditation

Question 6 – OTQ

According to Cousins, which ONE of the following is a 'spoke' of the 'supply wheel?'

A   Corporate and supply strategy

B   Organisation culture

C   Purchasing

D   Relationships

Question 7 – Woodsy (Case style)

Woodsy is a garden furniture manufacturing company, which employs 30 people. It buys its timber in uncut form from a local timber merchant, and stores the timber in a covered area to dry out and season before use. Often this takes up to two years, and the wood yard takes up so much space that the production area is restricted.

The product range offered by the company is limited to the manufacture of garden seats and tables because the owner-manager, Bill Thompson, has expanded the business by concentrating on the sale of these items and has given little thought to alternative products. Bill is more of a craftsman than a manager, and the manufacturing area is anything but streamlined. Employees work on individual units at their own pace, using little more than a circular saw and a mallet and wooden pegs to assemble the finished product. The quality of the finished items is generally good but relatively expensive because of the production methods employed.

Marketing has, to date, been felt to be unnecessary because the premises stand on a busy road intersection and the company's products are on permanent display to passing traffic. Also, satisfied customers have passed on their recommendations to new customers. But things have changed. New competitors have entered the marketplace and Bill has found that orders are falling off. Competitors offer a much wider range of garden furniture and Bill is aware that he may need to increase his product range, in order to compete. As the owner-manager, Bill is always very busy and, despite working long hours, finds that there is never enough time in the day to attend to everything. His foreman is a worthy individual but, like Bill, is a craftsman and not very good at man-management. The overall effect is that the workmen are left very much to their own devices. As they are paid by the hour rather than by the piece, they have little incentive to drive themselves very hard.

Tasks:

(a) Explain what is meant by the terms 'value chain' and 'value chain analysis'?

(7 minutes)

(b) Use a diagram to give a brief explanation of the two different categories of activities that Porter describes.

(8 minutes)

(c) Analyse the activities in the value chain to identify the key problems facing Woodsy.

(10 minutes)

(d) Based on your analysis, prepare a set of recommendations for Bill Thompson to assist in a more efficient and effective operation of his business

(10 minutes)

(Total: 35 minutes)

Test your understanding answers

Test your understanding 1

The operations function in manufacturing electric pumps is concerned with converting raw materials into a finished product and delivering them to the customer. Operations therefore covers the following areas:

- **Purchasing**. The purchasing department are responsible for obtaining raw materials and parts from suppliers.

- **Production**. The production function converts the raw materials and assembles parts and components into finished products. Without more information about the nature of the pumps that the company produces, it is not possible to suggest what type of production process the company uses.

- **Production planning and control**. This function is concerned with scheduling production, and making sure that the materials, labour, machinery and other resources are available to manufacture the pumps. Production control involves monitoring production flow and dealing with any problems, hold-ups and bottlenecks that might arise.

- **Product design or engineering**. There will probably also be a separate section within operations that provides technical expertise. These experts might be responsible for new product design.

- **Inventory management**. Raw materials and finished goods inventory must be stored or warehoused.

- **Logistics**. Manufactured pumps must be distributed to customers. The customers for pumps will be industrial buyers, and the task of delivering them will probably be included within the operations function.

Test your understanding 2

		Advantages	Disadvantages
(i)	**Single sourcing**	• Better communication • Economies of scale • Better production quality, lower variability • Possible source of competitive advantage since can build relationship with single supplier.	• Risk to security of supply since rely on one supplier • Few competitive pressures may reduce incentive for supplier to perform well • The supplier is in a powerful position and may increase prices or reduce quality
(ii)	**Multiple sourcing**	• Greater security of supply • Pressure on suppliers to be competitive • Buyer remains in touch with supply market	• Economies of scale may be lost • This is a traditional price-based strategy but it may not result in good relationships • Suppliers may display less commitment/ quality may be poorer
(iii)	**Delegated sourcing**	• The 1st tier supplier may be able to negotiate economies of scale • May result in the optimum mix of suppliers being used • Organisation delegates responsibility to the 1st tier supplier thus freeing up staff time	• 1st tier supplier is in a powerful position • Organisation may have little knowledge with regards to the 2nd tier suppliers, e.g. quality, work practices
(iv)	**Parallel sourcing**	• May blend the best bits of each strategy	• Quite difficult to manage

Test your understanding 3

Sustainability may result in a number of benefits to the firm:

Improved operational efficiency

Practices associated with sustainability include reducing waste, improved energy and water consumption and the sale of by-products that were previously a cost of disposal. These practices will contribute to improved long-term performance.

External stakeholder support

Sustainable development should help the company to portray a positive image and can result in enhanced relationships with external stakeholders, e.g. the local community may view the operations more positively if sustainable practices are used.

Internal stakeholder support

Sustainability can enhance relationships with the organisation's workforce. The organisation may use its sustainability policy as a tool for attracting and retaining the best employees. Employee motivation may increase if employees are involved in sustainability discussions and a positive culture should be shaped.

Source of competitive advantage

Sustainability may result in competitive advantage if:

- new business opportunities are exploited
- market share increases due to customers' needs being met and brand loyalty increasing.

Required by legislation

Legislation/regulation has increased in recent years and has resulted in many companies implementing policies for sustainable development. For example, three new pieces of legislation were introduced in the UK in 2008; the Climate Change Act, the Energy Act and the Planning Act.

Question 1 – OTQ

The correct answer is A

Question 2 – OTQ

The correct answer is C

Question 3 – OTQ

The correct answer is D

Question 4 – OTQ

The correct answer is A

Question 5 – OTQ

The correct answer is A

Question 6 – OTQ

The correct answer is D

Question 7 – Woodsy (Case style)

(a) **'Value chain'** describes the full range of activities which are required to bring a product or service from conception, through the intermediary of production, delivery to final consumers, and final disposal after use. It is a way of looking at a business as a chain of activities that transform inputs into outputs that customers value. Customer value derives from three basic sources:

- activities that differentiate the product

- activities that lower its cost

- activities that meet the customer's need quickly.

The value chain includes a profit margin since a mark-up above the cost of providing a firm's value-adding activities is normally part of the price paid by the buyer – creating value that exceeds cost so as to generate a return for the effort.

'**Value chain analysis**' views the organisation as a sequential process of value-creating activities, and attempts to understand how a business creates customer value by examining the contributions of different activities within the business to that value. Value activities are the physically and technologically distinct activities that an organisation performs. Value analysis recognises that an organisation is much more than a random collection of machinery, money and people. These resources are of no value unless they are organised into structures, routines and systems, which ensure that the products or services that are valued by the final consumer are the ones that are produced.

(b) Porter describes two different categories of activities.

The primary activities, in the lower half of the value chain are grouped into five main areas:

- Inbound logistics are the activities concerned with receiving, storing and handling raw material inputs.

- Operations are concerned with the transformation of the raw material inputs into finished goods or services. The activities include assembly, testing, packing and equipment maintenance.

- Outbound logistics are concerned with the storing, distributing and delivering the finished goods to the customers.

- Marketing and sales are responsible for communication with the customers e.g. advertising, pricing and promotion.

- Service covers all of the activities that occur after the point of sale e.g. installation, repair and maintenance.

Alongside all of these primary activities are the secondary, or support, activities of procurement, technology development, human resource management and firm infrastructure. Each of these cuts across all of the primary activities, as in the case of procurement where at each stage items are acquired to aid the primary functions.

(c) The key problem areas are as follows:

- Inbound logistics – Woodsy has problems with the procurement of the raw materials, labour and machinery. The company is buying its raw materials two years in advance of using it. This must be tying up capital that could be used to purchase new machinery and tools. Storing the timber entails large amounts of money being tied up in stocks, which are prone to damage, restrict the production area and is very slow moving. The workmen are being paid by the hour rather than by the piece and this means that they have little incentive to work harder.

- Operations are concerned with the transformation of the raw material inputs into finished goods or services. At Woodsy, employees work at their own pace on the assembly of the garden seats and tables, using very basic tools. The production methods used make the finished product relatively expensive. The linkages between the support activities are also causing some problems. Both the owner and the foreman have no man-management skills. Technological development is non-existent and the company needs re-structuring.

- Outbound logistics are concerned with storing, distributing and delivering the finished goods to the customers. Woodsy does not seem to have a system for distributing and delivering its goods.

- Marketing and sales are responsible for communication with the customers e.g. advertising, pricing and promotion. This seems to be non-existent at Woodsy as, in the past, satisfied customers have passed on their recommendations to new customers. The company relies on its position on a busy road intersection to displays its products, for customers to carry away themselves.

(d) For Bill Thompson, the main task is to decide how individual activities might be changed to reduce costs of operation or to improve the value of the organisation's offerings. The recommendations would include the following:

- The business needs managing full-time. A new manager, or assistant manager, could encourage Bill to streamline the manufacturing process, introduce new technologies and new production and administrative systems. He or she could also negotiate new payment methods to give the workforce an incentive to work harder.

- To increase the production area, the alternative strategies that the company could explore include storing the timber elsewhere, or purchasing it after it has dried out and seasoned.

- Holding high levels of finished goods might give a faster customer response time but will probably add to the total cost of operations.

- The purchase of more expensive power tools and equipment may lead to cost savings and quality improvements in the manufacturing process.

- The company needs a marketing and sales department to research the market, inform the customers about the product, persuade them to buy it and enable them to do so. The product range may need to be extended and alternative outlets for the products sought.

Tools and Techniques of Operations Management

Chapter learning objectives

Lead	Component
D2. Apply tools and techniques of operations management.	(a) Apply the tools and concepts of operations management to deliver sustainable performance.
	(b) Explain how relationships with the supply chain can be managed.

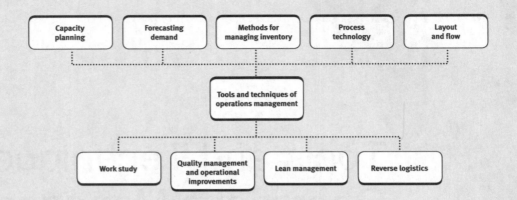

1 Capacity Planning

Balancing demand and productive capacity is a key challenge in operations.

Capacity planning aims to balance customer demand with production capability. There are three possible approaches to capacity planning:

- **Level capacity plan** – maintains production activity at a constant rate. A simple approach but can result in a build up of inventory or in stock outs.

- **Chase demand plan** – matches production with demand. Will require a flexible approach to production and a good forecasting system.

- **Demand management planning** – attempts to influence demand to smooth variations above or below capacity e.g. supermarkets may offer discounted ice-cream during the winter period in order to keep demand stable.

Illustration 1 – Capacity planning at Ikea

In reality, most organisations combine several approaches when managing capacity. For example, the world's largest furniture retailer, Ikea:

- has large warehouses containing goods that have yet to be ordered

- extended opening times over the Christmas period to cater for an increase in demand

- uses price cutting in order to shift products that have gone out of fashion.

Test your understanding 1

Describe the ways in which an organisation may respond to variations in demand for its products.

2 Forecasting Demand

2.1 Introduction

Demand forecasting is needed for a number of reasons:

- It assists in workforce scheduling and production planning.

- It helps in decision making and control.

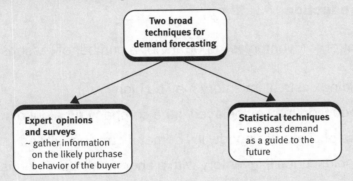

There are a number of techniques which fall under each of these broad methods.

2.2 Expert opinions and surveys

Technique	Explanation
Expert opinion poll	Product experts are asked to give their opinion about likely demand for a given product in future periods. Can be very subjective and experts may have a range of opinions.
Delphi technique	A variation on the expert opinion poll. A group of experts is questioned repeatedly until the responses are the same/ similar. Participants are supplied with responses to previous questions and such feedback may result in the expert revising their opinion.
Customer survey	Customers are surveyed in order to ascertain their demand for a future period. All customers may be surveyed or a sample taken (less costly but also less accurate).

2.3 Statistical techniques

Technique	Explanation
Time series analysis	Past data is analysed to determine the trend in demand and any seasonal variation. This information can then be used to predict future demand.
Regression analysis	A graph of past demand against time is plotted and the straight line of best fit is found. This is then used to predict demand in future periods. Only effective if there is a strong correlation between demand and time.

3 Methods for Managing Inventory

3.1 Introduction

The control of inventory is important for a number of reasons:

- Holding costs of inventory may be high
- Production may be delayed if the company runs out of raw materials
- Loss of customer goodwill if demand can't be fulfilled
- Obsolescence if inventory with a short shelf life is not used or sold

Therefore, it is important for a company to choose an appropriate inventory management system. There are **three main types of system** available. Each system will be reviewed in turn.

3.2 Continuous inventory system

A **continuous inventory system** keeps the level of inventory under continual review. Each new addition and withdrawal is recorded as it occurs. A pre-determined quantity of inventory is ordered when the inventory level falls to a re-order level.

The **economic order quantity** (EOQ) model can be used to establish the optimum re-order quantity. This model will minimise the total inventory costs.

EOQ model

Imagine that a firm sells A units a year and sales are constant. If it retails the product at a price p, its turnover will be pA. The firm purchases stock at a wholesale price of w, sells it and, when stock has fallen to zero, obtains more stock. If the firm orders an amount Q, the stock level of the firm will follow the profile shown in the diagram below, where Q has been assumed to be 10 and stock usage is one unit a period. From the diagram it follows that the average stock level will be Q/2, in this case five units.

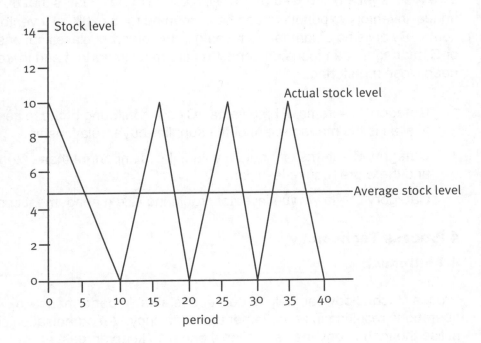

Total inventory costs are minimised when the combined cost of ordering inventory and holding inventory each period (each year) is minimised. To decide what to do, we must look at the demand and costs:

C = ordering cost per order event (fixed cost to place an order, not per unit)
H = holding cost per unit per unit of time e.g. per year
Q = is the reorder quantity, i.e. the EOQ
A = total sales demand per annum

The equation below, which you will not need to derive or use, is the so-called economic order quantity or EOQ

$$Q = \sqrt{\frac{2AC}{H}} = EOQ$$

3.3 Periodic inventory (or bin) system

The periodic inventory system does not keep inventory levels under continual review. Instead, inventory is checked on a regular basis and a variable order is placed depending on the usage during the period.

3.4 ABC system

The ABC system is based on Pareto's law. This law states that 80% of annual inventory expenditure can be accounted for by 20% of inventory items. By dividing a company's inventory into different classifications - A, B or C, managers can focus on items that are most important and therefore need close monitoring.

- Category A – items of high value. Close monitoring of these items is vital as is the management of the supplier-buyer relationship.

- Category B – items of medium value. Less important than category A and therefore require less control.

- Category C – low value inventory requiring little management control.

4 Process Technology

4.1 Introduction

Process technology can help to deliver sustainable performance in operations resulting in improvements in efficiency. An organisation should utilise the technology that is available and also keep abreast of technological developments in order to sustain competitive advantage.

There are many different types of process technology. Some common examples are discussed below.

4.2 Computer-integrated manufacturing (CIM)

Most modern manufacturing processes now utilise computer-aided design (**CAD**) and computer-aided manufacturing (**CAM**) operations. CAD and CAM allow flexible manufacturing as they enable computerised machines to perform a variety of functions. They also help an organisation:

- provide flexibility to meet customer requirements
- eliminate mistakes
- reduce material wastage.

These advances work towards **world class manufacturing**. When CAD and CAM are integrated it is possible to achieve computer-integrated manufacturing (**CIM**) whereby a system directs data flow whilst also directing the processing and movements of material.

World class manufacturing

World class manufacturing is concerned with achieving significant improvements in quality, lead times, flexibility and customer satisfaction. Core features include:

- a strong customer focus
- a flexible approach to responding to customer needs.

4.3 Flexible manufacturing systems (FMS)

A **FMS** is a highly automated manufacturing system, which is computer controlled and is capable of producing a large number of parts in a flexible manner, reacting to both predicted and unpredicted changes.

The main **benefit** is that dedicated output can be produced quickly in response to specific orders, giving a high level of customer focus and responsiveness.

The main **features** include:

- The ability to change quickly from one job to another.
- Fast response times.
- Small batch production.

The main **disadvantage** of a FMS is that there is a cost to the enhanced flexibility. Traditional production lines are very efficient at making single products cheaply and benefit from economies of scale and specialisation.

4.4 Computer numerical control (CNC)

With CNC a computer converts the design produced by CAD into numbers. The numbers can be considered to be the co-ordinates of a graph and they control the exact movements of the machine allowing the creation of almost any desired pattern or shape.

The **advantages** of CNC machinery are huge:

- No human could possibly control the precise movements that these machines will make over and over again.

- One skilled operator can perform the duties of several people thus reducing labour costs.

Whilst people in most walks of life have never heard of the term, CNC has touched almost every form of manufacturing process in one way or another.

4.5 Automated guided vehicles (AGV)

AGVs are fully automated transport systems using unmanned vehicles. AGVs safely transport all kinds of products without human intervention within production, warehousing and distribution environments. An example would be an automated forklift truck.

Illustration 2 – AGVs at Toyota in Kentucky

The Toyota manufacturing plant in Kentucky, USA, makes 1.8 million parts per year. These parts were previously transported by manned tow tractors. However, these were inefficient making frequent stops and there was often damage to material due to bangs and other human error. The Kentucky plant has now implemented the use of AGVs in this area and has saved almost $1 million and 400 worker days per annum as a result.

4.6 Robots

The use of robots can now be seen as a method of gaining competitive advantage. Companies such as Google, Amazon and Apple spend millions on robotics each year.

Illustration 3

In 2014, Apple invested $10.5 billion in factory robots to help produce iPads, iPhones and other gadgets. Google had a busy 2013 acquiring eight robotic engineering companies and in 2012 Amazon bought the robot manufacturer, Kiva. Their robots help improve warehouse efficiency by bringing the product shelves to the workers.

4.7 Decision making systems

A hierarchy of systems can assist in the decision making process:

- **Executive information systems (EIS)** – provide senior level managers with strategic level information to help them to make strategic decisions. Information can be presented in a user friendly format, e.g. graphs, pie charts.

- **Management information systems (MIS)** – provide middle managers with information to monitor and control the organisation's activities and to report this to senior managers, e.g. budgeting and control systems.

- **Transaction processing systems (TPS)** – these major applications carry out essential, routine processing of day to day transactional data. They are sometimes referred to as data processing systems. Examples include payroll or stock control systems.

- **Decision support systems (DSS)** – provide managers with information to support one off decisions. Uses complex mathematical models to allow managers to carry out complex 'what-if' analysis.

4.8 Expert systems

Expert systems stimulate the problem-solving techniques of human experts, by applying human expertise and knowledge to a range of specific problems about a particular area of expertise.

Test your understanding 2
Identify the benefits of good MIS and EIS

4.9 Material requirement planning (MRP)

One important aspect of operations management is to ensure that materials are ready when they are needed.

MRP is a computerised system for planning the requirements for raw materials, work-in-progress and finished items.

Functions include:

- Identifying firm orders and forecasting future orders with confidence.
- Using orders to determine quantities of material required.

- Determining the timing of material requirement.
- Calculating purchase orders based on stock levels.
- Automatically placing purchase orders.
- Scheduling materials for future production.

Benefits of MRP

- Improved forecasting.
- Improved ability to meet orders leading to increased customer satisfaction.
- Reduced stock holding.
- The MRP schedule can be amended quickly if demand estimates change since the system is computerised.
- System can warn of purchasing or production problems due to bottlenecks or delays in the supply chain.
- A close relationship tends to be built with suppliers (it is consistent with just-in-time – see discussion in section 7).

However, MRP will not be suitable if it is not possible to predict sales in advance.

5 Layout and Flow

Layout and flow is a big design consideration in operations management:

- It can affect the total distance travelled by material, people or information as they move through the operation.
- It can affect quality, e.g. if material is continually passed from one part of the operation to another there will be many points at which damage can occur.
- It will affect throughput time.

There are a number of approaches to layout.

 A **fixed position layout** involves the movement of employees and machines to the product (which remains stationary). In this type of layout, the material or major components remain in a fixed location, and tools, machinery and employees as well as other pieces of material are brought to this location.

This approach tends to be used when the cost of moving employees and machines is less than the cost of moving the product (perhaps because it is very heavy or bulky).

Another technique that can be used is cellular manufacturing. This technique can reduce the complexity of process layouts.

With **cellular manufacturing** work units are arranged in a sequence that supports a smooth flow of materials and components through the production processes with minimal transport or delay.

Rather than processing multiple parts before sending them on to the next machine or process step, cellular manufacturing aims to move products through the manufacturing process one-piece at a time, at a rate determined by customers' needs. Cellular manufacturing can also provide companies with the flexibility to vary product type or features on the production line in response to specific customer demands.

To make the cellular design work, an organisation must often replace large, high volume production machines with small, flexible, 'right-sized' machines to fit well in the process 'cell'. This transformation often shifts worker responsibilities from watching a single machine, to managing multiple machines in a production cell. This is often accompanied by a shift to semi-autonomous team working.

6 Work Study

The theorist, **Taylor**, was one of the first people to study the work process scientifically.

- Taylor believed that by analysing work in a scientific manner, the **'One Best Way'** to perform a task could be found.
- By organising work in the most efficient way, the organisation's productivity will be increased and this will enable the organisation to reward its employees with the remuneration they desire.
- He concluded that workers are motivated by obtaining the highest possible remuneration (money).

Steps in scientific management

Taylor's scientific management consisted of four principles:

- Work methods should be based on the scientific study of the task, i.e. they should be planned in a way to maximise productivity. This often involves breaking the work down into separate functions.

- Select, train and develop the most suitable person for each job, i.e. scientific management of staff.

- Managers must provide detailed instructions to workers to ensure work is carried out in a scientific way.

- Divide work between managers and workers – managers apply scientific principles to planning and supervising the work and workers carry out the task.

Taylorism today

With modern trends including the need for flexible working, teamwork and multi-skilling, it would be easy to dismiss Taylorism as outdated. However, it is still relevant in many areas, e.g. call centres.

Pig iron study

Taylor suggested that if workers were moving 12.5 tonnes of pig iron per day, and they could be incentivised (by money) to try to move 47.5 tonnes per day, left to their own devices they would probably become exhausted and fail to reach their goal.

However, by first conducting experiments to determine the amount of resting that was necessary, the worker's manager could determine the optimal time of lifting and resting so that workers could lift 47.5 tonnes per day without tiring.

Interestingly, only 1/8 of pig iron workers were capable of doing this. They were not extraordinary people but their physical capabilities were suited to moving pig iron. This led Taylor to suggest that workers should be selected according to how well they are suited to a job.

7 Quality Management and Operational Improvements

7.1 Introduction to quality

Quality is one of the most important and far-reaching issues in modern organisations.

The term is difficult to define and often means different things in different organisations. However, the need to **satisfy customer's needs** is critical to most definitions of quality.

What is quality?

In order to control and improve quality, it must first be defined. Most dictionaries define quality as 'the degree of excellence' but this leaves one having to define what is meant by 'excellence'. Who defines what is excellent and by what standards is it measured? In response to this problem, a number of different definitions of quality have been developed.

In an industrial context, quality is defined in a functional way. Here, quality means that a product is made free from errors and according to its design specifications, within an acceptable production tolerance level.

Such an approach also emphasises that every unit produced should meet the design specifications, so the idea of consistency becomes important. Note that consistency is a key aspect of quality standards such as the ISO 9000 series.

This still leaves a problem, however. How should standards and specifications be set? Who decides what an 'acceptable' tolerance level should be?

An alternative approach to defining quality is thus to focus on the user.

- Japanese companies found the definition of quality as 'the degree of conformance to a standard' too narrow and consequently started to use a new definition of quality as 'user satisfaction'.

- Juran defines quality as 'fitness for use' (1988).

In these definitions, customer requirements and customer satisfaction are the main factors. If an organisation can meet the requirements of its customers, customers will presumably be satisfied. The ability to define accurately the needs related to design, performance, price, safety, delivery, and other business activities and processes will place an organisation ahead of its competitors in the market.

Taking these definitions together, Ken Holmes (Total Quality Management) has defined quality as 'the totality of features and characteristics of a product or service which bears on its ability to meet stated or implied needs'.

Quality is also normally seen in relation to price, and customers judge the quality of a product in relation to the price they have to pay. Customers will accept a product of lower design quality provided that the price is lower than the price of a better-quality alternative.

Test your understanding 3

Explain the reasons why quality may be important to an organisation.

The growth of global companies has resulted in dramatic improvements in the quality of products and services. Much of this impetus can be attributed to the efforts of Japanese manufacturing companies.

7.2 Key writers on quality

Key writers on quality

There are a number of key writers on quality:

Writer	Main contribution
W.Edward Deming	Believed: • managers should set up and then **continuously improve** the systems in which people work • managers should work with employees to gain feedback from those who do the job • workers should be trained in quality to identify what needs changing and how. Deming was credited with the creation of TQM in Japan.
Joseph M. Juran	• Drew on Pareto principle and stated that **85% of quality problems are due to the systems that employees work within rather than the employees themselves**. • Therefore, need to develop key projects for dealing with quality problems rather than concentrating on employee motivation. • Also believed that anyone affected by the product is considered a customer, so introduced the idea of internal as well as external customers.
Phillip P. Crosby	• Introduced the concept of '**zero defects**'. • Believed that prevention is key and that the importance of quality is measured by the cost of not having quality.

7.3 Methods of quality measurement

There are four types of quality cost:

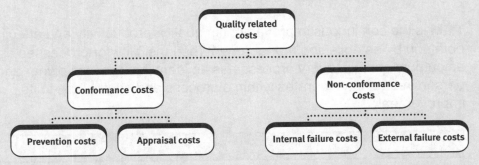

- **Prevention costs** – cost of preventing defects before they occur. For example:
  - Designing products and services with built in quality.
  - Training employees in the best ways to do their job.

- **Appraisal costs** – the cost of quality inspection and testing to ensure products/services conform to quality requirements.

- **Internal failure costs** – the costs arising from a failure to meet quality standards. Occurs **before** the product/service reaches the customer. For example:
  - Cost of re-working/scrapping parts.
  - Re-inspection costs.
  - Lower selling prices for sub-quality goods.

- **External failure costs** – the costs arising from a failure to meet quality standards. Occurs **after** the product/service reaches the customer. For example:
  - Costs of recalling and correcting products.
  - Cost of lost goodwill.

7.4 Approaches to operational improvement through quality management

There are two broad quality management approaches:

- total quality management (TQM)
- quality control (QC).

Each of these will be discussed in turn.

Total quality management (TQM)

Introduction

Total quality management (TQM) is a philosophy of quality management that originated in Japan in the 1950s.

TQM is the continuous improvement in quality, productivity and effectiveness obtained by establishing management responsibility for processes as well as outputs. In this, every process has an identified process owner and every person in an entity operates within a process and contributes to its improvement.

> ### Illustration 4
>
> ### A TQM success story
>
> Corning Inc is the world leader in speciality glass and ceramics. This is partly due to the implementation of a TQM approach. In 1983 the CEO announced a $1.6 billion investment in TQM. After several years of intensive training and a decade of applying the TQM approach, all of Corning's employees had bought into the quality concept. They knew the lingo – continuous improvement, empowerment, customer focus, management by prevention and they witnessed the impact of the firm's techniques as profits soared.
>
> ### An example of TQM failure
>
> British Telecom launched a total quality program in the late 1980s. This resulted in the company getting bogged down in its quality processes and bureaucracy. The company failed to focus on its customers and later decided to dismantle its TQM program. This was at great cost to the company and they have failed to make a full recovery.

Fundamental features of TQM

Prevention of errors before they occur – the aim of TQM is to get things 'right first time'. TQM will result in an increase in prevention costs, e.g. quality design of systems and products, but internal and external failure costs will fall.

Continual improvement – quality management is not a one-off process, but is the continuous examination and improvement of processes.

Real participation by all – the 'total' in TQM means that everyone in the value chain is involved in the process, including:

- Employees – they are expected to seek out, identify and correct quality problems. Teamwork will be vital.

- Suppliers – quality and reliability of suppliers will play a vital role (TQM and JIT often go hand in hand).

- Customers – the goal is to identify and meet the needs of the customer.

Commitment of senior management – management must be fully committed and encourage everyone else to become quality conscious.

TQM Techniques

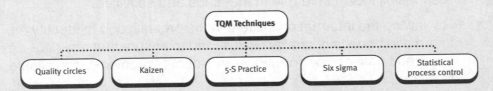

Each of these will be explored in turn.

Quality circles

A **quality circle** is a small group of employees, with a range of skills from all levels of the organisation. They meet voluntarily on a regular basis to discuss quality issues and to develop solutions to real problems.

Advantages include:

- Improvements in quality, leading to greater customer satisfaction and improved productivity.

- A culture of continuous improvement is encouraged.

- Employees at operational level will form part of the quality circle. They often have a better understanding of quality problems than their superiors/managers and their participation will increase commitment to and ownership of problems.

- The group approach helps to foster organisational unity.

- Using interdisciplinary teams helps staff to gain a better perspective of the whole organisation and their part within it.

Encouraging the development and use of quality circles

Putting the idea of quality circles into practice can be very difficult. There are a number of ways in which firms can encourage the development of the use of quality circles:

- Ensuring that there is high profile executive commitment to support the initiative.

- Ensuring that staff members have the training in problem solving and analysis which they need to identify problems and develop workable solutions.

- Ensuring that staff members who are involved in quality circles are free to spend the time necessary away from their day-to-day responsibilities to take part in meetings and activities.

- Reviewing the information system in the organisation to identify the information needs of quality circles, and to ensure that any data required to assess performance and identify problems is available to them.

- Demonstrating that the senior management of the organisation takes the process seriously and takes any action to resolve problems which is identified as necessary by quality circles.

- Developing a culture in the organisation that allows possible changes to be tested out, allowing for the possibility of mistakes.

- Providing training for all staff to increase awareness of the importance and value of quality circles.

Kaizen

Kaizen is a Japanese term for the philosophy of continuous improvement in performance in all areas of an organisation's operations.

Features include:

- Involves all levels of employees.

- Everyone is encouraged to come up with small improvement suggestions on a regular basis.

- Suggestions are not limited to a particular area, such as production or marketing, but look at all areas of the business.

- Setting standards and then continually improving those standards.

- Training and resources should be provided for employees in order for them to meet the standards set.

Illustration 5

Many Japanese companies have introduced a Kaizen approach:

- In companies such as Toyota and Canon, a total of 60–70 suggestions per employee per year are written down and shared.

- It is not unusual for over 90% of those suggestions to be implemented.

- In one US plant, 7,000 Toyota employees submitted over 75,000 suggestions, of which 99% were implemented.

There are a number of Kaizen tools:

Tool	Explanation
Plan-Do-Check-Act (PDCA) cycle	A cycle that encourages key stages to continuous improvement: • Plan: Plan activities • Do: Implement the plan • Check: Check the results • Act: Improve the process
The fishbone diagram	• A cause and effect diagram used to analyse all the contributory causes that contribute to a single effect. • A line is drawn indicating a route of continuous improvement and off this line 'fish bones' will splinter indicating problems that may be encountered.
The Pareto rule	• Pareto identified that 80% of the country's wealth was held by 20% of the population. • Similarly 80/20 classifications occurred regularly in most other areas. • The 'rule' encourages a focus of effort on the important 20% in order to be effective.
The five why process	• Examine issues by constantly asking 'why' until the real issue is identified. • First developed at Toyota; it encourages employee problem solving.

5–S practice

The 5–S practice is an approach to achieving an organised, clean and standardised workplace.

The 5–S practice is often part of a Kaizen approach.

The 5Ss are Japanese words but can be easily translated and understood.

The 5Ss

Word	Meaning	Example
Seiri	Sort	Eliminate unnecessary items, e.g. old, unwanted files.
Seiton	Organise	A structured filing system – 'a place for everything and everything in its place'.
Seiso	Clean	Clean work station regularly
Seiketsu	Standardise	Alphabetic filing system
Shitsuke	Discipline	Do not slip back into old habits.

Six sigma

This quality management programme was pioneered in the 1980s by Motorola, a multinational telecommunications company now best known for its mobile phones and tablet pcs.

The aim of the approach is to achieve a reduction in the number of faults that go beyond an accepted tolerance limit through the use of statistical techniques.

The sigma stands for standard deviation. For reasons that need not be explained here, it can be demonstrated that, **if the error rate lies beyond the sixth sigma of probability, there will be fewer than 3.4 defects in every one million.**

This is almost perfection. Customers will have a reason to complain fewer than four times in a million.

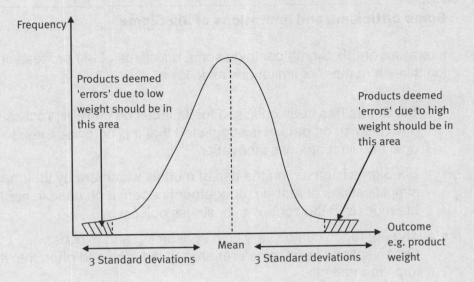

In order to do things right first time with no (or very few) defects, a key emphasis of the Six Sigma approach is to identify root problems and address them.

Further aspects of Six Sigma

Key requirements for successful Six Sigma implementation

There are a number of key requirements for the implementation of Six Sigma.

- Six Sigma should be focused on the customer and based on the level of performance acceptable to the customer.

- Six Sigma targets for a process should be related to the main drivers of performance.

- To maximise savings, Six Sigma needs to be part of a wider performance management programme which is linked to the strategy of the organisation. It should not be just about doing things better but about doing things differently.

- Senior managers within the organisation have a key role in driving the process.

- Training and education about the process throughout the organisation are essential for success.

- Six Sigma sets a tight target, but accepts some failure – the target is not zero defects.

Some criticisms and limitations of Six Sigma

Literature on Six Sigma contains some criticisms of the process and identifies a number of limitations as follows.

- Six Sigma has been criticised for its focus on current processes and reliance on data. It is suggested that this could become too rigid and limit process innovation.

- Six Sigma is based on the use of models which are by their nature simplifications of real life. Judgement needs to be used in applying the models in the context of business objectives.

- The approach can be very time consuming and expensive. Organisations need to be prepared to put time and effort into its implementation.

- The culture of the organisation must be supportive – not all organisations are ready for such a scientific process.

- The process is heavily data-driven. This can be a strength, but can become over-bureaucratic.

- Six Sigma can give all parts of the organisation a common language for process improvement, but it is important to ensure that this does not become jargon but is expressed in terms specific to the organisation and its business.

- There is an underlying assumption in Six Sigma that the existing business processes meet customers' expectations. It does not ask whether it is the right process.

Statistical process control

This technique is explored here since it shares many similarities with six sigma.

Statistical process control may be used when a large number of similar items (such as Mars Bars or car doors) are being produced. Every process is subject to variability, i.e. it is not possible to put exactly the same amount of chocolate in each Mars Bar or make every car door exactly the same width. The variability present is measured and compared to a target value.

- As per six sigma, the upper and lower limits will be three standard deviations away from the expected value (mean).

- All points outside the control limits should be investigated and corrective action taken.

Illustration 6 – Statistical process control

The following statistical control chart shows the size of a product (this may be an important aspect of product conformance) against time.

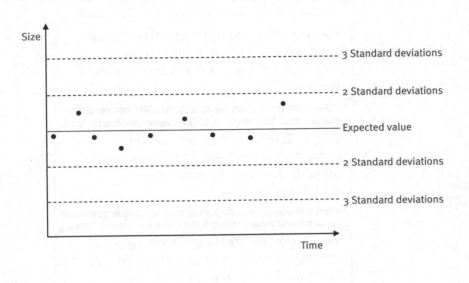

Implementation of a TQM approach

The implementation of a TQM approach may involve the following steps:

> **Step 1: Senior management consultancy –** Managers must be committed to the programme and should undergo quality training

> **Step 2: Establish a quality steering committee –** The committee will guide the company through the process of implementing TQM

> **Step 3: Presentations and training –** The steering committee should communicate the benefits of the change programme to employees in order to gain buy-in

> **Step 4: Establish quality circles –** This will involve employees in the process of quality improvement

> **Step 5: Documentation –** The actions carried out should be clearly documented

> **Step 6: Monitor progress –** Actual results should be monitored against the standard set

Test your understanding 4

Discuss some of the common reasons for the failure of TQM programmes.

Quality control (QC)

Quality control (QC) involves a number of routine steps which measure and control the quality of the product/ service as it is developed.

Purpose/uses of quality control

Quality control is essentially about monitoring whether products/services/processes are being done to the standard required.

As well as testing whether materials or products comply with stated quality levels, QC can also be used to test the following:

- whether procedure/process manuals are being adhered to
- whether actions are in line with best practice guidance
- staff competence, such as knowledge, skills, experience, and qualifications
- "soft" elements such as motivation and team working

The steps in quality control

A typical QC process will involve the following steps:

(1) Setting standards

In order to implement an effective QC program, an enterprise must first decide which specific standards the product or service must meet.

One aspect of defining quality is the idea of consistency but most organisations do not produce identical products or services so must decide what constitutes a "quality" product and what is not. This can often incorporate a range of factors

Note: these are usually linked to customer service agreements – what does the customer consider to be acceptable (or better)?

(2) Sampling

It is not practical in most industries to test every unit so a sample needs to be selected. Key processes should take priority in deciding where to test.

This could involve sampling at different stages in the process – raw materials ("receiving inspection"), work in progress ("floor inspection") and finished goods prior to distribution to customers ("final inspection"). For example, a set percentage of units from each batch of ready meals produced for a supermarket chain may be selected for testing prior to sending to the customer.

Note: Statistical methods may be used that can link sample sizes to an acceptable probability of defective units not being detected and ultimately reaching customers.

(3) Inspection/testing

Units are then tested against the criteria established in step 1 and results reported to management.

(4) Action

Corrective action must be decided upon and taken – for example, defective units must be repaired or rejected and poor service repeated at no charge until the customer is satisfied.

Linked to these is the need to understand why problems have occurred so steps to reduce or eliminate errors can be implemented.

(5) Further testing

QC process must be ongoing to ensure that remedial efforts, if required, have produced satisfactory results and to immediately detect recurrences.

8 Lean Management

8.1 Introduction

As the name suggests, lean management is a philosophy that aims to **systematically eliminate waste**.

In this section we will look first at manufacturing contexts but then we will consider how the same principles can be applied within service organisations.

> **Illustration 7**
>
> 60 years ago, the cars that Toyota was making were uncompetitive in both cost and quality terms. In a bid to catch up with its American competitors, it developed lean production. Lean production helped Toyota to become what it is now – the biggest car manufacturer in the world.

8.2 Wastes to be eliminated

- **Inventory** – holding or purchasing unnecessary raw materials, work-in-progress and finished goods.
- **Waiting** – time delays/idle time when value is not added to the product.
- **Defective units** – production of a part that is scrapped or requires rework.
- **Effort** – actions of people/equipment that do not add value.
- **Transportation** – delays in transportation or unnecessary handling.
- **Over-processing** – unnecessary steps that do not add value.
- **Over-production** – production ahead of demand.

8.3 Characteristics of lean production

- **Improved production scheduling** – production is initiated by customer demand rather than ability and capacity to produce, i.e. production is demand-pull, not supply-push.
- **Small batch production or continuous production** – production is based on customer demand, resulting in highly flexible and responsive processes.
- **Economies of scope** – lean production is only achieved where 'economies of scope' make it economical to produce small batches of a variety of products with the same machines. This is in stark contrast with traditional manufacturing and its emphasis on economies of scale.

- **Continuous improvement** – the company continually finds ways to reduce process times:
  - A multi-skilled, trained workforce provides flexibility.
  - The machines, tools and people used to make an item are located close together.
  - Quality at source reduces re-working.
  - A clean and orderly workplace.
- **Zero inventory** – JIT purchasing eliminates waste.
- **Zero waiting time** – JIT production means that the work performed at each stage of the process is dictated solely by the demand for materials for the next stage, thus reducing lead time.

Illustration 8 – Reverse Engineering

IBM regularly compares part counts, bills of materials, standard versus custom part usage, and estimated processing costs by tearing down competitor products as soon as they are available.

Through such tear-downs during the heyday of the dot matrix printer, IBM learned that the printer made by the Epson, its initial supplier, was exceedingly complicated with more than 150 parts. IBM launched a team with a simplification goal and knocked the part count down to 62, cutting assembly from thirty minutes to only three.

8.4 The six core techniques of lean manufacturing

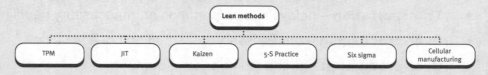

Just-in-time (JIT) and total productive maintenance (TPM) will be discussed in more detail below.

8.5 Total productive maintenance (TPM)

TPM engages all levels and functions of the organisation in maintenance. Workers are trained to take care of the equipment over its entire useful life.

Illustration 9 – TPM

Pulling the cord, called 'andcan', is part of Toyota's lean production system. An employee who notices a problem, pulls the cord to stop the production line. This will prompt fellow workers to gather round and to solve the problem.

Workers at the Toyota plant in Georgetown, Kentucky, pull the cord 2,000 times a week and their care is what makes Toyota one of the most desired and reliable brands in the US. In contrast, workers at Ford's plant in Michigan pull the cord only twice a week.

In 1998 it took Ford 50% more hours to make a car than Toyota. Toyota's lean system means that it has been able to produce cars more cheaply, and to a higher quality, than Ford.

TPM

The major factors that need to be considered in order to implement TPM are:

- training

- equipment maintenance

- planning

- having an adequate budget in place.

TPM should reduce equipment breakdowns, enhance equipment capability and improve safety and environmental factors.

8.6 Just-in-time (JIT)

Most inventory management systems assume that it is necessary to hold some inventory. An alternative view is that inventory is wasteful and adds no value to operations.

Just-in-time (JIT) is a system whose objective it is to produce or procure products or components as they are required by the customer or for use, rather than for inventory. This means that inventory levels of raw materials, work-in-progress and finished goods can be kept to a minimum.

JIT applies to both production within an organisation and to purchasing from external suppliers:

JIT purchasing is a method of purchasing that involves ordering materials only when customers place an order. When the goods are received, they go straight into production.

JIT production is a production system that is driven by demand for the finished products (a 'pull' system), whereby each component on a production line is produced only when needed for the next stage.

Illustration 10

Toyota pioneered the JIT manufacturing system, in which suppliers send parts daily – or several times a day – and are notified electronically when the assembly line is running out.

More than 400 trucks a day come in and out of Toyota's Georgetown plant in the USA, with a separate logistics company organising the shipment from Toyota's 300 suppliers – most located in neighbouring states within half a day's drive of the plant.

Toyota aims to build long-term relationships with its suppliers, many of whom it has a stake in, and says it now produces 80% of its parts within North America.

Requirements for successful operation of a JIT system

- **High quality and reliability** – disruptions create hold ups in the entire system and must be avoided. The emphasis is on getting the work 'right first time':
    - Highly skilled and well trained staff should be used.
    - Machinery must be fully maintained.
    - Long-term links should be established with suppliers in order to ensure a reliable and high quality service.

- **Elimination of non-value added activities** – value is only being added whilst a product is being processed. For example, value is not added whilst storing the products and therefore inventory levels should be minimised.

- **Speed of throughput** – the speed of production should match the rate at which customers demand the product. Production runs should be shorter with smaller stocks of finished goods.

- **Flexibility** – a flexible production system is needed in order to be able to respond immediately to customer orders:

  - The system should be capable of switching from making one product to making another.

  - The workforce should be dedicated and have the appropriate skills. JIT is an organisational culture and the concept should be adopted by everyone.

  - Management should allow the work teams to use their initiative and to deal with problems as they arise.

- **Lower costs** – another objective of JIT is to reduce costs by:

  - Raising quality and eliminating waste.

  - Achieving faster throughput.

  - Minimising inventory levels.

Illustration 11

The Impact of JIT

- Under JIT, a buyer can reduce the number of suppliers. GM, the US car manufacturer, reduced their suppliers by 50%.

- Westinghouse Electric Company has reduced their inventories by 45% and plant stockouts by 95%.

- The pharmaceutical company, Warner-Lambert has replaced its costly batch production by a JIT-based controlled process. Suppliers are also chosen because of close proximity to the plant. Long-term contracts and single sourcing is advocated to strengthen buyer-supplier relationships and tends to result in a higher quality product. Inventory problems are shifted back onto suppliers, with deliveries being as required.

- The luxury car manufacturer, Jaguar, when it analysed the cause of its customer complaints, compiled a list of 150 areas of faults. Some 60% of them turned out to be faulty components from suppliers. One month the company returned 22,000 different components to suppliers. Suppliers were brought on to the multi-disciplinary task forces the company established to tackle each of the common faults, establishing and testing a cure and implementing it as quickly as possible. Jaguar directors chaired the task force of the 12 most serious faults, but in one case the task force was chaired by the supplier's representative.

Test your understanding 5

Explain the advantages and disadvantages to an organisation of operating a JIT system.

Supplier relationships and JIT

As mentioned previously, many of the steps taken to improve the supply chain (and hence profitability) involve improving the relationship between the manufacturer and its suppliers.

This will be of particular importance in a company operating a JIT system.

The advantages to a JIT company of developing close supplier relationships are as follows:

- **No rejects/returns** – a strong relationship should help to improve the quality of supplies. This should minimise production delays since there will be less inspection, fewer returns and less reworking of goods.

- **On-time deliveries** – the development of close working relationships should help to guarantee on-time deliveries of supplies.

- **Low inventory** – suppliers can be relied upon for frequent deliveries of small quantities of material to the company, ensuring that each delivery is just enough to meet the immediate production schedule.

- **Close proximity** – the supplier/ portfolio of suppliers will be located close to the manufacturing plant. This will reduce delivery times and costs.

Test your understanding 6

What is the main principle difference between MRP and JIT?

8.7 Criticisms and limitations of lean manufacturing

- **High initial outlay** – It might involve a large amount of initial expenditure to switch from 'traditional' production systems to a system based on cellular manufacturing. All the tools and equipment needed to manufacture a product need to be re-located to the same area of the factory floor. Employees need to be trained in multiple skills.

- **Requires a change in culture** – Lean manufacturing, like TQM, is a philosophy or culture of working, and it might be difficult for management and employees to acquire this culture. Employees might not be prepared to give the necessary commitment.

- **Part adoption** – It might be tempting for companies to select some elements of lean manufacturing (such as production based on cellular manufacturing), but not to adopt others (such as empowering employees to make on-the-spot decisions).

- **Cost may exceed benefit** – In practice, the expected benefits of lean manufacturing (lower costs and shorter cycle times) have not always materialised, or might not have been as large as expected.

8.8 Application of lean techniques to services

Toyota pioneered the concept of a 'lean' operating system and it has now been implemented in countless manufacturing companies. Lean techniques can also be applied to service companies. The six core methods will still apply, although the use of the methods will be different.

With service operations, a lean approach often focuses on improving the customer experience.

Certain distinguishing features affect the application of lean techniques to services:

- Service organisations tend to be **more labour intensive**, so a lean approach to services could involve a mixture of cutting staffing levels, reducing wasted time and reducing mistakes.

  For example, a teller in a bank may spend only 6 out of 8 hours in day in direct customer service, and the remaining 2 hours are wasted in 1–2 minute segments. Rather than letting unplanned activities fill the void, a priority list of service support tasks such as restocking supplies, following a standardised procedure, can be used to not only reduce waste but also help eliminate other sources of poor service quality.

- Services are **intangible** and it is more difficult to measure their quality than it is for a physical product.

  Attempts to improve time efficiency may have an adverse effect on quality that could be difficult to quantify.

- Services are **consumed immediately** and cannot be stored.

  Matching staff levels to demand for services is critical to avoid wasted time.

- **Customers participate directly in the delivery process**, so firms must evaluate their services from the customer's perspective.

  The customer, when evaluating the quality of the service will take into account the face-to-face contact and the social skills of those providing the service. Again there is a danger that efficiency gains may compromise customer service.

Illustration 12 – Lean management in the NHS

Within the NHS in England lean thinking and Six Sigma have been used to reduce waiting times for patients.

Lean thinking looks to improve the flow in a patient journey and reduce waste while Six Sigma has been used to uncover root problems to ensure things are done right first time.

NHS leaders and staff previously had not fully understood how patients and their information (referrals, appointments, X-rays, pathology specimens, reports, coding information etc) flowed through their organisations and departments. Managers and clinicians tried to optimise their organisational or departmental activity and costs, with no reference to the bottleneck in the system that governs the rate at which patients and information flow along the system or pathways of care.

Accident and Emergency (A&E)

For example, in A&E, lean management approaches identified the bottleneck as the rate of arrival of patients in ambulances and the rate at which junior doctors could assess them and initiate treatment plans. To address this patient journeys were analysed to identify common processes, skill requirements and cycle times. As a result patients were split into two groups:

- Patients with minor conditions have a huge variety and range of conditions but all require a quick simple process to sort them out by experienced staff with minimal equipment. Processing the majority of patients in less than 20 minutes improves the overall time in A&E for the vast majority of patients.

- The major injury and resuscitation patients are fewer in number, but require different skills and technology and have much longer cycle times.

Mixing minors with majors is like putting a lorry into the fast lane on a motorway. It slows the speed of the whole motorway.

Processing pathology specimens

In 2007, turnaround times in pathology at Hereford Hospital were reduced by 40% in 7 days by improving the flow of the specimens through the department and eliminating wasteful activities, such as unnecessary staff movements like searching for things. A key change here was having dedicated staff man the specimen reception. This enabled staff to start processing specimens as soon as they arrived, rather than waiting for someone from a lab to come and see if any had arrived.

The reduction in processing times resulted in estimated savings of £365,000 a year because inpatients could be discharged quicker, shortening length of stay and creating extra capacity in the hospital.

Test your understanding 7

Explain how the six core methods of lean manufacturing can be applied to a call centre.

8.9 The lean supply chain

The lean supply chain

The main objective of a lean supply chain is to completely remove waste in order to achieve competitive advantage through a reduction in costs and an improvement in quality. Other benefits are:

- reduced inventories (and thus increased cash flows and profits)

- shorter lead times, and thus faster deliveries to customers

- few bottlenecks, so better utilisation of resources, and further improvements in profit,

- few quality problems, so less re-work, lower costs of quality failures, and happier customers.

However, disadvantages include the potential for large, powerful customers to dominate the supply chain and an over-emphasis on cost reduction rather than quality improvement.

9 Reverse Logistics

9.1 Introduction

Reverse logistics is the return of unwanted or surplus goods, materials or equipment back to the organisation for reuse, recycling or disposal.

The emergence of internet selling (some internet retailers estimate returns of 50%) and shorter product life cycles has led to many organisations focusing on their reverse logistics capability.

9.2 Reasons for returns

The main reasons are as follows:

- The **customer is not satisfied** with the product and takes advantage of the organisation's return policy.

- **Installation or usage problems** – a common problem if installation or usage is complicated, for example with IT equipment.

- **Warranty claims** for defective products or parts.

- Some manufacturers allow the **return of unsold stock** by retailers, for example this is common practice in the book industry.

- **Manufacturer recall** program due to faults.

9.3 Attacking the returns challenge

This is a critical area of supply chain management. Steps should be taken to:

- **minimise returns**, for example through the production of good quality products or parts, which meet customer requirements and have clear guidelines for installation and usage.

- **ensure the possible reuse or recycling of material**. This is closely linked to CSR but should contribute to increased profitability.

Techniques include:

- Root cause analysis to understand the reasons for returns.

- Creation of profit centres around the returns process to focus organisations on maximising the price that they will get for any returns.

- Separation of the supply chain into separate forward and reverse logistics.

- Centralising the returns centre to improve the speed and efficiency of handling returns.

- Outsourcing the returns process to a competent and dedicated provider.

- The use of state-of-the-art information technology such as enterprise resource planning (ERP) which supports reverse logistics processes.

The use of these techniques should reduce costs, improve customer service and increase revenue.

Illustration 13 – Reverse logistics at Estee Lauder

A good example of a complete reverse logistics program is a project by cosmetics manufacturer Estee Lauder. The firm used to dump $60 million of its products into landfills each year, destroying more than a third of the name brand cosmetics returned by retailers.

Estee Lauder made a small investment of $1.3 million to build its reverse logistics system and apparently recovered its investment in the first year.

Estee Lauder has reduced its production and inventory levels through its increased ability to put returned goods back on the market and the availability of better data on the reasons for returns. In the first year Estee Lauder was able to evaluate 24 per cent more returned products, redistribute 150 per cent more of its returns, reduce the destroyed products from 37 per cent to 27 per cent and save about $0.5 million on labour costs.

10 Chapter Summary

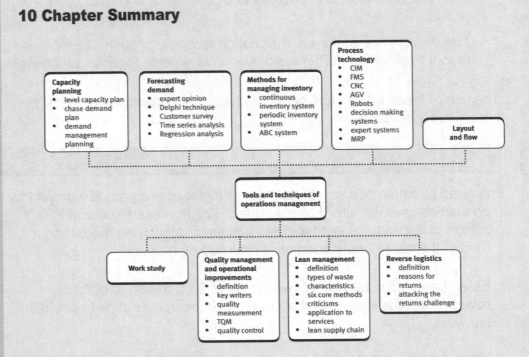

11 Practice questions

Question 1 – OTQ

Which one of the following is an advantage of a flexible manufacturing system?

A   A firm can make bespoke products in response to differing customer needs

B   The system allows management to identify and remove constraints within the system

C   The number of employees can be increased or reduced to fit with existing needs

D   It integrates data from all operations within an organisation

Question 2 – OTQ

An inventory system that records each new addition and withdrawal as it occurs is known as:

A   a Just-In-Time system

B   an ABC system

C   a periodic inventory system

D   a continuous inventory system

Question 3 – OTQ

An ABC system refers to:

A   an inventory management system that aims to eliminate or minimise inventory levels

B   accuracy, benefit and cost effectiveness of the inventory management system

C   an inventory management system that concentrates effort on the most important items

D   a system used to manage relationships with suppliers

Question 4 – OTQ

What is the likely error rate if it lies beyond the sixth sigma of probability?

A   1 defect in 100,000

B   3.2 defects in 600,000

C   3.4 defects in 1,000,000

D   4 defects in 6,000,000

Question 5 – OTQ

Which writer on TQM advocated a zero defects philosophy?

A   Deming

B   Peters

C   Crosby

D   Juran

Question 6 – OTQ

The six core methods of lean manufacturing include cellular manufacturing, six sigma, JIT, Kaizen, TPM and:

A   benchmarking

B   TQM

C   MRP

D   the 5-S practice

Question 7 – Quality circles (Case style)

The production director in a large manufacturing company wants to introduce quality circles into the company's factories, because he has heard of their success in several Japanese companies. He asks for your advice about introducing a system of quality circles, and he tells you: 'My objectives in wanting to introduce these circles are to arrive at decisions for change in product designs and production methods and to get a maximum degree of acceptance. Quality circles can improve quality, productivity, interdepartmental communication, teamwork, team spirit. They can reduce costs and absenteeism and create more job satisfaction. I want them.'

Task:

The production director asks you to explain whether you can foresee any problems with introducing quality circles, and how you would set about implementing a programme for setting them up and using them.

(15 minutes)

Test your understanding answers

Test your understanding 1

Adjustments to workforce capacity to influence supply

- hiring and layoffs
- use of overtime working
- use of part-time or casual labour
- developing a multi-skilled, flexible workforce.

Outsourcing to another provider to help meet temporary increases in demand.

Flexible inventory levels – inventory can be built up in periods of slack and then used to fill demand during periods of high demand.

Pricing and promotion – to smooth peaks and troughs in demand.

Test your understanding 2

The value of having good **MIS** includes:

- Potentially more effective operations and improved management control.
- More complete information available to managers to improve decision making.
- Improved satisfaction and motivation amongst managers.
- Better information leading to improved budgetary control, stock control, improved forecasting etc.

The value of having good **EIS** includes:

- Ability to make informed and potentially significant, decisions of strategic value.
- Maintaining a competitive advantage over rival companies who do not make this investment.
- Improved ability to recognise opportunities or external challenges.
- Ability to track key performance indicators (KPIs) meaning that monitoring and control at strategic level is more effective.

Test your understanding 3

Higher quality can help to increase revenue and reduce costs:

- Higher quality improves the perceived image of a product or service. As a result, more customers will be willing to buy the product/ service and may also be willing to pay more for the product/ service.

- A higher volume of sales may result in lower unit costs due to economies of scale.

- Higher quality in manufacturing should result in lower waste and defective rates, which will reduce production costs.

- The need for inspection and testing should be reduced, also reducing costs.

- The volume of customer complaints should fall and warranty claims should be lower. This will reduce costs.

- Better quality in production should lead to shorter processing times. This will reduce costs.

Test your understanding 4

Tail off – after an initial burst of enthusiasm, top management fails to maintain interest and support.

Deflection – other initiatives or problems deflect attention from TQM.

Lack of buy-in – managers pay only 'lip service' to the principles of worker involvement and communication.

Rejection – TQM does not fit in with the organisational culture and is therefore rejected.

Test your understanding 5

Advantages of JIT

- Lower stock holding costs means a reduction in storage space which saves rent and insurance costs.

- As stock is only obtained when it is needed, less working capital is tied up in stock.

- There is less likelihood of stock perishing, becoming obsolete or out of date.

- Avoids the build-up of unsold finished products that can occur with sudden changes in demand.

- Less time is spent checking and re-working the products as the emphasis is on getting the work right first time.

The result is that costs should fall and quality should increase. This should improve the company's competitive advantage.

Disadvantages of JIT

- There is little room for mistakes as little stock is kept for re-working a faulty product.

- Production is very reliant on suppliers and if stock is not delivered on time or is not of a high enough quality, the whole production schedule can be delayed.

- There is no spare finished product available to meet unexpected orders, because all products are made to meet actual orders.

- It may be difficult for managers to empower employees to embrace the concept and culture.

- It won't be suitable for all companies. For example, supermarkets must have a supply of inventory.

- It can be difficult to apply to the service industry. However, in the service industry a JIT approach may focus on eliminating queues, which are wasteful of customers' time.

Test your understanding 6

JIT is a pull-based system which responds to customer demand. In contrast, MRP is a push-based system which tends to use stock as buffers between the different elements of the system such as purchasing, production and sales.

Test your understanding 7

JIT – planning and forecasting can be used to manage demand. This will ensure that there is an appropriate number of staff to minimise queuing times (these waste customer's time but also give them an adverse impression about the quality of the service) but that staff idle time is also kept to a minimum. Well trained staff should be able to meet the customers' needs effectively and efficiently and a well organised work area should be able to reduce the amount of time that customers are on hold for.

Kaizen – this might be used to reduce customer waiting times. Some call centres use electronic wall boards. These show information, such as the number of customers waiting, and can be used to reduce this waiting time for customers.

5-S practice – this model can be used to organise the surroundings of the call centre office. All of the materials the employee uses should be organised and within reach without having to leave the area. This should allow the call centre staff to talk on the phone, access the computer and view any other documents, all without moving from their desk.

TPM – call centre staff should be trained to take care of their equipment and will be able to solve common problems themselves, e.g. with their phone/computer.

Cellular manufacturing – rather than placing pieces of equipment such as postage machines, photocopiers, fax machines and file drawers throughout the area for everyone to use (and wait on), consider placing these together in a U shaped cell to minimise movement.

Six sigma – It is more difficult to define a fault in a service company but it can be thought of as not fulfilling the needs of the customer. Well trained, experienced staff will have the ability to put the customer first and to achieve the low level of 'faults' required by six sigma.

Question 1 – OTQ

The correct answer is A

Question 2 – OTQ

The correct answer is D

Question 3 – OTQ

The correct answer is C

Question 4 – OTQ

The correct answer is C

Question 5 – OTQ

The correct answer is C

Question 6 – OTQ

The correct answer is D

Question 7 – Quality circles (Case style)

Quality circles are a method of trying to encourage innovative ideas in production, and by involving employees they are likely to improve the prospects for acceptance of changes in products and working methods.

The production director should be advised that the nature of the changes recommended by the quality circle will depend on the range of skills and experience of the circle members. The wider their skills are, and the broader their experience, the more significant and far-reaching will be the changes they might suggest. Groups of workers with similar skills are more likely to make suggestions for limited changes, within the sphere of their own work experience. What range of skills should the circles have?

The 'terms of reference' of the circles should be made clear. Are they to recommend changes to senior management, or will they have the authority to decide changes, and make them?

Since the purpose of quality circles is to encourage innovation, the co-operation of employees will be crucial. The plans for setting up quality circles should therefore be discussed with the employees who will provide membership of the circles.

Possible problems with the introduction of quality circles might be:

(a) not enough support from top management.

(b) no co-operation from middle management.

(c) poor choice of circle leaders.

(d) insufficient training of circle members.

(e) unwillingness to participate among employees.

(f) individual talkers dominate the circle.

(g) poor communication.

The keys to a successful programme are:

(a) creating a proper atmosphere in which to launch them – a positive approach and good publicity.

(b) giving circle member adequate training in quality circle techniques.

(c) introducing circles slowly, one or two at a time, instead of setting up too many all at once. Learning from experience. Getting employees to accept the value of circles from their experience and observations over time.

(d) full support from top management.

(e) an enthusiastic 'facilitator' – a manager in charge of making the circles a success.

(f) setting up a good system for following up and evaluating proposals for change.

(g) giving recognition to circle members – for instance, rewards for successful changes.

Introduction to Marketing

Chapter learning objectives

Lead	Component
E1. Demonstrate the purpose of the marketing function and its relationship with other parts of the organisation.	(a) Apply the marketing concept and principles in a range of organisational contexts. (b) Apply the elements of the marketing mix.
E2. Apply tools and techniques to formulate the organisation's marketing strategies, including the collection, analysis and application of big data.	(a) Apply the main techniques of marketing.

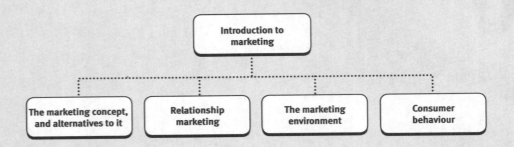

1 Introduction

- Organisations are increasingly recognising the importance of marketing's role and its contribution in achieving sustainable growth and profitability. It can be a key driver of competitive advantage. Marketing is not simply promotion but is a much broader concept.

- This chapter introduces what is meant by marketing. The following two chapters describe the marketing tools that an organisation may use to compete.

In the UK, the Chartered Institute of Marketing (CIM) defines marketing as:

"The management process responsible for identifying, anticipating and satisfying customer requirements profitably."

The organisation will first understand the needs of the customer and will then adopt a strategy producing products with the benefits and features to fulfil these needs.

2 The Marketing Concept, and the Alternatives to it

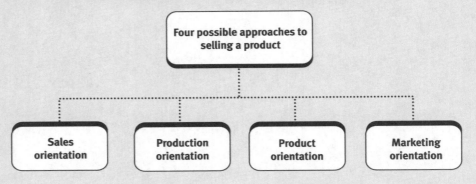

A marketing orientated business is one that has adopted a marketing concept (philosophy). However, a number of other 'orientations' – sales, production and product – may be adopted. Before explaining the marketing concept each of these alternatives will be introduced.

2.1 Sales orientation

- The major task of management is to use persuasive communication and aggressive promotional policies to entice the customer.

- The sales team and the sales manager are the focal point of the business.

- The belief is that a good sales team can sell anything to anybody.

Test your understanding 1

Explain the types of organisation that adopt a sales orientation.

Drawbacks of the sales orientation

- There is no systematic attempt to identify customer needs, or to create products that satisfy them.

- As a result, the organisation has to rely on intensive sales techniques.

2.2 Production orientation

The main focus is on production efficiencies and low costs.

Illustration 1 – Production orientation

In America and Europe, the production orientation was a popular approach until the 1930s. Up until then, there was a general shortage of goods relative to demand and a lack of competition resulted in a seller's market.

During periods of shortages, a production orientation sometimes returns to an industry sector. Normally the UK honey industry is typified by a marketing orientation (see below), where customer needs are prioritised. However, a poor summer in the UK in 2008 resulted in a honey shortage since worker bees don't forage as much in the rain or cold weather. This resulted in producers simply trying to harvest and produce as much honey as possible, a production orientation.

Drawbacks of the production orientation

- If production exceeds demand, too much may be produced and left unsold.

- The approach does not take account of customer preferences and the low cost may be associated with lower quality.

2.3 Product orientation

The business centres its activities on continually improving and refining its products, assuming that customers simply want the best quality for their money.

Drawbacks of the product orientation

The business concentrates on its products and, as a result, the product may or may not fulfil customer requirements.

Illustration 2 – Product orientation

Sir Clive Sinclair's business adopted a product orientation. Some of his products proved extremely popular. For example, The Spectrum computer released in 1981 was very cheap and powerful for its day.

Other products were not such a success: The Sinclair C5, a road hugging vehicle that could reach speeds of 15mph. When it was released in 1985, it was billed as the last word in futuristic transport. However, it was rumoured to be powered by a washing machine motor and was so small that driving it was dangerous. The product was consigned to the commercial scrapheap after just ten months.

2.4 Marketing orientation

Understand customer's **needs** .... Product **benefits and features** should fulfil needs

All of the approaches reviewed so far have potential drawbacks. The best approach that an organisation can adopt is a marketing orientation.

Benefits of the marketing orientation

Where an organisation is able to meet its customers' needs efficiently and effectively, its ability to gain an advantage over its competitors will be increased.

Benefits of a marketing orientation

As CIM point out:

"It is all about getting the right product or service to the customer at the right price, in the right place, at the right time. Business history and current practice both remind us that without proper marketing, companies cannot get close to customers and satisfy their needs. And if they don't, a competitor surely will."

Test your understanding 2

Car manufacturers must adapt their strategy to reflect changing customer needs. For example:

- In the 1980's some car manufacturers targeted young upwardly-mobile professionals (yuppies).

- In the early 21st century, car manufacturers targeting families have had to recognise the changing needs of the modern family.

Using the example of a car, explain the needs of the two groups above. Describe what features and benefits manufacturers have included in their cars in order to fulfil the needs of these customers.

Who is responsible for marketing?

Satisfying customers is at the heart of marketing. Who then assumes responsibility for this important function? Possibly the marketing department or the sales force? True, such personnel can have an influence on customer satisfaction, but marketing as a philosophy is wider than this narrow group of employees. Employees outside the marketing department or sales force can also play an important role in determining customer satisfaction.

Marketing is more than a range of techniques that enables the company to determine customer requirements. It can be better understood as a shared business ethos. The marketing concept is a philosophy that places customers central to all organisational activities. The long-term strategies of an organisation might be centred on profit maximisation, market share growth, or growth in real terms but none of this can be achieved without satisfying customers.

Without customers there would be no business.

3 Relationship Marketing

Customer retention is a critical issue for many businesses.

Reasons why customers are lost
Customers may be lost for a number of reasons: • unhelpful staff • poor quality of service • inappropriate prices • lack of customer care.

Relationship marketing is the technique of maintaining and exploiting the firm's customer base as a means of developing new business opportunities.

Transaction marketing	Relationship marketing
• concentrates on the product • little knowledge of the customer • product quality a key issue • little effort on customer retention	• concentrates on retention and loyalty • considerable customer commitment • considerable customer contact • emphasis on quality service

4 The Marketing Environment

4.1 Different levels in the marketing environment

The marketing environment is the content in which the organisation exists. The environment can have a considerable impact on the organisation and exists at three levels.

The macro environment

This includes all the factors that influence an organisation but are **outside of their control**. Organisations will need flexible marketing practices to respond to this dynamic environment.

Test your understanding 3

The factors in the macro environment are realistically out of the organisation's control, however is there any way an organisation may seek to exercise some influence?

The micro environment

This includes all the factors that can influence an organisation, but the organisation has some opportunity to **exercise influence**. It consists of the organisation's stakeholders, such as suppliers and customers.

The internal environment

This includes all the factors that are internal to the organisation and are therefore potentially **all controllable** including its human resources, finance available and assets.

4.2 PEST(EL) analysis

One popular technique for analysing the **macro** environment is PEST(EL) analysis.

This analysis divides the business environment into six related sub-systems – Political, Economic, Social, Technical, Environmental/Ecological factors and Legal. Each of these factors can be applied to the marketing function.

Political

Political factors can have a direct effect on the way a business operates. Decisions made by government affect our everyday lives.

For example, the instability of many governments in less developed countries has led a number of companies to question the wisdom of marketing in those countries.

Economic

All businesses are affected by economical factors nationally and globally. For example, within the UK, the climate of the economy can dictate how consumers behave within society.

Test your understanding 4

Describe the changes that may be made to the marketing approach of a supermarket if the country goes into recession.

Social

Forces within society such as family, friends and the media affect our attitude, interests and opinions and, in turn, will influence our purchases.

For example, within the UK people's attitudes are changing towards their diet and health. Over the last 10 years, the UK has seen an increase in the number of people joining fitness clubs and a massive increase in demand for organic food.

Social factors

According to Johnson and Scholes the following social influences should be monitored:

- **Population demographics** – a term used to describe the composition of the population in any given area, whether a region, a country or an area within a country.

- **Income distribution** – will provide the marketer with some indication of the size of the target markets. Most developed countries, like the UK, have a relatively even distribution spread. However, this is not the case in other nations.

- **Social mobility** – the marketer should be aware of social classes and the distribution among them. The marketer can use this knowledge to promote products to distinct social classes within the market.

- **Lifestyle changes** – refer to our attitudes and opinions to things like social values, credit, health and women. Our attitudes have changed in recent years and this information is vital for the marketer.

- **Consumerism** – one of the social trends in recent years has been the rise of consumerism. This trend has increased to such an extent that governments have been pressured to design laws that protect the rights of the consumer.

- **Levels of education** – the level of education has increased dramatically over the last few years. There is now a larger proportion of the population in higher education than ever before.

Technical

This is an area in which change takes place very rapidly and the organisation needs to be constantly aware of what is going on.

For example, new technology has resulted in the production of new products, such as hybrid cars. These cars have improved fuel economy and reduced emissions.

Ecological

These have become increasingly important in recent years and influence a marketing orientated organisation in a number of ways.

For example, pressure on natural resources has influenced the products offered by some industry sectors, e.g. the fishing industry.

Legal

Regulations governing businesses are widespread; they include those on health and safety, information disclosure, the dismissal of employees, vehicle emissions, the use of pesticides and many more.

For example, the UK smoking ban in public places has resulted in UK tobacco companies exploring new products, such as the legal, electronic cigarette (although these may also be banned in public in the near future), and new markets outside of the UK.

5 Consumer Behaviour

5.1 Introduction

The marketing concept means that organisations need to understand their customers before marketing plans can be developed, or attempts made to improve customer satisfaction.

5.2 Factors affecting buying decisions

Lancaster and Withey concluded that there are three key factors that influence the purchasing decision:

Factor	Examples
(1) Socio/ cultural influences	• **Reference groups** such as school friends or work colleagues e.g. it is a bold person who reads the Sun in an office full of FT readers • **Role modelling** e.g. a young mother would be influenced to make certain buying decisions, such as a push chair, due to her role • **Family** e.g. the influence of 'pester power' may result in child dominant decisions. • **Culture** e.g. beliefs and values may influence whether or not meat is bought by a household.

(2) Personal influences	• Age • Family status • Occupation • Economic circumstances • Lifestyle e.g. a young single male in his 20s, with a high level of disposable income, is likely to purchase a different type of car to a man in his 30s with a growing family.
(3) Psychological influences	• Motivation • Perception • Learning • Beliefs and attitudes e.g. Individuals will be motivated by different needs. Some buyers may be motivated by superb customer service and would not return to a restaurant unless this is received.

Social interaction theory states that an individual's behaviour may depend on what he or she perceives others in society to be doing. The social influence of others therefore impacts on a person's buying habits.

5.3 The stages in the buying process

Lancaster and Withey concluded that customers go through a five stage decision-making process in any purchase. This is summarised in the diagram below:

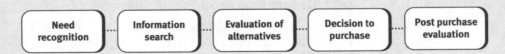

Stage 1: Need (problem) recognition

The consumer identifies the need or the problem and the firm must use appropriate promotional tools to convince the customer that their product could be the answer.

Illustration 3

Marketers have recognised that the cheap coffee that was once bought from a supermarket or a cafe is not going to satisfy the needs of increasingly discerning buyers who seek a coffee that suits their particular tastes, lifestyle and budget. In addition, a growing awareness of ethical trading and healthy living has contributed to the development of coffee to cater for these increasingly complex needs.

Starbucks is one company that has successfully understood these needs. Its cafes sell a huge range of coffees and other beverages and the company also sells its own-branded quality coffee in UK supermarkets.

Stage 2: Information search

Once a need has been recognised buyers will look for information regarding which products may satisfy their needs.

Test your understanding 5

Explain what information sources are likely to be used by a buyer when seeking out information about the alternative ways in which they can satisfy their needs.

Stage 3: Evaluation of alternatives

The consumer compares various brands and products in order to make a choice. The organisation needs to understand the basis of this choice (e.g. price, quality, design, branding etc).

Stage 4: Decision to purchase

This stage is where the customer actually makes a purchase choice.

The final decision to purchase may involve a large number of people, known as the decision-making unit (DMU). The DMU is made up of six groups:

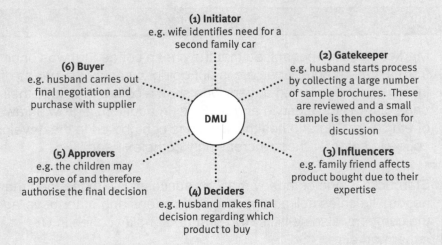

(1) Initiator
e.g. wife identifies need for a second family car

(2) Gatekeeper
e.g. husband starts process by collecting a large number of sample brochures. These are reviewed and a small sample is then chosen for discussion

(6) Buyer
e.g. husband carries out final negotiation and purchase with supplier

DMU

(3) Influencers
e.g. family friend affects product bought due to their expertise

(5) Approvers
e.g. the children may approve of and therefore authorise the final decision

(4) Deciders
e.g. husband makes final decision regarding which product to buy

Stage 5: Post-purchase evaluation

The consumer will assess whether they are satisfied with their purchase decision.

Satisfied customers will act as one of the best forms of promotion: a customer spending just $20 in a restaurant on a first visit could be worth thousands of pounds over the next few years.

The company may seek customer feedback.

Evaluation of 5-stage process

The five-stage model implies that customers pass through all stages in every purchase. However, in more routine purchases, customers often skip or reverse some of the stages.

For example, a student buying a favourite hamburger would recognise the need (hunger) and go right to the purchasing decision, skipping information search and evaluation. However, the model is very useful when understanding any purchase that requires some thought and deliberation.

5.4 Buyer behaviour

> ### Buyer behaviour
>
> Rationally consumer behaviour can be understood in terms of:
>
> - **Relevance** – if a product or service is being purchased for the first time the consumer will be highly involved. The consumer will take more time and effort to make a choice as a way of compensating for their inexperience or minimising the risk. Consumers will also spend more time gathering and processing information for decisions that are important for them.
>
> - **Frequency** – if by comparison, the consumption is repetitive by nature, possibly purchased frequently and has a low price, the consumer will give the purchase little conscious attention and have low involvement in the process. (The purchaser will, after all have experienced the good or service many times previously).
>
> - **Freedom** – a less voluntary or involuntary consumption. It may be seen as something unavoidable possibly if there is little choice between brands, for example the purchasing process is refilling a car with fuel.
>
> - **Influence** – here the issue is the susceptibility of the consumer to influence by others because the consumer might be purchasing on behalf of the family as a whole or the business they work for.

5.5 Theories of consumer behaviour

The following theories should help to guide marketing practices:

- **Cognitive paradigm theory** – the theory is based on the idea that a purchase is an outcome of problem-solving. The consumer receives and makes sense of considerable quantities of information before choosing between products.

- **The learned behaviour theory** – consumers learn from past satisfying or unsatisfying purchases and therefore make shortcuts with future routine/habitual purchases.

- **Habitual decision making** – consumers make decisions based on loyalty, inertia or satisfying behaviour (i.e. the first product is good enough even if a better solution exists).

5.6 Types of buyer behaviour

Buyer behaviour will be influenced by the type of consumer good:

Type of consumer good	Meaning	Factors influencing the purchase
Fast moving consumer good (FMCG)	• Relatively cheap • Purchased on a regular basis e.g. bread, baked beans	• Habitual purchases – often involves very little decision making by buyer • Advertising, branding and packaging will be important.
Durable goods	• Relatively expensive • Not purchased on a regular basis e.g. TV, computer, car	• Fashion • New technical features • Old product wearing out

6 Chapter summary

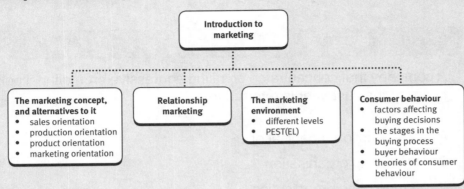

7 Practice questions

Question 1 – OTQ

A company that concentrates on using aggressive promotional policies to entice the customer is referred to as:

A   a production organisation

B   a learning organisation

C   a marketing organisation

D   a sales organisation

Question 2 – OTQ

Which one of the following is a drawback of the production orientation?

A   The business concentrates on its products but the product may not fulfil the customer's needs

B   The organisation relies on sales techniques to sell its products

C   Low cost may be associated with low quality

D   High volume production results in economies of scale

Question 3 – OTQ

Which one of the following is not one of the accepted headings included in PESTEL analysis?

A   Economic

B   Taxation

C   Social

D   Technical

Question 4 – OTQ

Harry is 12 years old. He is a keen Manchester United supporter and in his spare time he plays football for his local team and is a scout member. Which one of the following would be least likely to be a reference group for Harry?

A   His teachers

B   One of the Manchester United players

C   The other members of his local football team

D   The other members of his scout group

Question 5 – OTQ

Which one of the following is an example of a durable good?

A   A games console

B   Milk

C   Tea bags

D   Shampoo

Question 6 – M Company (Case style)

Background

M Company began over a century ago as a small family-run business, selling its own-branded clothing, food and drink. The company has grown rapidly over the past 30 years and now has a prominent position on the high street of many of the country's towns and cities.

Challenges

Until recently, the company had a strong reputation and was well known for quality products at affordable prices. However, the situation has changed dramatically as new entrants have taken market share away from M company.

Sales and profits have fallen over each of the three past consecutive years and there is concern that the company may make a loss in the forthcoming year.

Potential adoption of a marketing orientation

After various attempts failed to improve matters, M company has recently appointed a management consultant to identify the reasons for the declining sales and the loss of customers.

The management consultant has concluded that the problem for M company is that it has never moved from being sales orientated to being marketing orientated and that is why it has lost touch with its customers. The consultant has recommended the adoption of a marketing orientation.

Tasks:

(a) Explain the difference between a company that concentrates on 'selling' its products and one that has adopted a marketing orientation. Explain the benefits to M company of adopting a marketing orientation.

(10 minutes)

(b) Explain, using examples, how M company's marketing function may use PEST(EL) analysis to understand its external environment.

(15 minutes)

(Total: 25 minutes)

Test your understanding answers

Test your understanding 1

A sales orientation has been adopted by a number of business sectors. For example:

- Organisations selling double glazing
- Organisations selling timeshare holidays

These organisations rely on persuasive and aggressive promotional policies to entice the customer.

Test your understanding 2

	Needs of target customer	Product features	Product benefits
1980's – some car manufacturers targeted yuppies	• A fast car • Cutting edge design • Car should enhance image	• Sporty design • Turbo engine • Other features such as an electrically operated roof and leather upholstery	• 0–60 mph in six seconds • Superb road handling
Early 21st century – some car manufacturers target families but have had to recognise their changing needs	• Value for money • Safety • Environmental friendliness • Low fuel consumption	• Air bags • Economical engine • Designed for safety and space	• Good safety record • Low fuel consumption and CO_2 emissions • Room for child seats

Test your understanding 3

An organisation may seek to influence laws by political lobbying or by being part of a trade organisation.

Test your understanding 4

The changing needs of the population must be reflected in the product offerings. For example:

- The supermarket may reduce its range of luxury items in favour of lower priced, basic products.

- Special offers may be made on products, for example, discounts, buy one get one free offers, additional loyalty points on products.

- The supermarket may introduce more 'restaurant style' meals to reflect the trend that fewer people are eating out.

Test your understanding 5

- **Personal experience** – the buyer may already have used the company's products.

- **Word-of-mouth** – for example, recommendations from friends regarding a restaurant.

- **Internet** – for example, websites such as Trip Advisor include user feedback on a large number of hotels.

- **Reference groups** – rather than referring to people we know, we may use various other reference groups to guide us, for example, what kind of shoes is our favourite celebrity wearing at the moment?

- **Reviews** – newspapers and consumer review sources such as Which? magazine.

Question 1 – OTQ

The correct answer is D

Question 2 – OTQ

The correct answer is C

Question 3 – OTQ

The correct answer is B

Question 4 – OTQ

The correct answer is A

Question 5 – OTQ

The correct answer is A

Question 6 – M Company (Case style)

(a) **Sales orientation**

A company that concentrates on 'selling' its products is said to be sales orientated. M company currently adopts a sales orientation.

The major task of M's management will be to use persuasive communication and aggressive promotional policies to entice the customer to buy its products.

The sales team and the sales manager will be the focal point of M company. There will be huge investment in the sales department, the belief being that a good sales team can sell anything to anybody.

Techniques such as personal selling and product promotion will be used to emphasise product differentiation and branding.

Drawbacks of the sales orientation

M company is losing customers and its sales and profits have fallen for each of the past three consecutive years. These problems may be largely due to the adoption of a sales orientation since:

– There is no systematic attempt by M company to identify customer's needs, or to create products that satisfy these needs.

– As a result, M company is having to rely on intensive sales techniques but these do not appear to be working.

Adoption of a marketing orientation

This orientation addresses the problems highlighted above.

If M company were to adopt a marketing orientation, they would begin by understanding the needs of the customer and would then adopt a strategy producing products with the benefits and features to fulfil these needs.

Benefits of a marketing orientation

If M company adopts a marketing orientation it will put its customer's needs first. If it is able to identify these needs and meet the needs efficiently and effectively, its ability to gain competitive advantage will increase.

(b) If M company is to turn itself around, not only will it have to understand its customer's needs but it will also need to understand the opportunities, challenges and risks presented by changes in the external environment. PEST(EL) analysis can be used to analyse the external environment. Each of these factors can be applied to M company's marketing function.

Political

Political factors will have a direct effect on the way in which M company operates.

For example, the government in the UK is currently encouraging sustainability in operations and the adoption of a healthy lifestyle by individuals. This may influence a decision by M company to reduce the amount of packaging in its products or to improve product labelling to clearly show the sugar, fat, salt and calorie content of their food products.

Economic

M company will be affected by national and global economic factors.

For example, if the country moves into recession, M company may decide to focus on selling cheaper products rather than luxury products.

Social

Forces within society such as family, friends and the media will influence the choices that individuals make.

For example, within the UK consumer's attitudes, with regards to the source of products, is changing. Ethical sourcing is becoming more important to individuals, e.g. with an increased emphasis on fair trade, a reduction in air miles and fair treatment of suppliers all being considered important. These factors will all influence the decisions taken by M company.

Technical

This is an area in which change takes place very rapidly and it is important for M company to monitor and react to these changes.

For example, new technology may allow existing products to be made more quickly and hence prices can be lowered.

Ecological

These have become increasingly important is recent years and M company must react to any ecological factors. For example, pressure on natural resources may influence the types of fish that M company sell or include in their products.

Legal

Regulations on businesses are widespread, including those on health and safety, information disclosure, the dismissal of employees and many more. For example, M company must clearly display product information on its goods, such as a list of ingredients on its packaged food.

If M company understands its customer's needs as well as its external environment, there is a good opportunity for the business to be turned around.

The Market Planning Process and the Marketing Mix

Chapter learning objectives

Lead	Component
E1. Demonstrate the purpose of the marketing function and its relationship with other parts of the organisation.	(a) Apply the marketing concept and principles in a range of organisational contexts. (b) Apply the elements of the marketing mix.
E2. Apply tools and techniques to formulate the organisation's marketing strategies, including the collection, analysis and application of big data.	(a) Apply the main techniques of marketing. (b) Explain the role of emerging technologies and media in marketing.

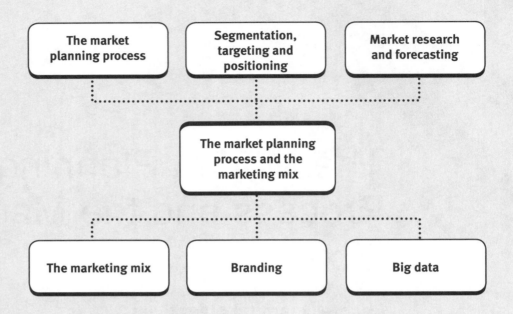

1 The Market Planning Process

A company may currently have a sales/production/product orientation and may want to adopt a marketing orientation. In order to do this, it will need to implement a strategic marketing action plan.

The following components should be included in this plan:

Step 1: Situation analysis

A number of techniques can be used:

SWOT analysis – the organisation needs to understand its own strengths and weaknesses together with an appreciation of the wider environment in which it operates (opportunities and threats).

PEST(EL) analysis – this technique was discussed in chapter 10. The organisation should review the macro environment for opportunities that may allow it to further meet their customers' needs. It should also monitor its competitors' strategies.

Step 2: Review corporate objectives/mission

The organisation may already have a mission statement and a set of corporate objectives in place. However, these should be reviewed to ensure that they are still relevant for the organisation.

Step 3: Set its marketing objectives

Marketing objectives should be consistent with the company's overall mission and objectives.

Marketing objectives should be SMART – specific, measurable, achievable, realistic and time bound, e.g. to achieve a 10% growth in sales in Europe in the next 12 months.

Step 4: Devise an appropriate marketing strategy

The organisation should consider the following:

- Segmentation – the market should be segmented, e.g. by age, social class or income. The needs of each segment should be established using market research.

- Targeting – the most attractive segments in terms of profitability and growth should be targeted using an appropriate marketing mix.

- Positioning – an appropriate positioning strategy, e.g. differentiation or cost leadership should be chosen for each market segment.

- Marketing mix – the organisation should use the marketing mix to determine the correct strategy for product, price, place and promotion.

Market research will be required to understand the organisation's activities and to provide a basis for effective marketing decisions to be made.

Note: Each of these ideas will be explored in more detail in the remainder of the chapter.

Step 5: Plan the marketing mix

The organisation must then plan the specific elements of the marketing mix into a marketing action plan.

The marketing action plan will form an important component of any business plan. The business plan has many objectives including:

- Securing external funding
- Measuring business success.

Step 6: Implementation

The marketing action plan should then be implemented.

Step 7: Review

The plan should also be monitored to gauge its success and to identify any necessary changes.

2 Segmentation, Targeting and Positioning

2.1 Market segmentation

Market segmentation is the sub-dividing of the market into homogenous groups to whom a separate marketing mix can be focused.

A market segment is a group of consumers with distinct, shared needs.

Why segment the market?

- Market segmentation allows companies to treat similar customers in similar ways.
- Each segment has slightly different needs which can be satisfied by offering each segment a slightly different marketing mix.
- The key objective is to say that people falling into a particular segment are more likely to purchase the product than most.
- The company will choose a particular segment or segments to target.

Criteria for market segments

Kotler suggested that segments must be:

- measurable
- accessible and
- substantial.

Criteria for segmentation

- **Measurable** – It must be possible to identify the number of buyers in each market segment so that their potential profitability can be assessed, e.g. the size of the segment of people aged 30–40, or who are married with children, can be accurately calculated but information about the number of people who are environmentally aware is not readily available.

- **Accessible** – It must be possible to reach the segment, e.g. some buyers in a market may be tied to suppliers by long-term supply contracts. Therefore, this market is not accessible.

- **Substantial** – The cost of targeting a particular segment must be less than the benefit. Small market segments may prove unprofitable.

Bases for segmentation

One form of segmentation may be enough, or a number of variables may be used, to define the target market exactly. Possible bases include:

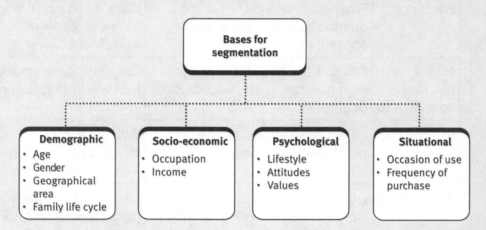

Bases for segmentation

Demographic

Market segments are frequently based on age, gender, geographical location or family life cycle.

This can be highly relevant with some products, for example, certain brands of breakfast cereal have regular sales to families with young children (e.g. Coco Pops), whereas other brands (e.g. Bran Flakes) sell almost entirely to adults.

In other areas, demographic influences seem to have little effect. For instance, own-label products are believed to sell equally to high and low income families and single people and across all age groups.

Family life cycle segmentation divides customers by their position in the family life cycle:

Life cycle stage	Characteristics	Examples of products purchased
Bachelor	Financially well off. Fashion opinion leaders. Recreation orientated.	Cars, holidays, basic furniture, kitchen equipment.
Newly married couple	Still financially well off. Very high purchase rate, especially of durables.	Cars, furniture, houses, holidays, refrigerators.
Full nest (i)	Liquid assets low. Home purchasing at a peak. Little money saving.	Washers, TVs, baby foods, toys, medicines.
Full nest (ii)	Better off. Some partners work. Some children work part time. Less influenced by advertising.	Larger size grocery packs, foods, cleaning materials, bicycles.
Full nest (iii)	Better off still. Purchasing durables.	New furniture, luxury appliances, recreational goods.
Empty nest (i)	Satisfied with financial position.	Travel, luxuries, home improvements.
Empty nest (ii)	Drastic cut in income. Stay at home.	Medicines, health aids.

Geo-demographic segmentation combines demographic and geographic variables. This is a recent, but powerful, development in which geographical segmentation is undertaken at a much more localised level and linked to other demographic factors.

Socio-economic

One of the most widely used forms of segmentation in the UK is socio-economic.

Class	Social status	Job descriptions
A	Upper middle class	Higher managerial, administrative and professional
B	Middle class	Middle management, administrative and professional
C1	Lower middle class	Supervisory, clerical, junior management, administrative staff
C2	Working class	Semi and unskilled manual jobs
D	Subsistence	Pensioners, widows, lowest grade workers

While such class-based systems may seem out of date, the model is still widely used, especially in advertising. Socio-economic class is closely correlated with press readership and viewing habits, and media planners use this fact to advertise in the most effective way to communicate with their target audience.

Psychological

Lifestyle segmentation may be used because people of similar age and socio-economic status may lead quite different lifestyles. Marketers have segmented the market using terms such as 'Yuppies' (young, upwardly-mobile professionals) and 'Dinkies' (double income, no kids).

Attitudes and values can be harder to measure but can prove to be a useful basis for segmentation, e.g. individuals may have a value based on caution and therefore purchase a safe, reliable car.

Situational (or behavioural)

Occasion of use – a product may be bought at different times for different uses. For example, workers may expect a lunchtime meal in a restaurant to be fast and good value for money, whereas those same individuals may be willing to pay more in the evening for a more relaxed dining experience.

Frequency of purchase – frequent buyers may be more demanding with regards to product features and may be more sensitive to price changes.

Customer loyalty – many organisation try to segment their markets into those where loyal (and hence valuable) customers can be found, compared to those segments with little or no customer loyalty.

Test your understanding 1

Explain five variables that you think would be useful as a basis for segmenting the market for cars.

Industrial segmentation

Industrial segmentation is different from that used in consumer marketing. The following factors influence the way industrial customers can be segmented:

Geographic is used as the basis for sales-force organisations.

Purchasing characteristics – is the classification of companies by factors such as average order size or the frequency with which they order.

Benefit – industrial purchasers have different benefit expectations to consumers. They may be orientated towards reliability, durability, versatility, safety, serviceability or ease of operation. They are always concerned with value for money.

Company type – industrial customers can be segmented according to the type of business they are, i.e. what they offer for sale. The range of products and services used in an industry will not vary too much from one company to another.

Company size – it is frequently useful to analyse marketing opportunities in terms of company size. A company supplying canteen foods would investigate size in terms of numbers of employees. Processed parts suppliers are interested in production rate, and lubricants suppliers would segment by numbers of machine tools.

2.2 Targeting

Targeting is the process of selecting the most lucrative market segment(s) for marketing the product.

Having segmented the market, the organisation can now decide how to respond to the differences in customer needs identified and will reach a conclusion as to which segments are worth targeting.

When evaluating potential target markets, the following issues should be considered:

- Size of segment
- Growth potential
- Profit potential
- Degree of competition
- Accessibility
- Barriers to entry

2.3 Positioning

Positioning involves the formulation of a definitive marketing strategy around which the product would be marketed to the target audience.

After the target market has been chosen, marketers will want to position their products in relation to the competitors for that segment. A variety of techniques are available.

For example, the market for package holidays can be split into a variety of different segments – the family market, the elderly market, the young singles market, the activity holiday market, the budget holiday market, etc.

It would be virtually impossible to provide one single holiday package that would satisfy all people in the above markets. Because the people in the different segments will have different needs and wants, a holiday company has a choice in terms of its marketing approach. It can go for:

- **Concentrated marketing** (sometimes referred to as niche or target marketing) specialises in one or two of the identified markets only, where a company knows it can compete successfully. For example, Saga holidays offers a variety of holidays for the older market niche only.

- **Differentiated marketing** (sometimes called segmented marketing) – the company makes several products each aimed at a separate target segment. For example, Virgin Holidays offers a variety of family holidays, honeymoon packages and city breaks, each of which is targeted at a different group. Many retailers have developed different brand formats to target different groups.

- **Undifferentiated marketing** (sometimes called mass marketing) – this is the delivery of a single product to the entire market. There is little concern for segmentation. The hope is that as many customers as possible will buy the product. When Henry Ford began manufacturing cars he offered any colour 'as long as it's black'.

Perceptual mapping

Perceptual mapping is used to chart consumers' perceptions of brands currently on offer and to identify opportunities for launching new brands or to reposition an existing brand. Marketers decide upon a competitive position that enables them to distinguish their own products from the offerings of their competition (hence the term 'positioning strategy').

The marketer would draw out the map and decide upon a label for each axis. They could be price (variable one) and quality (variable two), or comfort (variable one) and price (variable two). The individual products are then mapped out next to each other. Any gaps (strategic spaces) could be regarded as possible areas for new products. The analysis below illustrates a local grocery market.

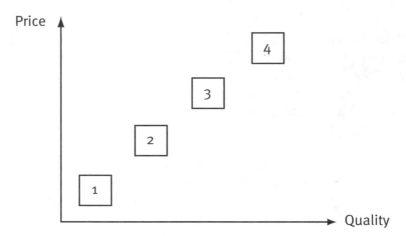

The two critical success factors here are price and quality. Of course, others, such as location, opening hours, marketing expenditure, and so on might be important too under some circumstances.

Group 1 are the price discounters. The business cuts cost wherever it can. Product ranges are restricted and there are few attempts to make the store decorative or service friendly.

Group 2 are the main market retailers. They compete on price, but offer more and better ranges, better customer service, and so on.

Group 3 offer a higher quality range, they do not attempt to compete on price at all.

Group 4 are delicatessens. They offer a superior service and specialist items. Prices are very high.

It is a great strategic mistake to try to position oneself where there are no customer groups. For example, several companies have tried to cross between groups 1 and 2, usually without success.

3 Market Research and Forecasting

3.1 Market research

Market research is the way in which organisations find out what their customers and potential customers need, want and care about.

It involves a number of data gathering techniques and methods of analysis:

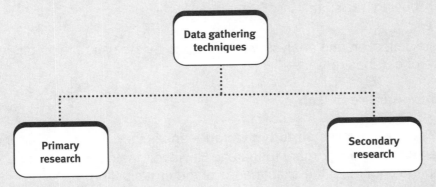

Primary research

This is **collected for the specific purpose of the research in question**. The organisation may enlist a specialist agency to carry out the research. Methods include:

- **Questionnaires** – A popular technique and can be done face to face, online, over the telephone or by self completion. Key information about the respondents will be obtained for segmentation purposes.

- **Focus groups** – consist of a group of approximately 8–10 people plus a trained moderator who leads a discussion on an issue about which the company wants to learn more, e.g. feedback on a new product.

- **Observation** – observational techniques can be used to understand behaviour, for example:
  - Many organisations will monitor their competitors through gathering brochures, monitoring websites and obtaining price lists. This will help the organisation to understand how its competitors are aiming to fulfil the needs of its customers.

  - In addition, the internet has allowed customer behaviour to be monitored, e.g. how many visits has a customer made to a website, have there been subsequent purchases, which pages did they review and in which order?

- **Interviews** – a similar approach to questionnaires but may be more detailed and open ended and may focus on a smaller group due to the time involved.

- **Experimentation** – similar to focus groups, in so much as users may discuss a product, but it does not require group discussion. For example, triad testing is where people are asked which of a given three items they prefer. If the three are brands of a given type, replies may show a great deal about which features of a product most influence the buying decision.

Data collection and analysis will be helped by the use of technology, e.g. the use of databases.

Secondary research

This is **data that is already available** and is therefore cheaper and quicker than carrying out primary research. However, the data may not be accurate and may not meet the exact needs of the organisation.

Test your understanding 2
Describe the sources of secondary research that may be available.

3.2 Forecasting

Forecasting will focus on sales potential.

The **sales potential** is an estimate of the part of the market that is within the possible reach of a product.

Estimates of sales potential are required to decide whether to invest money in the development or promotion of a new or improved product. The forecasting of sales potential can be based on:

- historical data, e.g. using techniques such as linear regression

- future demand, e.g. using:
  - a survey of buyers' intentions
  - sales force/other expert's estimates.

Forecasting

The determination of the future profitability of a chosen target segment is the critical element for marketing success. Sales forecasting may utilise a variety of sources, rely on hard facts and subjective views as well as use technology and gut feeling to reveal what is essentially an unknown future to the marketer.

Market demand (total market potential)

This approach uses a combination of variables in simple formulaic structure to determine the future market potential. Variables are:

- Size of customer group
- Time period
- Geographical area
- Market environment.

Area demand (area market potential)

This is an identical approach but on a smaller geographic scale.

Industry sales and market share

Determination of industry size and the company's relative sales will provide an analysis of market share that can be used to extrapolate income based on projected growth in the marketplace over the future time period.

Survey of buyers' intentions

Survey of a small group of potential customers, and their reaction to a marketing mix provides some general indication of the likely uptake of a full marketing strategy in the future.

Sales force opinions

Since the sales team is close to the customer, they will provide an expert view on the potential future success of a new product.

Expert opinions

Independent experts offer an unbiased view of future environmental conditions, particularly economic change, that affects consumer confidence and buyer behaviour.

Past sales analysis

Trend analysis, including seasonal elements smoothed through time series analysis, could be used as the basis for forecasts.

Market tests

There are a variety of market tests including the launch of a trial product in a localised area or the use of market research to elicit possible buyer responses to a new product. This could be the same as a survey of buyers' intentions.

4 The Marketing Mix

4.1 Introduction

Once the positioning strategy has been arrived at, the marketing mix will be formulated.

By blending the different 'P's' of the marketing mix together the organisation aims to satisfy customer's needs profitably.

The traditional marketing mix (4P's):	Elements
Product	Quality, design, durability, packaging, range of sizes/ options, after-sales service, warranties, brand image.
Place	Where to sell the goods, distribution channels and coverage, stock levels, warehouse locations.
Promotion	Advertising, personal selling, public relations, sales promotion, sponsorship, direct marketing, e.g. direct mail and telephone marketing.
Price	Price level, discounts, credit policy, payment methods.

Additional 3P's for the service industry:	
People	Relates to both staff, who will have a high level of customer contact in the service industry (staff will need to be motivated to support the firm's external marketing activities), and customer's whose needs must be monitored (e.g. supermarkets use customer loyalty cards).
Processes	These are the systems through which the service is delivered, e.g. teaching methods used in a university, speed and friendliness of service in a restaurant.
Physical evidence	Required to make the intangible service more tangible, e.g. brochures, testimonials, appearance of staff and of the environment.

The extension of the traditional marketing mix to include the three additional P's acknowledges that there are fundamental differences between products and services and therefore services marketing assumes a different emphasis to product marketing.

Features of service organisations

Service industries have certain distinguishing features that should be considered:

- Services are **intangible** and it is more difficult to measure their quality than it is for a physical product.
- Services are consumed immediately and **cannot be stored**.
- **Customers participate directly in the delivery process** (in contrast to a manufacturing organisation where production and purchase are usually physically separated).
- The customer when evaluating the quality of the service will take into account the **face-to-face contact** and the social skills of those providing the service.
- Service organisations tend to be **more labour intensive**.

Test your understanding 3 – Case style question

H Company, a High Street clothing retailer, designs and sells clothing. Until recently, the company was well-known for quality clothing at an affordable price, but the situation has changed dramatically as new entrants to the market have rapidly taken market share away from H Company.

One marketing analyst has commented that the problem for H Company is that it has never moved from being sales orientated to being marketing orientated and that this is why it has lost touch with its customers.

Task:

Explain how the management in H Company could make use of the traditional marketing mix to help regain its competitive position in the clothing market.

(15 minutes)

Link between the marketing mix and positioning

The marketing mix is essentially the working out of the tactical details of the positioning strategy. An organisation should ensure that all of the above elements are consistent with each other.

For example, a firm that decides to go for a strategy of differentiation through high quality, knows that it must produce high quality products, charge a relatively high price, distribute through high-class dealers and advertise in high quality magazines.

Each element of the traditional marketing mix will now be reviewed in turn:

4.2 Product

4.2.1 Introduction

A product can be a physical commodity, a service or an experience. It has two important roles in the marketing mix:

* It plays a key role in satisfying the customer's needs.

* Product differentiation is an important part of competitive strategy.

4.2.2 Product portfolio

A product portfolio is a collection of products or services an organisation provides to its customers.

After determining the main target markets and the type of product(s) it will offer, the organisation needs to determine the variety and assortment of those products.

The following are the elements of a typical product portfolio:

- **Product item**: This is the individual product, e.g. a specific model of phone or a brand of washing powder. The organisation will usually sell a variety of product items.

- **Product line**: This is a collection of product items that are closely related. For example, The Campbell Soup Company sells many types of soup.

- **Product mix**: This is the total range of product lines that a company has to offer. It consists of:
  - **Width** – the number of product lines. For example, Apple sell computers, i-pods, phones and accessories.
  - **Depth** – the number of product items within each product line. For example, Apple sell a large variety of i-pods.

Different ways of defining a product

The product can be viewed or defined in a number of different ways:

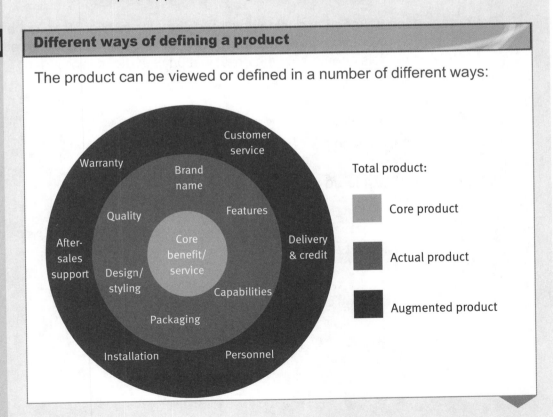

The core product – what is the buyer really buying? The core product refers to the use, benefit or problem solving service that the consumer is really buying when purchasing the product, i.e. the need that is being fulfilled.

The actual product is the tangible product or intangible service that serves as the medium for receiving core product benefits.

The augmented product consists of the measures taken to help the consumer put the actual product to sustained use, including installation, delivery and credit, warranties, and after-sales service.

An automobile offers personal transportation (core product), has many different features and attributes (actual product), and may include a manufacturer's warranty or dealer's discounted service contract (augmented product).

A product, therefore, is more than a simple set of tangible features. Consumers tend to see products as complex bundles of benefits that satisfy their needs. Most important is how the customer perceives the product. They are looking at factors such as aesthetics and styling, durability, brand image, packaging, service and warranty, any of which might be enough to set the product apart from its competitors.

The organisation will need to decide how much funding to allocate to each product, e.g. for promotion, further research and development, branding etc. The following models should help the organisation with these investment decisions:

- the product life-cycle
- the Boston Consulting Group (BCG) matrix.

Note: Branding is explored further in Section 5.

4.2.3 The product life-cycle

Most products go through a number of stages in their existence:

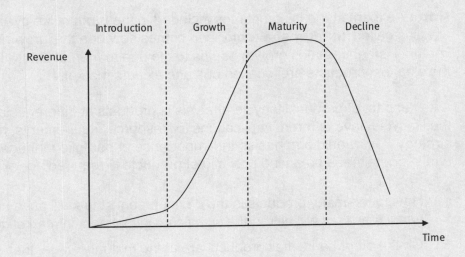

The marketing mix will change over time as the product goes into different stages of its 'life'. For example:

- When a product is in the 'growth' stage, the marketing mix may emphasise the development of sales outlets and advertising.

- In the maturity stage, there may be an increased emphasis/investment in product quality and design.

- To postpone decline, prices may be reduced and advertising increased.

Stage 1: Introduction – A small number of individuals will be prepared to pay a high price for a new, innovative product, e.g. the latest mobile phone model. High marketing costs are likely.

Stage 2: Growth – Revenue and profit grow as production and interest in the product increases. Prices may fall due to economies of scale and increased competitive pressure. The firm will seek to differentiate its product and brand.

Stage 3: Maturity – This is the longest and most successful stage of the life cycle. Purchases settle down into a pattern of repeat or replacement purchasing. Growth slows or halts due to high levels of competition. The price may be cut in order to attract a new group of customers.

Stage 4: Decline – Few people will purchase the product at the end of the life cycle as superior alternatives replace it and promotional activity will drop. The firm will look to exit the market and find profitable alternatives.

Note: An extra stage is sometimes included in the product life-cycle. This stage is called **'market shakeout'** and comes between the 'growth' and 'maturity' stages. Sales growth begins to dip due to market saturation and the weakest products are 'shaken out' and exit the market.

A key aspect of product lifecycle analysis is products at different stages in the lifecycle have different implications for resource requirements, risk and strategy. This would emphasise the importance of portfolio management and suggest that a balanced portfolio of products is required, for example:

- Having too many products in the development stage will put a strain on finance as they will all require significant investment in marketing.

- On the other hand, if all products are at the maturity stage, then there may be a question mark over the firm's long term future – how long will it be before they move into the decline phase?

4.2.4 Product Portfolio Theory – Boston Consulting Group (BCG)

The BCG diagram plots all products in a portfolio according to the:

- growth rate of the market served and
- the market share held.

The matrix allows a firm to:

- visualise a diverse range of products together to consider the overall cash flow surplus or deficit within the portfolio
- to help to decide whether a change in the mix of products is required.

This analysis classifies products into one of four categories with the following implications:

Boston Consulting Group Growth / Share Matrix

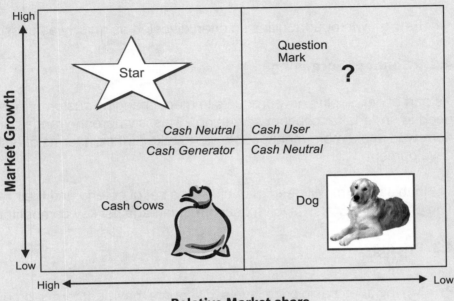

Cash cows (high market share, low market growth)

- These products generate cash for investment elsewhere in the portfolio.
- Investment tends to be low and the product is simply 'harvested' or milked of cash.

Stars (high market share, high market growth)

- Investment needed to maintain market share but is worth it since the market is growing.
- Will become tomorrow's cash cows.

Question marks (low market share, high market growth)

- Also known as a problem child. A choice must be made:
  - business may invest (e.g. in promotion, product modification) to increase market share or

- may divest if insufficient funds are available and/or better investment decisions exists.

- Cash user overall.

Dogs (low market share, low market growth)

- Few growth opportunities so often divested as quickly as possible.

4.2.5 Concept Screening

As part of developing new products to meet changing customer needs, firms need to undertake "concept screening". This is where the range of ideas is narrowed into a more manageable set to take further in terms of testing and development.

To do this the firm will need to decide on a set of criteria and their ranking. The process may also involve benchmarking against key competitors.

4.3 Pricing

Pricing includes basic price levels, discounts, payment terms, credit policy etc.

4.3.1 Factors influencing price; the 3 C's

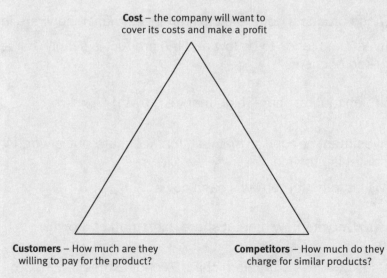

Ultimately the organisation must address the issue of whether customers believe the price is fair and commensurate with the quality of the product or service.

4.3.2 Pricing strategies

The pricing strategy should not be made in isolation. It is important that the company considers:

The positioning strategy

A large, well established business is better able to compete on price due to:

- **economies of scale**, i.e. average unit cost falls as the scale of production increases
- **the experience curve**, i.e. average unit cost falls due to learning from past experiences.

For other companies, it may be more advisable to add value to their products so differentiating it from the competitors' offering. Some companies use "**perceived quality pricing**", where a high price is set to reinforce a high quality image.

The product's stage in the product life-cycle.

> **Test your understanding 4**
>
> For each of the four stages of the product life-cycle describe the pricing considerations.

Two forms of pricing might be applied, particularly in the introduction stage of the product life-cycle, namely:

- **Skim pricing** – a high price is set initially to benefit from those who want to be early adopters of a product.
- **Penetration pricing** – a low price is set initially in order to gain rapid growth in market share.

The nature of the competition

If the competitor is a price leader, pricing levels may be determined by **follow the leader pricing**. So, for instance, if the largest oil company cuts the price of fuel, others are likely to follow suit

If, on the other hand, a company may find itself to be in the fortunate position of being the sole producer of a product due to a monopoly 'know-how', resources or raw materials. This company will therefore have more scope to charge **high prices** for its product, perhaps based on a **cost-plus** approach

Corporate objectives

Pricing can be linked to promotion – this may lead to **loss leader pricing** (i.e. products are sold at a loss) of certain products in order to generate customer loyalty or more sales of other products. This is particular popular in pricing consumables in a supermarket.

Alternatively pricing can be used as a competitive weapon – **low prices** may be charged in order to crush competitors rather than achieve returns in revenue.

The nature of the market

Some markets can be segmented in such a way that transfers between segments are impossible, or at least very difficult. This allows firms to charge different prices for the same product in different segments, a strategy known as **price discrimination.** For example, there can be a big difference between peak and off-peak rail fares.

A related concept is that of **variable pricing**, which involves adjusting prices to increase demand in off-peak periods in the hope of stimulating demand and generating revenue. For example, many bars have a "happy hour" early evening when there would otherwise be fewer customers.

Product portfolio considerations

The price of one product may affect the demand for another so pricing strategies are linked. For example, the price of a water filter jug may be relatively low but the company expects to boost its profits through the sale of additional (relatively expensive) replacement filters.

4.4 Promotion

Introduction

 Promotion includes the tools available to communicate with the customer and potential customers.

The organisation must first attempt to understand what the customer sees as the main benefits of their product or service and will then focus on these aspects using promotion.

Communications can take many forms and generally operate at one of three levels:

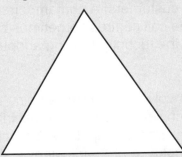

Mass Media - non personal and aimed at whole market segment, eg advertising

Personal and direct - typically one way communication with a customer, eg by letter

Personal and interactive - involves a one to one dialogue between the salesperson and the potential customer

Interactive marketing

Prof. John Deighton (1996) first defined interactive marketing as "the ability to address the customer, remember what the customer says and address the customer again in a way that illustrates that we remember what the customer has told us."

For organisations of any size to 'remember' what the customer has said and then 'communicate' with them is realistically only possible by use of the Internet. Thus IT allows customer information to be collected online and communication made either by e-mail or by 'remembering' when a customer logs on to the company website in future.

Developments in other communication technologies, specifically cable, satellite and digital technologies have also provided a platform for another form of home shopping via the television. Advantages over web-based selling include complete user familiarity with the equipment (the TV) and the ability to extensively demonstrate/advertise the products visually on a dedicated channel.

Telephone technology is not new but ownership is more widespread than ever. Within the UK, virtually all businesses, most homes and increasingly all teenagers and adults have a telephone. This provides the potential for contact to be made by telemarketing to stimulate product interest, sell directly or arrange for a visit to be made by a salesperson. There has, of late, been great emphasis in providing specialist training for telesales personnel including coaching on accent and responses to questions raised by customers. A contemporary trend is also the development of large call centres sometimes based overseas. ('M-marketing' refers to the technique being adopted using mobile telephones.)

This type of selling involves the initiative being taken by the vendor and is unsolicited. As such it may be unwelcome, intrusive even and naturally ethical concerns can surface. Impolite approaches or 'pushy' sales techniques being employed are particularly distasteful.

Promotional tools and the promotional mix

An organisation's **promotional mix** comprises the blend of promotional tools that a company uses to promote its products to existing and potential customers.

There are a number of promotional tools available:

- **Advertising** – e.g. using TV, radio, newspapers, billboards or the Internet.

- **Sales promotions** – e.g. product discounts, coupons, buy one get one free (BOGOF) offers.

- **Public relations** – news items in the media, e.g. a press release on the company's newest product.

- **Personal selling** – direct one to one contact with a potential customer, e.g. telesales.

- **Direct mail** – traditional mail or email sent to potential customers.

Test your understanding 5

Identify the advantages and disadvantages of following methods of promotion:

(a) Advertising

(b) Personal selling

(c) Public relations

(d) Sales promotion

(e) Direct mail

Advertising

There are two polar opposite views on advertising:

- Advertising is ineffective and a waste of money, only adding to company (and hence customer) costs. Brands such as Body Shop and Pizza Express do not see a need to use advertising in their promotional campaigns relying instead on other sources of information in order to form positive attitudes towards their products. In any case some might think that advertising demeans a particular product or company. In some cases, advertising may seem unethical. Lancaster and Withey (2005) conclude that some brands may be strong enough to sell on their own merits only if they are long established and have strong brand-loyal users.

- Advertising is so powerful and effective as to be essential. Consumers, it could be argued, will rarely purchase unadvertised brands so by not advertising, a company will be at serious disadvantage compared to its competitors. The results of advertising campaigns have been undeniably successful including those for brands such as Walkers Crisps, Strongbow cider and French Connection.

New forms of marketing communication

Three relatively new forms of marketing communication include viral, guerrilla and experiential marketing:

- **Viral** marketing – encourages individuals to pass on a marketing message to others, so creating exponential growth in the message's exposure in the same way computer viruses grow.

Illustration 1 – Viral marketing

A good example of viral marketing is a Nike video of footballer Ronaldinho putting on a new pair of boots and then juggling a ball for three minutes. The video was posted on YouTube and to date over 30 million people have got to know about the video and so have been exposed to Nike's promotion of their products.

Advantages	Disadvantages
• Can reach a mass audience quickly. • Can be a relatively cheap form of promotion compared with traditional promotional techniques. • Can create a buzz and hence be very effective.	• Can require high initial investment. • No guarantee that the campaign will go viral. • Can also work quickly to spread negative statements about the organisation.

- **Guerrilla marketing** – relies on well thought out, highly focused and often unconventional attacks on key targets.

Illustration 2 – Guerrilla marketing

A good example of guerrilla marketing is when a leading men's magazine projected the image of the model Gail Porter on the Houses of Parliament in London. It was a stunt that was talked about by a huge number of people. It was an attempt to get people to vote for the magazine's 'world's sexiest women' poll and the results were outstanding.

Advantages	Disadvantages
• As with viral marketing, it can be a relatively cheap form of promotion compared with traditional promotional techniques – if done well it should gain maximum results from minimum resources. • Helps the organisation to stand out and differentiates its marketing message from that of its competitors. • As with viral marketing, it can create a buzz and result in word of mouth generation.	• Requires a greater level of dedication and energy than traditional marketing. • Is not a quick fix – it will take time to see results. • Can be highly criticised and may even result in legal action.

- **Experiential marketing** – an interactive marketing experience aimed at stimulating all the senses, e.g. road shows, street theatre, product trials. The next time the consumer sees the product, it should trigger a range of positive memories making it the first choice.

Illustration 3 – Experiential marketing

Dove body products has a long running campaign for real beauty, challenging the stereotypical model of beauty. This has included building an online sharing community, emotive photography, road shows and in store sampling.

Advantages	Disadvantages
• Differentiates the product from the competition. • Possible to create a good campaign without a big budget. • Drives customer brand loyalty to targeted demographics. • Opportunity to meet customers face to face and interact with them.	• May get lots of negative word of mouth publicity. • Can be a waste of time and money if people only remember the experience and not what is being marketed.

Digital marketing

Digital marketing is the promotion of products or brands via one or more forms of electronic media, for example using email, mobile phones or social media.

Digital marketing monitors things such as what is being viewed, how often and for how long, sales conversions and what content does and doesn't work.

Advantages	Disadvantages
• Reduced costs. • Greater engagement with customers and improved meeting of needs. • Real time results, measurement and refinement of strategy. • Brand development. • Greater exposure. • Opportunity for viral marketing.	• Can take time to realise measurable success. • Consumers may ignore the advertising due to the vast amounts of digital marketing information that exists. • Negative feedback may damage reputation. • Digital marketing is not yet embraced by all people.

E-marketing

E-marketing

The internet can be used as a method of promotion but can also be used in other parts of the marketing mix, e.g. it can act as a distribution channel in 'place'.

In recent years, there has been a huge increase in online marketing and a move away from traditional media.

Advantages of using the internet to sell products	Disadvantages of using the internet to sell products
Global access to customers	Cost of set-up and maintenance
Internet presence not governed by organisational size	Possible credit card fraud
A new method of distribution	Possible virus infection
Information is delivered free to customers	Potential for hacking

Intimate customer relationship possible	Risk of losing confidential customer information
It provides sophisticated segmentation opportunities	Site may fail
	Inability to find site using search engine/poorly designed site

Can meet the customer's specific requirements

Rapid response times

Good quality, up to date content

Security of information

Characterisitcs of a good website

Allows customer feedback

Allows online trading

Quick download time

Easy to navigate site

Social Media Marketing (SMM)

Related to digital marketing, social media marketing refers to the process of gaining traffic or attention through social media sites.

The main attractions of using social media sites for marketing are as follows:

- The sheer number of people who use the sites - Facebook has over 1 billion users, Twitter 600 million, LinkedIn 250 million and Instagram over 200 million users. This gives the possibility of reaching large numbers of potential customers at a lower cost than if conventional channels were used.

- Using social marketing to deal with immediate customer complaints or queries directly – e.g. via a facebook page.

- It can be a very simple way of gaining an online presence.

- Particularly relevant if firms want to target younger people – for example, 74% of Twitter users (who disclose their age) are under the age of 26.

Using Facebook for marketing

Facebook offers a vast number of explicit and implicit marketing channels – most of which are viral. These include the following:

- Facebook pages – here a business can include logos, photos and text explaining what the firm does.

  If customers can be encouraged to become "fans", then any interaction they have with the page (e.g. a poll) effectively creates a news story that can be sponsored and then communicated to their friends and contacts.

  For example, Starbucks has over 27 million fans on Facebook.

  People can be encouraged to become fans by offering them benefits if they do so – e.g. Redbull, an energy drink, offers fans access to videos of motor racing (a sport they sponsor), web TV and a range of games.

  Friends and fans can be encouraged to comment or post photos of themselves using the company's products, thus creating more stories that will be communicated.

- Adverts – a firm can name its campaign, select its budget and set the schedule for the campaign.

  This will ensure the advert is shown to the specific market segment targeted (e.g. people who live in California in the USA who have stated that they like cooking in their profiles). Firms can try different adverts and measure relative performance.

- Events – Facebook events, such as product launches can be quickly communicated to potential customers.

  For example, in 2011 Ford released details of their new Explorer SUV vehicle by revealing it first on Facebook. As people commented on it the news spread. Ford estimated that the Facebook launch drove a 104% increase in online shopping activity for the SUV, in contrast to 14% after a SuperBowl TV advert. In a survey of Facebook fans exposed to the campaign, 77% said the Facebook reveal had positively impacted their shopping considerations.

- Market research

    Polls offer an easy way for marketers to quickly conduct research within their targeted audience. Results are streamed in real time to a dashboard that allows marketers to break down results by gender and age.

    Threadless is a community-based online t-shirt company. They invite artists to create t-shirt designs and then sell the ones selected by fans.

Postmodern marketing

Postmodern marketing is a philosophical approach to marketing which focuses on how individual customers prefer to be communicated with.

It uses a range of techniques to:

- stay nimble
- be reactive and
- shift with customers.

Interactivity, one-to-one communication and new media are all inherent in the postmodern approach.

4.5 Place

Introduction

Place involves more than just the location of factories, offices or sales outlets. It also includes distribution channels and coverage, stock levels, types of transportation vehicle, warehouse locations etc.

Distribution

Distribution involves getting the right products to the right people at the right time.

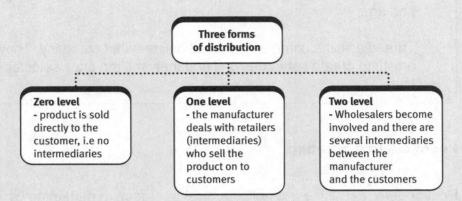

Direct marketing may be used for zero level distribution. One and two level distribution involve two types of marketing:

- A '**pull**' strategy means massive advertising to create consumer demand and this demand more or less forces the retailers to include this product in their assortment (not having this product in stock means disgruntled consumers that may go elsewhere to shop).

- A '**push**' strategy means that the producer does not try to create consumer demand through heavy advertising, but instead offers high margins to the trade channel members (retailers and wholesalers) and expects that in return they will actively promote and market the product.

Note: These strategies can also be called push and pull **promotion**.

5 Branding

5.1 Introduction

A **brand** is a name, symbol, term, mark or design that enables customers to identify and distinguish the products of one supplier from those offered by competitors.

Brands can vary from company names (e.g. Volvo) to logos (e.g. the Nike 'tick' symbol) to product names or even to the people themselves (e.g. David Beckham)

The Chartered Institute of Marketing (CIM) identify certain attributes of brands as follows:

- people use brands to make statements about themselves
- good brands reduce the risk of poor product choice
- brands can be a key asset for a business
- brands are the reason consumers choose one company over another
- although intangible, brands can be of substantial value
- strong brands can positively influence share performance
- brands can command higher prices

Brand equity is the premium that customers are prepared to pay for a brand compared to a similar, generic product.

Illustration 4 – Leading UK brands

The following is a list of the leading UK brands:

Brand	Rank	Category
Google	1	Internet – General
Microsoft	2	Technology – Computer hardware and software
Mercedes-Benz	3	Automotive – Vehicle manufacturer
BBC	4	Media – TV stations
British Airways	5	Travel – Airlines
Royal Doulton	6	Household – General
BMW	7	Automotive – Vehicle manufacturer
Bosch	8	Household – Appliances
Nike	9	Sportswear and equipment
Sony	10	Technology – General
Apple	11	Technology – Computer hardware and software
Duracell	12	Household – General consumables
Jaguar	13	Automotive – Vehicle manufacturer
Coca-cola	14	Drinks – Carbonated soft drinks
AA	15	Automotive – General
Lego	16	Leisure and Entertainment – Games & toys

Marks & Spencer	17	Retail – General
Thorntons	18	Food – chocolate and confectionery
Cadbury	19	Food – chocolate and confectionery
Hilton	20	Travel – Hotels and resorts

5.2 Characteristics of a strong brand

- **Consistency:** This is crucial to the development of the brand. For example, McDonalds manage to achieve consistency through standardisation.

- **A distinctive name:** The name should have positive associations with the product. For example 'Flash' sounds like it will clean thoroughly whereas the 'Nova' car was very unpopular in Spain since 'Nova', in Spanish, means 'doesn't work'.

- **Distinctive product features:** These will help to prompt instant recognition. For example, the Cadbury Chocolate Orange has a distinctive 'orange shape' design which makes it recognisable and Coca Cola has a distinctive image that is also instantly recognisable.

5.3 Brand management

Brand management is the development and implementation of a strategy with the long-term objective of putting a brand at the forefront of consumer's minds.

Developing and maintaining a brand can be expensive. However, a strong brand can enhance profitability.

The value of a brand is based on the extent to which it has:

- High loyalty.
- Name awareness.
- Perceived quality.
- Strong personality association.
- Other attributes such as patents and trademarks.

It is very important that brand value is protected:

- Low quality, counterfeit goods can erode the genuine brand's kudos and exclusivity

- There is a risk of some brands becoming a generic term – for example, aspirin and shredded wheat were once brands but were eventually declared to be generic terms.

- Adverse publicity can seriously undermine the values associated with a brand. For example, Body Shop will vigorously challenge any accusations that its products are not as ethical as they would like you to believe.

- Some firms have made the mistake of using exclusive brands on inferior goods hoping the brand would enhance perceived value. Unfortunately the reverse happened and the value of the brand was compromised.

Benefits of effective brand management

- **Improved profitability** – effective brand management should translate into improved profit potential.

- **Valuable asset** – although intangible, brands can be of substantial value.

- **Higher prices** – a strong brand will create the opportunity to create higher prices than competitors.

- **Method of differentiation** – a brand can distinguish an organisation from its competitors acting as a source of competitive advantage.

- **Way of connecting with customers** – brands can connect with customers in a deep way resulting in high levels of customer loyalty.

- **Assists with other marketing practices** – the brand should assist with other marketing practices, e.g. advertising by establishing a bond of trust which can be built upon.

- **Customer loyalty** – effective brand management should add to grand loyalty, repeat sales and habitual buying

Brand strategies (Kotler)

Kotler identified 5 brand strategies:

(1) Line extensions

   –   an existing brand is applied to new variants/products within the same product category

   –   e.g. Ford Fusion and Ford Focus are both small cars

(2) Brand extensions

   –   an existing brand is applied to products in a new product category

   –   e.g. Honda cars and motorcycles

(3) Multibrands

   –   having many different brands in the same product category

   –   e.g. Kellogs breakfast cereals include Cornflakes, Frosties, Special K, etc

(4) New brands

   –   new brands are created for new products and/or markets, usually because existing brands are not deemed suitable.

   –   e.g. when the banking arm of the Prudential expanded into internet banking they created a new brand, Egg Banking

(5) Cobrands

   –   two brands are combined in an offer so the brands reinforce each other.

   –   e.g. Dell Computers with Intel Processors

6 Big Data

As discussed in chapter 7, Big Data management involves using sophisticated systems to gather, store and analyse large volumes of data in a variety of structured and unstructured formats. In addition to traditional data from internal sources such as sales history, preferences, order frequency and pricing information, companies can also gather information from external sources such as websites, trade publications and social networks.

In the digital age, companies gather data about their customers from a huge range of sources. Sophisticated analysis using Big Data technologies enables some companies to more accurately predict demand for their products and services which can have several internal business benefits such as improved inventory management.

The use of Big Data analytics to predict customer demand can help to improve the customer experience in the following ways:

- Collating and analysing these large volumes of information allows companies to gain a variety of insights into customer behaviour and this can help to **more accurately predict customer demand**. These demand forecasts may be in terms of volume but also the type of products required and this is beneficial to company planning but can also help the company to improve aspects of the customer experience.

- In terms of volume predictions, these can help to ensure that a company will always have **sufficient inventory to satisfy demand**. This will mean that customers do not need to wait to receive their goods which is likely to be a key part of their shopping experience.

- Furthermore companies can use the information and insights to **understand which products and features are most popular with customers**. This can inform product re-design to ensure that any revisions are in line with customer preferences.

- Retail businesses can also use data regarding customer purchases and therefore likely future demand for goods to influence store layout and help to **create an enjoyable shopping experience**.

Illustration 5 – How Avis Budget uses Big Data in marketing

Car rental giant Avis Budget has launched a new marketing services organisation fuelled by Big Data analytics to better serve its customers. They recognised that rental companies offer similar cars in similar locations at similar rates – and that makes a very competitive environment. Their aim was to differentiate themselves based on customer service and customer experience. This differentiation has been driven, in part, by Big Data. Data is analysed to better understand customers' needs, preferences and intent to rent.

7 Chapter summary

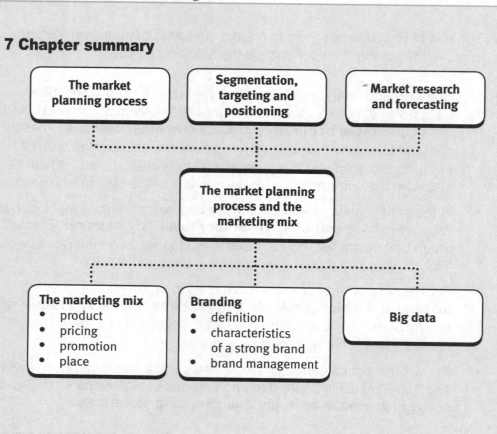

8 Practice questions

Question 1 – OTQ

In marketing 'skim pricing' reflects:

A   full recovery of costs only

B   a promotional device to entice customers into the store

C   high prices but low profit due to fixed costs

D   a competitive strategy to deny the competitors opportunities to enter a market

Question 2 – OTQ

Undifferentiated marketing involves an organisation in offering:

A   products based on market research

B   a single product to the market as a whole

C   multiple products to the market as a whole

D   single products to segmented markets

Question 3 – OTQ

Segmentation involves identifying target market which must be:

A   measurable, accessible and substantial

B   acceptable, feasible and suitable

C   undeveloped, undiscovered and undifferentiated

D   aligned to core competences

Question 4 – OTQ

Companies with high costs will find it difficult to compete on the basis of price and would be well advised to:

A   compete on the Internet

B   develop brand loyalty amongst customers

C   employ high pressure sales techniques

D   develop new products

Question 5 – OTQ

Which one of the following phrases explains concentrated marketing?

A   The company produces one product for a number of different market segments

B   The company introduces several versions of the product aimed at several market segments

C   The company produces one product for a mass market

D   The company produces one product for a single segment of the marketplace

Question 6 – OTQ

A promotional pull policy will lead to:

A   high advertising costs

B   price reduction to entice customers

C   a focus on maximising channels of distribution.

D   product breadth and depth decisions

Question 7 – Johnson, Halifax and Company (Case style)

Background

Johnson, Halifax and Company are a long-established medium-sized training practice operating in a large industrial city, in the country of Wetland. The practice had developed a stable and profitable client base between 20 and 30 years ago providing advice on corporate presentations and media skills, along with the usual steady income stream from general staff training. During this period the practice's main clientele had been owner-managed manufacturing and retail businesses within the city and its suburbs. The partners had never actively sought out business and new clients had arrived on the basis of recommendations and personal contacts. In summary, the practice was seen to be the natural supplier of training services to the small and medium-sized business sector of the city. Over the years, Johnson, Halifax and Company have become conservative in approach and inflexible.

Recession

The last two recessions led to a massive shake-out in the manufacturing businesses in the city. Many of these businesses closed, and with restructuring in the manufacturing sector, there were numerous mergers and acquisitions. Understandably as headquarters were relocated and businesses were taken over, the practice began to lose clients as they moved to larger training practices in order to streamline their training. In addition, many of these companies ran their own training departments.

Response to recession

In response, Johnson, Halifax and Company attempted to attract new business by focusing on the smaller services sector. This approach brought them into direct conflict with the small training companies. The result was not the success they had hoped for. The very wide range of small clients did not present the opportunities for economy of delivery, and the intense fee competition was producing a large amount of smaller profit margin contracts.

By the end of 20X9, the partnership was only just breaking even financially. The long delayed economic recovery was not bringing them the rewards they had hoped for. Although the older partners recognised the problems they were undecided as to the way forward. The younger members of the practice were beginning to voice their discontent.

Action required

One in particular, Dominic Gower, was proposing a more proactive role for the firm. His main concern was that the partnership needed to go out and market itself. It was not enough to be technically proficient. It needed new and profitable business, particularly in the current turbulent and competitive environment. The managing partner agreed that something needed to be done urgently if the firm was to see prosperous times again and decided to encourage Gower to develop his ideas.

Tasks:

(a) Explain the need to adopt a marketing-orientated stance to the management of the partnership and suggest a possible approach to the development of a partnership marketing plan.

(20 minutes)

(b) Explain the differences that are likely to arise between the marketing of consumer products and the marketing of services?

(15 minutes)

(Total: 35 minutes)

Question 8 – Vitac (Case style)

Background

Vitac Corporation is a medium-sized regional company producing and distributing fruit-flavoured, carbonated drinks. In recent years, it has seen a rapid decline in its sales to local stores and supermarkets. There are two main reasons for its poor performance. First, the major corporations who sell cola drinks have developed global brands which are now capturing the youth market in search of 'sophisticated' products. Secondly, the sales outlets are no longer willing to provide shelf space to products which are not brand leaders, or potential leaders, in the product category.

The managing director (MD) of Vitac believes that the company needs a drastic turnaround if it is to survive. The soft drinks industry has become too competitive, and the bottling technology too expensive to warrant new investment. However, the company feels that its greatest strength is its knowledge of and access to distribution channels, and therefore its opinion is that it should stay within the food and drinks industry.

New product

Whilst on a fact-finding mission to the USA, the MD was attracted by a new chocolate confectionery product named 'EnerCan' which claims to provide high energy content but low fat. This seems to be a successful combination of attributes for those consumers, mainly active participants in sporting activities, who are concerned with their diet but enjoy an occasional treat. EnerCan has been developed and is owned by a relatively-unknown confectionery company in California. The company has agreed to provide Vitac with a licensing contract for manufacture and sale of the product within Vitac's own country.

Marketing of Enercan

The MD is convinced that the secret to success will be in the marketing of the product. The company has suffered in its drinks business because it did not develop a distinctive and successful brand. EnerCan is also unknown in Vitac's own country. In order to get national recognition and acceptance from the major retail outlets, the product will need considerable promotional support. As the company has very little experience or expertise in promotional activity it was decided to use a marketing consultancy to provide guidance in developing a promotional plan.

Vitac, being a medium-sized company, has only a limited budget. It will have to focus upon a new and national market instead of its traditional, regional stronghold. It has to develop a new brand in a product area with which it is not familiar. Before committing itself to a national launch of EnerCan, Vitac has decided to trial the product launch in a test market.

Role

You have been appointed to act as business consultant in the marketing consultancy team assisting Vitac.

Tasks:

(a) Prepare notes for the management of Vitac recommending and justifying the types of promotional activity that could be used to support the new product launch.

(20 minutes)

(b) Explain the factors which need to be considered to ensure that the test market produces results which can be reliably used prior to the national launch?

(15 minutes)

(Total: 35 minutes)

Test your understanding answers

Test your understanding 1

Gender

It would be useful to segment the market based on gender. Females may prefer a car that is smaller, is available in bright colours and comes with fashionable accessories. Males, on the other hand, may prefer a more masculine looking and powerful car.

Age

The age of the consumer will be of upmost importance. Teenage drivers may prefer a cheaper model, whereas drivers in their 20s, with more disposable income, may prefer a more expensive and stylish model.

Lifestyle

There may be a number of different lifestyles that could be targeted. Each group will have quite different needs, e.g. a leisure user may be more interested in the style and design of the car where as a commuter may want a safe, reliable car.

Income

The level of income will impact the make and the model that the user can afford and any optional extras that may be purchased.

Family life cycle

The life cycle stage will be important, e.g. bachelors may prefer a higher priced, sporty, stylish model where as those with a young and growing family may prefer a safe, reliable and family orientated people carrier.

Test your understanding 2

- Market research agency data, e.g. Mintel produce periodic sector reports on market intelligence.

- The Internet.

- Universities typically have databases allowing for research and analysis of customer behaviour.

- Companies' Annual Reports and Accounts.

- Professional and trade associations.

- Trade and technical journals.

- National media.

Test your understanding 3 – Case style question

The marketing mix aims to match the products being sold by the company with the needs of the particular market segment that H Company have decided to target. The main elements of the mix are as follows.

Product

If H Company has already carried out some market research into what kind of products its customers want, these products should be available in its stores. For a clothes retailer this will include looking not only at what styles to offer, but also considering things like sizes, colours, fabrics, etc. An additional point is to note that these things are likely to change on a fairly frequent basis, so H Company should always be trying to look ahead.

Price

In the past, H Company has attempted to sell quality clothing at affordable prices. This may now have to be reviewed. The research carried out by the company may lead it to attempt to go upmarket, the higher quality/design of its clothes leading to higher prices, or it may go downmarket, by reducing innovative design/using cheaper fabrics with a consequent reduction in price if customers feel that the company is not offering them anything extra for their money.

Place

The place commonly refers to where the products are available to consumers. For a clothes retailer such as H Company, this would have traditionally been via retail outlets. Based on the results of market research, H Company will have to decide on the best way to retail their clothes. Various possibilities exist, amongst these are:

- Expanding the number of shops in the High Street.

- Expanding the number of shops on retail parks.

- Expanding the number of in-store displays in departments stores (within e.g. Debenhams etc.).

- Setting up an Internet website.

The place must be linked in with the other elements of the marketing mix, for example if H Company is trying to appeal to a more exclusive clientele then having its own range of shops in prestigious locations would be sensible. Alternatively, if the company wants to appeal to a more mainstream customer base then having the clothes sold in department stores would be more appropriate.

Promotion

The promotional part of the mix refers to how the potential customer is made aware of the products. The first consideration is looking at where to advertise. Clothes have traditionally been advertised through magazines and newspapers. If H Company goes down this route, then they should advertise in appropriate publications that are likely to be seen by their target customers. An increasingly popular approach particularly for clothes aimed at the upper end of the market is that of endorsement by celebrities. Clothes might be loaned/given to people in the public eye, thus generating positive publicity.

All of the above elements must be blended together so that the product, price, place and promotion appeal to the market segments identified by H Company.

Test your understanding 4

- **Introduction**

  High prices might be charged, because the product is new and supply is limited. Initial set up costs also need to be recovered.

- **Growth**

  Competition between rival producers intensifies so prices will reduce in the hope of penetrating the existing market and either retaining or increasing market share at the expense of competitors.

- **Maturity**

  Prices fall mainly in order to beat competitors but the experience curve and scale economies should come into play. Market segments are sought where higher prices can be charged.

- **Decline**

  The product declines into obsolescence so it may even be sold off below cost price to clear stocks and exit the market.

Two forms of pricing might also be applied, particularly in the introduction stage of the product life cycle, namely:

- Price skimming reflecting high prices but low profit due to high fixed costs.

- Penetration pricing, deliberately entering a market at a low price to build market share and pricing so as to deny the competitors those opportunities.

Test your understanding 5

Method	Advantages	Disadvantages
(a) Advertising	• Reach a large number of potential customers. • Low cost for each potential customer.	• Total cost can be very high. • Difficult to evaluate effectiveness.
(b) Personal selling	• Can focus on needs of individual customer. • A talented salesperson can be very persuasive.	• Can be seen as pushy. • High cost per potential customer.
(c) Public relations	• Low or no cost. • Can be targeted. • Unbiased opinion.	• Negative review may damage reputation.
(d) Sales promotion	• Can help gain new users. • Counteract competition. • Clear out surplus stock.	• Can be costly. • May not win customer loyalty.
(e) Direct mail	• Personalised targeting of an individual. • Test market before a full roll out. • Less competitor visibility.	• Negative associations. • Can be costly.

Question 1 – OTQ

The correct answer is C

Question 2 – OTQ

The correct answer is B

Question 3 – OTQ

The correct answer is A

Question 4 – OTQ

The correct answer is B

Question 5 – OTQ

The correct answer is D

Question 6 – OTQ

The correct answer is A

Question 7 – Johnson, Halifax and Company (Case style)

(a) Adopting a marketing orientation

Johnson, Halifax and Company need to perform better and more cost-effectively than their competitors; forcing them to be more flexible and responsive to client needs. In order to satisfy them, the needs of the clients must be analysed and understood by the partnership.

Marketing plan for the partnership

Step 1: Situation analysis – an initial assessment of the current position of the partnership will be performed as part of the marketing plan. This will involve why and where there has been a deteriorating change in the client base in recent years. One reason is the economic downturn within the region that Johnson operates in.

Another reason may be that they are offering the wrong types of training, i.e. not meeting the demands of their customers. One of the main problems identified by the company is that it appears to be 'stuck in the middle': in other words, its services are not priced cheaply enough to appeal to small companies whilst at the same time it does not have the range of services required by larger companies.

Step 2: Set corporate objectives – the partnership did enjoy past success but there is no indication that there is a mission statement or set of corporate objectives in place. Even if there is, these should be reviewed to make sure that they are still relevant.

Step 3: Set marketing objectives – these should be set in relation to the marketing objectives.

Step 4: Devise an appropriate strategy – this will involve:

- Segmentation – the market should be segmented, e.g. by size of client, and the needs of each segment should be established.
- Targeting – the most profitable segment(s) should be targeted using an appropriate marketing mix.
- Positioning – a strategy of differentiation or cost leadership should be chosen for each segment.

Step 5: Marketing mix – a plan for the development of the marketing mix needs to be adopted for Johnson and Halifax to achieve its plans.

Product (i.e. the development of new services)

In the light of newly-established customer requirements, new products or services need to be developed, possibly forced by the changing requirements of the local economy. Johnson will need to carry out some kind of research in order to establish what these needs are and then segment the market to decide which training courses they will provide. These new services will have to be closely monitored and may have to be regularly updated.

Price

Prices charged by the firm will obviously have to be competitive but will equally have to be reflective of the business segment they are operating within, and its specific competitiveness. It may prove necessary to run free 'taster' courses so that potential clients can see what the company is like.

Distribution channel (i.e. place)

If the firm has a great deal of flexibility in its distribution of services, then it should gain a competitive advantage quickly. At the moment Johnson appears to be tied to its current geographical region.

The partnership should take advantage of any available IT systems such as the Internet to help gain a competitive advantage.

Promotional activity

The use of good quality communication will be crucial in an attempt to target appropriate clients. Media considerations are relevant (e.g. where and when to advertise), however it should be remembered that there may only be one person within a company who decides on the company's training needs, these people should be identified and contacted with a view to building a long-term relationship.

Step 6: Implementation and control – The marketing plan should then be implemented. The plan should also be monitored to gauge its success and to identify any necessary changes.

(b) Service industries face different problems to production industries for the following reasons:

Intangibility

In a service industry, it is difficult to judge quality because it is difficult to sample a service.

It is difficult for customers to examine a service in advance. However, in a production business, such as the manufacture of cars, the sampling will be achieved by test driving the vehicle. Steps can be taken to make the service more tangible, e.g. physical evidence such as brochures can be used.

Inseparability

The service is often inseparable from the individual delivering the service. Clients could easily become disappointed if they discover that the work carried out on their behalf is not performed by the person with whom the contract was negotiated. Partners therefore need to maintain enough interest in the work performed to ensure that personal contact with the client is maintained. The marketing of a product is different, as the item or goods will be purchased from the seller.

Heterogeneity

As a result of inseparability, the service will vary from one occasion to the next. To ensure consistency, the firm needs to maintain the training of personnel as well as ensuring quality standards are adhered to. However, in the production of, say a motor car, each vehicle will conform exactly to its specification.

Perishability

Services cannot be stored; sale and consumption take place at the same time. To ensure that assets are utilised effectively, steps can be taken to manage this problem, e.g. off-peak discounts or using temporary staff to solve the problem of fluctuating demand. Products, on the other hand, can be stored (even if only for a limited period).

Differentiation

As most training firms offer similar services to their clients it is important to gain a competitive advantage by offering a slightly different service which is relevant to the needs of the particular clients served. This could include aspects such as personal involvement by all staff, follow-up contacts, experience and the use of high technology equipment. The differentiation of a product refers to the specific attributes enforced by that firm and therefore is easy to undertake.

Ownership

Consumers may find it difficult to value a service since there is no transfer of ownership.

Question 8 – Vitac (Case style)

(a) Introduction

The company has acquired an interest in a product that is new to the market, and is proposing to market this product via the major retail outlets to a specific target group, namely sports participants.

Promotional vehicles

The key objective during the trial period is to create awareness within the target market. The focus of the promotion will be on the different types and styles of promotion to be used to obtain the appropriate responses from the target market. These will vary from conventional advertising to sales and public relations.

With a limited promotional budget the company could concentrate on a 'push' strategy which influences the retail outlets to stock and display the products.

In attempting to influence the target consumers a key strategy would be to encourage them to try the product initially.

Due to the inherent high costs, it is not realistic to expect wide-scale consumer advertising on television and through the mass print media. This strategy would not be specifically targeting the chosen market segment.

The preferred choices would include a balanced selection of the following.

- **Advertising**. Dependent upon the budget available, advertising should focus on advertisements or editorials placed in one or two specialist magazines. These magazines would be those that are commonly read by the target market – sports enthusiasts. The advertising should be supported with point-of-sale material to draw potential consumers' attention and encourage trial purchase.

- **Sales promotions** could be both trade and consumer led.

- **Trade promotions**. It is essential that retailers both stock the product and provide excellent shelf display. To generate a 'push' approach to promotion, it may be possible to provide retailers with inducements in the form of customer prizes and discounts. Without retailer commitment, it is unlikely that the product launch will be successful.

- **Customer promotions**. This will need significant expenditure on sales promotional material which would include a mixture of the following:
    - In-store trials
    - Coupon offers
    - Initial price reductions.

All of the above might help to stimulate demand and make the product recognisable. Attractive packaging of the product will in itself help stimulate product interest and create brand awareness. The following could also be tried:

- **Public relations**. It could be beneficial to use one or two well-known sports personalities to recommend the product. Though it might appear to be expensive this could provide exposure significantly cheaper than could otherwise be obtained from conventional media. Additionally the product could be trialled at prestigious sports meetings, international athletics meetings, cycling events, tennis tournaments, etc. The product image would reach the target audience and it would be promoted in a superior environment

- **Sales**. The sales force will need to be sufficiently skilled and committed, being able to operate at a national level to obtain wide geographical coverage. Although this approach may be expensive it will be far more cost effective than attempting a nationwide television campaign. The sales force will have the task of persuading retailers to accept the product, and providing merchandising support. They will handle most of the problems at the product's launch.

Conclusion

With the restrictions of a limited budget, expenditure should be directed at those areas which will accurately reach the target market and encourage participation in the trial.

On this basis, the promotional emphasis should be on a 'push' strategy as opposed to a 'pull' strategy. To measure how well the campaign is progressing, control systems should be implemented. The systems should ensure that the use of the limited money available achieves the desired objectives.

(b) **Definition of a test market**

A test market is often used prior to the launch of fast-moving consumer goods. It enables the company to identify any operational problems that may occur and to fine tune its marketing activities.

The company has the benefit that it can save considerable amounts of money which would have been lost if the mistakes had occurred at the national level.

Factors to consider

The following factors should all be taken into consideration before deciding upon a test market area. If the test is to provide guidance for a future national launch, the results should be based upon reliable sets of data.

- **Comparable test areas**. The test market area should provide a good indication as to how the market throughout the whole country will behave. It would be of little use if the results from the test market misrepresented the true state of the total market. The test market area must be representative of the total market in terms of demographics – income, social class, age and any other parameter which would help determine purchase activity.

- **Comparable distribution channels**. The distribution channels, including the sales outlets, should be comparable with the rest of the country. It is pointless if small retailers dominate the test area whereas in the rest of the country the multiple supermarkets are dominant.

- **Isolation of test area**. The area should be reasonably isolated so that outsiders coming into the test area do not influence test results.

- **Comparability of promotional media**. If the national promotional emphasis were to be radio then there ought to be a local radio station available.

- **Control markets**. There should be a control market just in case extraneous activities might falsify the results, e.g. a strike at a major employer within the test area.

- **Test period**. The test period should be long enough to enable reliable results to be obtained, in this case time for a repurchase after the initial trial. However, the test period must not be so long that it alerts competitors.

12

Further Aspects of Marketing

Chapter learning objectives

Lead	Component
E1. Demonstrate the purpose of the marketing function and its relationship with other parts of the organisation.	(a) Apply the marketing concept and principles in a range of organisational contexts. (b) Apply the elements of the marketing mix.
E2. Apply tools and techniques to formulate the organisation's marketing strategies, including the collection, analysis and application of big data.	(a) Apply the main techniques of marketing. (b) Explain the role of emerging technologies and media in marketing.

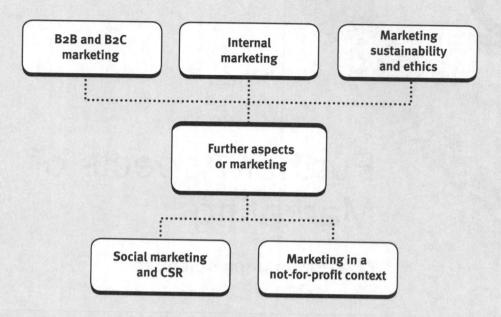

1 Business to Business (B2B) and Business to Consumer (B2C) Marketing

1.1 Definitions

- **B2B marketing** – targeting goods and services at businesses that will use the products to produce the goods or services that they sell.

- **B2C marketing** – the market for products and services bought by individuals for their own use or for their family's use. As mentioned in Chapter 10, consumer goods fall under two categories; durable goods and fast moving consumer goods.

1.2 Features of B2B marketing

- **Derived demand** – demand for the product is derived from consumer demand.

- **Fewer buyers** – the number of buyers for an industrial good is generally smaller than for a consumer good. Therefore, it is very important to know each customer (there may be several people associated with the buying process within an organisation) and to understand their individual requirements. It is important for the buyer to understand the business objectives of the seller and to demonstrate to them how their product or service can help them to achieve these objectives.

- **High purchasing power** – each industrial buyer tends to have a higher purchasing power than consumers. The financial value of organisational purchase orders will be much larger and the frequency much lower. Therefore, it is important to maintain close contact with customers.

- **Closer relationships between buyers and sellers** – as mentioned above, this is because there are fewer buyers with higher purchasing power in B2B marketing compared to B2C marketing. Customer relationships are extremely valuable and need to be managed. An organisation's brand identity most likely will be created based on the personal relationships developed.

- **Technical complexity** – There is often a greater degree of technical complexity in B2B marketing. Given the size of orders and the requirements for consistent quality, agreements may be made between organisations for the supply of products or services over a number of years. The negotiation process may be quite lengthy.

Test your understanding 1

On what basis are B2B purchasing decisions made?

Buying decisions with B2B

Business-to-business (B2B) marketing differs from business-to-consumer (B2C) marketing in a number of key respects, not least the fact that the purchaser makes buying decisions for organisational rather than personal reasons. In addition, several individuals and groups are involved in the B2B buying decision including:

- **Initiators** who start the buying process. (For example, a department who identifies a need to replace a piece of equipment.)

- **Influencers** who affect the buying decision often based on their particular technical expertise.

- **Buyers** who raise orders and sanction payment, although they may enter into negotiation, they may be guided heavily by others in the organisation.

- **Users** who ultimately operate the equipment (using the earlier example).

There may be others (dependent upon the organisation) who will have further roles such as Deciders, Approvers and Gatekeepers.

2 Internal Marketing

This is the means of applying the philosophy and practices of marketing to the people who serve the external customers so that:

- The best possible people can be employed and retained.

- The employees will do the best possible work.

Internal marketing is essentially the process of motivating and training employees so as to support the organisation's external marketing activities.

Employee's efforts to achieve marketing goals should be recognised and rewarded.

Implications of internal marketing

- The company may have a strong marketing strategy but without their employee's support, it will not be effective.

- If advertising promises are not kept through the services and the products provided, eventually the company's reputation will suffer and the customers will stop buying.

- For the firm to deliver consistently high quality, everyone must practise a customer orientation. This will require investment in employee quality and performance.

- Internal marketing will be of particular importance in service companies which tend to be more customer-facing.

3 Marketing Sustainability and Ethics

3.1 Marketing sustainability

Marketing could be accused of encouraging a throwaway society, which is good for increasing sales, but less **sustainable** for the environment.

The general public has become increasingly aware of ecological issues and, more importantly, some segments have shown a greater willingness and ability to spend their money in a way which minimises ecological harm.

Benefits of sustainability

- Many markets are characterised by segments that are prepared to pay a premium for a product that has been produced in an ecologically sound manner.

> **Illustration 1**
>
> Some companies, such as Organic Paint Company, have developed valuable niches on this basis. What starts off as a 'deep green' niche soon expands into a larger 'pale green' segment of customers who prefer ecologically sound products but are unwilling to pay such a high premium price.

- Being green may actually save the company money.
- A company which adopts environmentally sensitive production methods ahead of compulsion can gain experience and hence competitive advantage ahead of other companies.

3.2 Ethics and marketing

We now turn our attention to the broader subject of **ethics**, and the responsibilities of marketers to act according to a set of shared values, rather than simply pursuing short-term profits.

Marketing's responsibility for customers' privacy and security

In a technological environment in which information about customers can be very quickly collected and disseminated, concerns have been expressed about the privacy of consumers and the security of data that is held about them.

Firms have a responsibility to respect customers' privacy and their personal data, and this moral responsibility is increasingly being enshrined in codes of conduct and legislation.

Marketing's responsibilities to vulnerable people

We have seen that the basic principles of marketing are based on the assumption that customers know what they want and are able to evaluate the extent to which a product will meet their needs.

Unfortunately, many people may not be able or willing to make a proper evaluation of a product and its likely impact on their physical and mental wellbeing.

Illustration 2 – O2's policies towards children

At the mobile phone company O_2, children were considered vulnerable, on account of the potential health risks and their uncritical acceptance of advertising claims. The company worked with the UK Home Office and children's charities to draw up a code of practice to regulate the provision of content on mobile phones, e.g. any commercial content rated '18' has to be behind content controls which can only be accessed by someone verified to be over 18. O_2 agreed to a policy of only advertising in magazines or between television programmes where more than 50 per cent of the audience is over 16.

Marketing's responsibility to employees

The marketing manager owes some responsibility for the welfare of employees. There is a widely held view that if employees are not happy with their jobs, customers will never be uppermost in their minds.

Illustration 3 – 24/7 society

One example which is currently exercising the minds of many marketing managers is the issue of 24/7 access to goods and services. What happens when a company's customers want access to its goods and services 24 hours a day, and when they want immediate access, not a promise of delivery tomorrow or some time in the future? One consequence is often stress at work for those who are charged with responding to a company's promises, which it must make if it is to stay alive in a competitive business environment. The 24/7 culture has had a big impact on employees' lifestyles, with many individuals having to adjust to varying and often unsocial shift patterns.

Marketing's responsibility for preserving the competitiveness of the market

Most business people would publicly acknowledge that competitive markets are a good thing, but quietly, many would be only too happy to come to an agreement with their competitors to limit the amount of competition between them.

For sellers, a cosy cartel between them will put less pressure on them to reduce costs. For buyers, the consequence would most likely be less choice and/ or higher prices. Is it responsible for marketers to seek to undermine the power of market forces?

Responsible communication

The final aspect of responsible marketing that we will consider is in respect of firms' communication. In an ideal world, a company would act responsibly, and communicate honestly with its customers and key stakeholders. Unfortunately, there are too many cases where a company acts in an irresponsible manner, and then uses communication dishonestly to try and portray itself as acting responsibly.

Illustration 4 – Responsible communication

Many bars used to promote a 'happy hour' period during which alcohol was sold at a reduced price. For pub operators, such promotions were vital to boosting turnover, especially if all bars in the area were offering equally low prices. However, the UK government recognised that these offers were contributing to an increase in 'binge drinkers' with town centres becoming noisy and violent areas at night-time, fuelled by excessive drinking. The use of such promotions was banned in the UK in 2008.

4 Social Marketing and Corporate Social Responsibility

4.1 Social marketing

Social marketing uses commercial marketing practices to achieve non-commercial goals, e.g. the solution of social and health problems.

Social marketing is based on the logic that if marketing techniques can encourage people to buy products such as a fizzy drink brand or a particular telephone handset, then it can also encourage people to adopt 'beneficial' behaviours for their own good and the good of others.

Merit goods are commodities that an individual or society should have on the basis that it is 'good' for them rather than ability or willingness to pay. Governments often provide merit goods 'free at the point of use' and then finances them through general taxation (e.g. in the UK access to health care is through the National Health Service).

Demerit goods are the exact opposite of merit goods and negative consequences can arise from their consumption for society as a whole, e.g. health implications of smoking, unwanted pregnancies.

Social marketing can be applied to promote merit goods and encourage society to avoid demerit goods, e.g. persuading people to give up smoking through the use of a powerful advertising campaign.

Understanding social marketing

According to the National Social Marketing Centre (2008) the following features and concepts are key to understanding social marketing:

- A strong customer orientation with importance attached to understanding where the customer is starting from, their knowledge, attitudes and beliefs, along with the social context in which they live and work.

- A clear focus on understanding existing behaviour and key influences upon it, and developing clear behavioural goals.

- Using a mix of different methods to achieve a particular behavioural goal.

- Audience segmentation to target efforts more effectively.

- Use of the 'exchange' concept (understanding what is being expected of an individual, and the real cost to them).

- Use of the 'competition' concept (understanding factors that impact on people and that compete for their attention and time).

4.2 Corporate social responsibility in a marketing context

As discussed, a marketing orientated firm will seek to produce and sell products that meet the needs of the customers. However, this policy may result in firms adopting policies which society, as a whole, view as irresponsible.

Test your understanding 2

Explain why a company may be deemed irresponsible for providing customers with products that meet their needs?

The basis of social responsibility is the premise that an organisation enjoys certain benefits of society and, in return, should engage in practices that supports rather than exploits society.

e.g

Illustration 5

The following are some of the companies that will have a responsibility that goes beyond their own profit motive:

- Tobacco companies
- Alcohol producers and retailers
- Gas and oil companies
- Car manufacturers
- Drug companies
- Media companies

4.3 Advantages to a company for adopting a socially responsible approach

- **Unique selling point** – the market for a particular product may be highly competitive. The support of socially valuable causes may allow a company to develop a unique identity for its products.

  Starbucks, for example, has managed to create a strong brand and a unique selling point in what is a saturated market by only using 'Fair Trade' coffee and supporting community projects.

- **Increased sales** – customers may be willing to pay more for a product bought from a responsible company rather than an irresponsible one.

  In 2008, for example, a UK TV program saw celebrity chefs on a crusade against intensive chicken farming. As a result of this campaign, sales rocketed for the more expensive, free range chickens.

- **Change before new legislation is introduced** – some companies may put new practices in place before new legislation is introduced. This may help the company to gain from positive publicity.

  Some UK pubs and restaurants, for example, introduced a smoking ban before the UK legislation banning smoking in enclosed public spaces, was introduced in July 2007.

- **Can reduce company costs** – many companies wrongly believe that social responsibility will increase costs but it can actually reduce them.

Illustration 6 – Marks & Spencer

In May 2008 Marks & Spencer (M&S) introduced a number of initiatives aimed at improving their image as a socially responsible retailer. These included an initiative to reduce the number of plastic carrier bags used by customers:

- The introduction of a 5p charge for its single use carrier bags, in all of its UK stores.

- All profits (1.85p per bag) raised from the sale of the 5p bags will be invested in 'Groundwork', a charity which creates and improves greener living space in the UK.

- Any unwanted or unused M&S carrier bags can be returned by customers to any M&S store for recycling.

- M&S were the first major UK food retailer to use a standard carrier bag made from 100% recycled plastic.

- The steps taken have not only helped M&S's image as a socially responsible retailer but they have also enabled the company to reduce their costs.

5 Marketing in a Not-for-Profit Context

5.1 Introduction

The not-for-profit (NFP) sector incorporates a diverse range of operations including:

- private sector organisations, e.g. charities, sports associations
- public sector organisations, e.g. healthcare, education.

Many such organisations have now adopted (and adapted) a marketing orientation.

Whilst private sector organisations may try to understand and meet the needs of their customers, NFP organisations will have the challenge of needing to reach several groups with their marketing efforts, for example:

- contributors of money
- customers (may be referred to as clients, patients etc)
- volunteers and other supporters.

5.2 Marketing for charities

Charities must focus on the needs and wants of all different customer groups:

- beneficiaries (users, clients, members, etc.),
- supporters, and
- regulators.

With thousands of charities worldwide, competition for voluntary giving is intense. Those charities employing the most appropriate marketing practices are most likely to attract the generosity of peoples' time and money for their particular cause. Branding in particular is important in communicating a particular charity's core values, and distinguishing it from another.

Test your understanding 3

First run in 1994, Cancer Research UK's Race for Life, is the largest women-only fundraising event. Women are invited (for a fee) to walk, jog or run 5k at a choice of hundreds of Race for Life events taking place each year. The event has been a huge marketing success with over 6 million participants and £493 million raised to date.

Required:

Explain, using examples, how Cancer Research UK (a not-for-profit organisation) has been able to use the traditional marketing mix to increase the success of its running series.

5.3 Marketing for the public sector

- Within the UK, political reforms have pushed the public sector into a more commercial and managerial style meaning some managers need to make marketing decisions.

- Specialist companies have been enlisted to carry out market research, e.g. on behalf of public sector bodies.

- Social problems concerning (say) the elderly or disabled may call for information about their opinions and circumstances to help inform policy decisions.

Illustration 7 – Public goods

A public good is a good:

- that individuals cannot be excluded from using
- where use by one individual does not reduce availability to others.

Examples of public goods include street lighting, national defence and lighthouses.

The 'free-rider' problem is associated with public goods, i.e. people not paying for the good may continue to access it. The government overcomes this problem by providing the good for free at the point of consumption but funds the provision of the good through taxation.

An important role of government will be to understand society's needs in terms of how much tax to charge and on which goods to spend the funds that are raised.

5.4 Marketing for NGOs

NGOs play an important role in international development by directing development funds from donors and agencies to the point of need, unconstrained by profit or politics.

NGOs use marketing to:

- find a position for themselves within the market
- distinguish client and donors needs
- formulate and communicate NGO requirements
- gain new supporters.

6 Chapter summary

B2B and B2C marketing
- definitions
- features

Internal marketing

Marketing sustainability and ethics

Further aspects or marketing

Social marketing and CSR
- social marketing
- CSR
- advantages CSR

Marketing in a not-for-profit context
- charities
- public sector
- NGOS

7 Practice questions

Question 1 – OTQ

Which one of the following is not a feature of business to business (B2B) marketing?

A Industrial buyers have a lower purchasing power than consumers

B A closer relationship between buyers and sellers than compared to business to consumer (B2C) marketing

C Fewer buyers than B2C marketing

D Demand for the product is derived from consumer demand

Question 2 – OTQ

Which one of the following statements is false with regards to the not-for-profit sector?

A Marketing is difficult because there is no marketplace within which customers can choose competing goods and services

B A desire to meet customer's needs is constrained by the requirements to meet wider social goals

C The not-for-profit sector will have a number of financial objectives and non-financial social objectives

D The not-for-profit sector is unable to successfully adopt marketing principles

Question 3 – OTQ

Internal marketing is about:

A fulfilling the needs of employees and managers

B ensuring employees are able to support the organisation's marketing activities

C promoting the company's products to employees in order to increase sales

D reducing expenditure on advertising

Question 4 – T Inc (Case style)

Background

Sam is the Chief Executive Officer (CEO) of T Inc, a tobacco company. He has traditional views about the purpose of business in general and his own organisation in particular. Though he is frequently pressured by a variety of groups and organisations that think he should run his organisation differently, he sticks firmly to the view that the overriding purpose of business is to make money for the shareholders.

Responsibility to stakeholders

His son, Frank, who is being coached to take over the CEO role, takes a very different perspective. In his view, T Inc has a responsibility to a wide range of stakeholders.

Tasks:

(a) Explain how:
  (i) Sam would justify his view that the overriding purpose of the business is to make money for the shareholders.

  (ii) Frank would justify his view that T Inc has a responsibility to a wide range of stakeholders.

(15 minutes)

(b) Describe the stages Frank should go through in determining the priority of the goals of T Inc when he becomes CEO.

(10 minutes)

(Total: 25 minutes)

Test your understanding answers

Test your understanding 1

A mixture of

- Economic/task factors (price, delivery, location, quality, reliability, customer care, after care, etc.)

- Non-task factors (personal risk or gain, previous decisions, politics, those influencing the purchaser, perception, etc.)

As a result, significant B2B marketing mix features include quality assurance, reliability, delivery, price and after sales service.

Test your understanding 2

- **Environmental impact** – the product may deplete natural resources or emit harmful gases. In 2008, the DIY store B&Q decided to end the sale of patio heaters due to their environmental impact.

- **Harmful product** – products such as addictive drugs, alcohol and fast food may fulfil a customer's short term needs but could result in long term damage.

- **Vulnerable consumers** – marketers have a responsibility towards vulnerable groups such as children who are unable to fully evaluate decisions. For example, in the UK in 2007, TV advertisements for unhealthy food were banned during kids TV programs.

- **Deceptive practices** – for example, a customer may perceive that a certain mobile phone deal fulfils their needs. However, not reading or understanding the small print may mean that they don't know what they are committing themselves to.

- **Labour practices** – for example, a customer may buy a product because it fulfils their need for good value. However, they may be unaware that the labour used to produce the product are paid a poor wage and are subject to substandard working conditions, e.g. in 2008 Primark, the UK clothing company, were found to be using Indian suppliers who sub-contracted the work to smaller suppliers who, in turn, relied on child labour.

Test your understanding 3

Product

- Brand image is bright and consistent.
- The product fulfils many women's need to keep fit whilst also fulfilling a need to raise money for charity.
- The distance, 5k, is challenging but manageable for most.

Price

- The fee is affordable for most women.
- The fee is higher than an average race entry but most women will be willing to pay more since the money is donated to a good cause.
- Women will also be encouraged to raise sponsorship money.

Promotion

- The product is promoted using adverts on TV, in women's magazines and in gyms.
- The website is easy to navigate, branding is consistent, on-line entry is available and the site contains helpful advice with regards to training and sponsorship.
- Celebrity endorsement has been used. Many popular women celebrities have completed the race.

Place

- A wide choice of accessible locations.
- Scenic locations making the event enjoyable.

Question 1 – OTQ

The correct answer is A

Question 2 – OTQ

The correct answer is D

Question 3 – OTQ

The correct answer is B

Question 4 – T Inc (Case style)

(a) (i) Stakeholders are any people or groups that have an interest in a particular organisation. Although there are a large number of stakeholder groups that might have an interest in a company, the most important group is usually seen as the shareholders.

Sam would argue that there are a number of reasons for this:

The reason why a company exists is to make money for its owners, i.e. for its shareholders. The company belongs to them and so they should always be given the highest priority.

Although there are other stakeholders such as employees, suppliers, etc. they are given their rewards through items such as high wages, bills being paid on time, etc. It is only possible to do these if the company is profitable, i.e. this is the same goal as keeping the shareholders happy.

(ii) Frank would argue that the responsibility of the company stretches to more than just the shareholders. For example:

T Inc could increase profitability at the expense of its employees (by paying them lower wages) or suppliers (by taking extended credit). Although these are both of benefit in the short term to the profits of the company and therefore to the shareholders, it is unlikely that they will bring long-term benefits.

The company is operating in the tobacco industry and as such is high profile. If the company is seen to be acting irresponsibly it might be forced by government to adopt certain procedures, which will lead to increased costs. It is therefore more sensible to consider the environment and local community since it is more cost effective in the long term.

Frank would argue that any modern organisation must see itself as being in co-operation with a large number of other people: suppliers, customers, employees, etc. If it views itself as purely catering to shareholders and the pursuit of profit it will be unlikely to be successful in the modern business environment.

(b) The process that Frank needs to go through in determining the priorities of stakeholders is sometimes known as stakeholder mapping.

Firstly, Frank will need to draw up a list of all stakeholders from both inside and outside the organisation.

Secondly, Frank should identify what each group wants from T Inc. For example:

- Shareholders want increased profits and dividends.

- Employees want increased wages and working conditions.

- Government wants taxes and some contribution towards healthcare costs from both T Inc and from their customers.

- Action groups might want T Inc to stop targeting young people for advertising campaigns.

- Political groups might want to ban/limit the use of T Inc's products through smoking bans (as was introduced in 2008 in the UK).

It can be seen from the above list that it is not possible to meet the expectations of each group since some are in direct opposition to others.

Thirdly, Frank should look at how much influence and power each group has. For example, shareholders (particularly institutional ones) can sell their shares and depress the share price if they are unhappy with the decisions being made by T Inc. As such they are powerful. On the other hand, low-grade employees may not have many other job opportunities so they have much less power to influence decisions.

Finally, Frank will have to set goals and objectives that meet the expectations of those groups with the most power whilst meeting the minimum requirements of each group with some power.

Introduction to Human Resource Management

Chapter learning objectives

Lead	Component
F1. Demonstrate the purpose of the human resource function and its relationships with other parts of the organisation.	(a) Explain the contribution of human resources to the sustainable delivery of the organisation's strategies. (b) Apply the elements of the HR cycle.
F2. Apply the tools and techniques of human resource management.	(a) Demonstrate the human resource activities associated with developing employees. (b) Demonstrate the role of the line manager in the implementation of human resource practices.

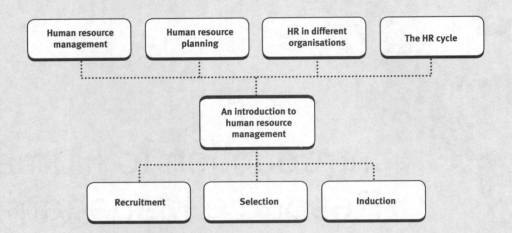

1 Introduction

Human resource management (HRM) can be viewed as a strategic approach to acquiring, developing, managing and motivating an organisation's key resource. This should help the organisation achieve its stated objectives through the best use of its employees.

Note that HRM is not simply a renaming of old "personnel" departments but a radical change in emphasis:

The role of personnel versus the role of HRM

Personnel	HRM
• The **traditional** approach to managing human resources.	• The **modern** approach to managing human resources.
• Concerned with **operational** matters, e.g. recruitment to fill a current vacancy.	• Concerned with **operational and strategic** matters, e.g. training to fulfil the current and future needs of the organisation.
• Employees seen as **costs**.	• Employees seen as **assets**.
• Employees motivated by **payment and coercion.**	• Employees motivated by **consent and involvement**.
• Line manager's role is more **transactional** with an emphasis on **negotiation**. Key managers are seen to be personnel and industrial relations specialists.	• Line manager's role is now one of **transformational leadership** with an emphasis on **facilitation**. Line managers are seen as key within a HR emphasis.

HRM can also be considered in terms of a hard or soft approach.

Hard HRM treats the employees simply as a resource of the business (like machinery and buildings). There is little empowerment of staff and pay is just enough to recruit and retain sufficient staff.

Soft HRM, on the other hand, treats employees as the most important resource in the business and as a source of competitive advantage. Employees are empowered and receive a competitive pay structure (including performance-related pay).

The Guest model of HRM

A HR strategy can only make sense when related to business objectives. One model that clearly demonstrates the relationship between HRM activities and strategy was proposed by David **Guest** (1997) and comprised six components:

(1) HRM strategy

(2) HRM practices

(3) a set of HRM outcomes

(4) behavioural outcomes

(5) a number of performance outcomes

(6) financial outcomes.

The central idea of the model is that HRM practices should be designed to lead a set of positive outcomes including high staff commitment and quality, and highly flexible employees. The main features are:

- a goal of binding employees to the organisation and obtaining behavioural outcomes of increased effort, co-operation, involvement and organisational citizenship

- high quality employees, involving workplace learning and the need for a capable, qualified, skilful workforce to produce high-quality services and products

- flexibility concerned with ensuring that workers are receptive to innovation and change and operation.

Outcomes 3–6 focus on the link between HRM and performance. According to the model, only when all three HRM outcomes, of commitment, quality and flexibility, are achieved, can behaviour change and superior performance outcomes be expected. These HRM goals are a 'package' and each is necessary to ensure superior performance and financial outcomes.

2 Human Resource Planning (HRP)

The organisation's **HR plan** is a strategy developed within the context of the organisation's corporate strategic plans.

- Its aim is to define and close the gap between the demand for labour and the supply of labour within the organisation.

- A typical HR plan looks forward 3–5 years and is a cyclical process.

Reasons for creating a HR plan
(1) To rationally plan recruitment
(2) To rationally forecast future costs to assist in budgeting and control
(3) To smooth change management in redeployment, redundancy etc.
(4) To assist in planning the education, development and training needs of staff
(5) To adapt more quickly to ever changing circumstances.

The stages of HRP are as follows:

Stage 1: Strategic analysis
- The organisation's strategic objectives will have implications regarding the number of employees and the skills required over the planning period (e.g. development of a new product or expansion into a new market)
- The broader strategic environment should also be considered (e.g. trends in population growth, pensions, education and employment rights of women)

Stage 2: Internal analysis
- An 'audit' of existing staff should be carried out to establish the current numbers and skills
- Also consider:
  - Turnover of staff and absenteeism
  - Overtime worked and periods of inactivity
  - Staff potential

Stage 3: Identify the gap between supply and demand
- Shortages or excesses in labour numbers and skills deficiencies should be identified

Stage 4: Put plans into place to close the gap

Adjustments for shortfall
- Internal: Transfers, promotions, training, job enlargement, overtime, reduce labour turnover
- External: Fill remaining needs externally. Consider suitability and availability of external resource

Adjustments for a surplus
Consider use of natural wastage, recruitment freeze, retirement, part time working and redundancy

Stage 5: Review
Measure the effective use of the human resource and their contribution towards the achievement of the organisation's objectives

Stage 4 of the HR plan

In stage four of HRP a number of plans will be created and used:

Recruitment plan	Numbers and types of people, when required, recruitment programme
Training plan	Number of trainees required and training programme
Redevelopment plan	Programme for transferring staff
Productivity plan	Setting targets and developing incentive schemes
Redundancy plan	Location, selection process, package details
Retention plan	Career development programmes

Test your understanding 1

Describe **four** problems in implementing the HR plan.

Test your understanding 2

How can an organisation plan rationally in an unstable environment?

3 HR in Different Organisations

Organisational HR practices inevitably vary dependent upon the individual size and culture of the organisation and availability of specialist HR or personnel managers to support management in carrying out their duties.

The need to respond to a fast moving environment has led to organisations moving from traditional hierarchies to adopting more flexible organisational structures including fluid matrix or project-based firms. Alongside these virtual or networked firms have grown up. Inevitably these non-traditional structures have presented new HR challenges and required managers to adapt traditional approaches to these local contexts.

Clearly HR thinking and practice needs to evolve in response to these challenges of flexibility and environmental uncertainty, specifically in the areas of:

- planning horizons
- staff appraisal where there may be no formal supervisor/subordinate reporting relations
- remuneration strategies where outputs are not easily attributable to individuals alone
- the structure of the workforce and the use of consultants and contractors
- development, promotion and succession planning.

New forms of organisation have resulted in changing HR needs. For example:

Project based teams

Employees are organised into work teams, e.g. for a particular project or customer group. HR implications:

- Multi-skilled employees are required.
- Intensive training will be needed.
- A movement away from traditional hierarchies to flatter structures.

Virtual organisations

Technology has resulted in the development of virtual organisations. Virtual teams work together using the internet, networked computers and teleconferencing.

This can bring huge benefits for the employer in terms of the flexibility to recruit the most talented individual for a particular role. However, it can also bring additional challenges with regards to HR since geographical spread will make all elements of HR (i.e. recruitment, selection, inductions, appraisals and training and development) more difficult.

4 The HR Cycle

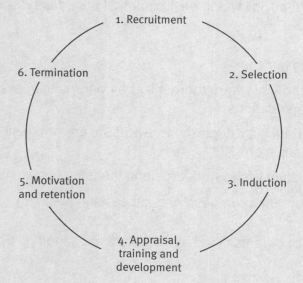

Each of these activities will be reviewed in turn. This chapter will focus on recruitment, selection and induction.

5 Recruitment

5.1 Introduction

Recruitment involves attracting a field of suitable candidates for the job.

The best recruitment campaign will attract a small number of highly suitable applicants, be cost effective, be speedy and show courtesy to all candidates.

5.2 Agree vacancy

When an employee leaves an organisation, the vacancy they leave presents an opportunity to the business to either reassess the requirements of the job, or to consider restructuring. The organisation could consider:

- analysing the role in more detail – what is its purpose? Has it changed? This could lead to:
  - not replacing the employee – could the vacant role be handled by existing staff through retraining, promotion or adjustment of workloads?
  - replacing the employee with a part-time worker – alternatives to full-time employment include home working, job-sharing or flexi-time contracts.

Assessing the need to recruit

When considering recruitment, there are two questions that managers must address. The first is whether there is really a job, and the second is whether there is someone suitable who is already employed by the organisation. There are many alternatives to recruitment, e.g.

- promotion of existing staff (upwards or laterally)
- secondment (temporary transfers to another department, office, plant or country) of existing staff, which may or may not become permanent
- closing the job down, by sharing out duties and responsibilities among existing staff
- rotating jobs among staff, so that the vacant job is covered by different staff, on a systematic basis over several months
- putting the job out to tender, using external contractors.

5.3 Job analysis

Job analysis is 'the process of collecting, analysing and setting out information about the content of jobs in order to provide the basis for a job description and data for recruitment, training, job evaluation and performance management. Job analysis concentrates on what job holders are expected to do.' **Armstrong**

Such an exercise is frequently necessary since all too few organisations have a precise picture of the work that people do to achieve organisational objectives.

Test your understanding 3

Explain the importance of job analysis for a large supermarket chain, such as Tesco.

Methods of analysing and defining roles would include:

- interview with existing post holder or supervisor
- direct observation
- questionnaires
- manager trying the job.

Competences are the critical skills, knowledge and attitudes that a job-holder must have to perform effectively. A competent individual will be more able to contribute effectively to the business almost as soon as they are appointed.

As such, it is important for an organisation to ensure that all staff are appropriately qualified and trained for their role in the organisation. Competency frameworks can help with this.

Competency frameworks attempt to identify all the competencies that are required by anyone taking on a particular role within the organisation.

A list of key competences is produced which can be used as a benchmark to either ensure that the correct individual is chosen for the role or as a way of checking that an existing member of staff has all the up to date skills needed for their role.

Most competency frameworks cover the following categories:

- communication skills
- people management
- team skills
- customer service skills
- results-orientation
- problem-solving skills.

Illustration 1

A research analyst working for the government might have the following factors within their competency framework (amongst others):

Delivery skills

- Focus
- Delivery skills
- Learning and improving

Intellectual capacity

- Critical analysis and decision making
- Constructive thinking

Interpersonal skills

- Developing constructive relationships
- Communicating with impact

Each competence will then be supported by a high level description. For example, 'Learning and improving' could be described as:

'Acknowledges own development needs and seeks new skills. Learns from others and adapts to new people and task needs.'

> ### Test your understanding 4 – OTQ
>
> Consider the following list:
>
> (i)   Attention to detail
>
> (ii)   Communication skills
>
> (iii) Computer skills
>
> (iv) Numeracy
>
> Which of these competences would be required by a typical accountant?
>
> A   (i) and (ii) only
>
> B   (ii), (iii) and (iv) only
>
> C   (ii) and (iv) only
>
> D   (i), (ii), (iii) and (iv)

Employers should regularly keep the competency frameworks updated for their employees and assess whether they still have the appropriate skills and abilities needed for their jobs. If not, the employer may wish to consider continuing professional development (CPD) which will involve employees attending training courses or reading technical information to update their skills.

Ensuring that employees have up to date skills will:

- minimise employee errors and mistakes
- improve customer service and satisfaction
- increase employee motivation, as they feel valued by the organisation.

5.4 Job descriptions

After a full job analysis has been carried out, a job description can be drawn up identifying the precise nature of the job in question.

> ### Test your understanding 5
>
> Prepare a job description for a London based role as a Finance Director in an internet media company which is about to become a public company.

Job descriptions

Most job descriptions include all of the following points.

- The title of the job and the name of the department in which it is situated.

- The purpose of the job, identifying its objectives in relationship to overall objectives.

- The position of the job in the organisation, indicating the relationships with other jobs and the chains of responsibility. For this purpose, many firms refer to existing organisation charts.

- Wage/salary range.

- Principal duties to be performed, with emphasis on key tasks, and limits to the jobholder's authority. Usually included under this heading is an indication of how the job differs from others in the organisation.

- A further breakdown of principal duties is made identifying specific tasks in terms of what precisely is done and in what manner, and with some explanation, both in terms of quantity and quality.

- Aspects of the 'job environment' should be considered. Descriptions should be made of how the organisation supports the job, in terms of management and the provision of key services. The working conditions should be considered in terms of both the physical environment and the social environment (is the job part of a group task?). The opportunities offered by the job should be identified; these are especially important in a recruitment exercise.

- No job description is complete without a full identification of the key difficulties likely to be encountered by the jobholder.

Most of the content of a job description will be generated by the line manager. However, an HR department can help through the use of standardised templates, discussions over grading and salary and the position of the role in the wider organisation.

5.5 Person specifications

The **person specification** defines the personal characteristics, qualifications and experience required by the job holder in order to do the job well. It therefore becomes a specification for the attributes sought in a successful candidate for the job, a blueprint for the perfect person to fill the role.

Rodgers recommended that the following categories should be covered in a person specification:

Category	Example
B – Background/circumstances	Details of previous work experience and circumstances, e.g. family background, criminal record.
A – Attainments	Details of qualifications and any relevant experience.
D – Disposition	The individual's goals and motivations, e.g. where do they see themselves in 5 years time?
P – Physical make-up	Appearance, speech, health and fitness may be important.
I – Interests	General interests and hobbies will be important, e.g. being a member of a football team demonstrates teamwork skills.
G – General intelligence	Not necessarily academic qualifications but may refer to practical intelligence, e.g. problem solving ability.
S – Special attributes	Skills such as the ability to speak another language or IT skills.

As with job analysis and job description, the prospective line manager is usually in the best position to construct a person specification but many managers will appreciate assistance here from HR specialists who may have more experience.

Fraser's 5-point plan

A similar blueprint was devised by **Fraser**. He referred to it as the Five Point Plan, to include the following considerations:

- **F**lexibility and adjustment – emotional stability, ability to get on with others and capacity for stress.
- **I**mpact on other people – appearance, speech and manner.
- **R**equired qualifications – education, training, and experience.
- **M**otivation – determination and achievement.
- **I**nnate abilities – 'brains', comprehension and aptitude for learning.

Illustration 2

Care must be taken not to transgress one of the laws relating to discrimination, as in the case of a job advertisement seeking 'a female Scottish cook and housekeeper', which was barred both on the grounds of race and sex discrimination.

Test your understanding 6

Are there any circumstances when discrimination on the basis of physical make-up is acceptable?

5.6 Source candidates

It is important to know where suitable candidates may be found, how to make contact with them and to secure their application. The following sources are available:

Source	Comment
Job centre	Free but may not find a suitable candidate.
Recruitment consultant	Reduces burden on employer and may be a source of expertise but expensive and may not understand the organisation's needs.
Job fair	Can meet people face to face but may not attract enough suitable candidates.
National press	Good coverage for national jobs but advertisements are expensive and short-lived.
Local newspaper	Useful for local staff and cheaper than national but may not attract sufficiently qualified people.
Internet	Good as long as target people are frequent internet users.
Radio and TV	Expensive but sometimes can produce a large number of suitable candidates.
Specialist journals	Already degree of selection but may contain many similar advertisements.

Sourcing candidates usually involves the HR department unless the firm is particularly small. Partly this is to ensure that any advertisements comply with any legal requirements on diversity and discrimination, but also because the HR department will have more experience of recruitment consultants and the different advertising media.

6 Selection

6.1 Introduction

Selection is aimed at choosing the best person for the job from the field of candidates sourced via recruitment.

Any selection process needs to ensure:

- **Reliability** – to give consistent results
- **Validity** – as a predictor of future performance
- **Fairness** – selection in a non-discriminatory way
- **Cost effectiveness** – in terms of manager's time and other options available.

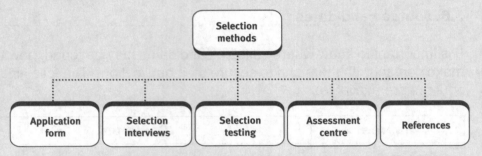

6.2 Application forms

Application forms are used to obtain relevant information about the applicant and allow for comparison with the person specification of the job. They should also give the applicants some ability to express themselves beyond the limited factual remit of the form. Their usefulness includes:

- eliminating unsatisfactory candidates
- saving interview time by selecting only the most suitable candidates for interview
- forming an initial personal record for an employee.

Application forms are likely to be standardised to some extent and hence will be produced by HR professionals with input from the line managers.

6.3 Selection interviews

Once a shortlist has been drawn up, the most common way of selecting a candidate is by interview. Their purpose is to:

- find the best person for the job (research shows that an interview used in isolation is unreliable as a selector but when used with other selection methods greater reliability is achieved)

- ensure the candidate understands what the job is and what the career prospects are

- make the candidate feel that they have been given fair treatment in the interview.

Line managers would normally expect to be part of the interviewing panel for new employees for their departments.

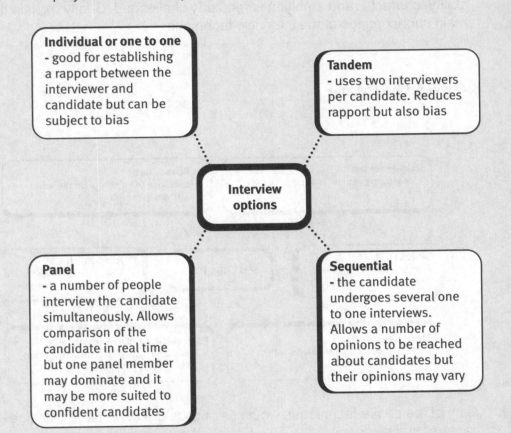

Individual or one to one
- good for establishing a rapport between the interviewer and candidate but can be subject to bias

Tandem
- uses two interviewers per candidate. Reduces rapport but also bias

Interview options

Panel
- a number of people interview the candidate simultaneously. Allows comparison of the candidate in real time but one panel member may dominate and it may be more suited to confident candidates

Sequential
- the candidate undergoes several one to one interviews. Allows a number of opinions to be reached about candidates but their opinions may vary

Advantages of selection interviews

- Places candidates at ease.

- Highly interactive, allowing flexible question and answers.

- Opportunities to use non-verbal communication.

- Opportunities to assess appearance, interpersonal and communication skills.

- Opportunities to evaluate rapport between the candidate and the potential colleagues/bosses.

Test your understanding 7

The validity of a face-to-face interview as a means of gauging a person's ability, character and ambition is regularly challenged. Briefly explain the main shortcomings of the interview technique.

6.4 Selection testing

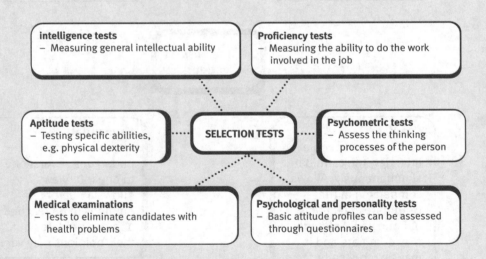

Many of the above techniques would lie outside the expertise of the line manager and so specialists would be called in to carry out the testing and feed back.

Psychometric testing

In the following extracts from an article by Bryan Appleyard the growth and usefulness of psychometric testing is reviewed:

Welcome to the weird world of psychometrics. If you want to work for a big company there's at least a 70% chance that before being given a job you will be subjected to a personality test by one of the big four – MBTI (Myers-Briggs Type Indicator), 16PF (16 personality factors), OPQ (occupational personality questionnaire) or Hogan – and an ability exam measuring verbal reasoning and numeracy.

These are basically IQ tests by another name...according to the Association of Graduate Recruiters, it's because nobody trusts university degrees any more. It has just issued a report saying degree standards are inconsistent and, as a result, companies are turning to psychometrics. But Ceri Roderick at occupation psychologists Pearn Kandola adds two other reasons. 'Companies want to know things like the motivational characteristics of recruits and the technology is now available to do these things.' There's also a fourth reason: the need to compete for quality recruits. 'There's a war for talent,' says Professor David Bartram of the British Psychological Society (BPS), 'companies are fighting to get the best people.' All of which means there is now a rapid proliferation of psychometrics consultancies, most of them offering candidates the chance to do all the tests online. . . .

Sceptics think the whole enterprise is misguided. In America a book – The Cult of Personality by Annie Murphy Paul – has cast doubt on the intellectual credibility of psychometrics…

In support of Paul's book the author Malcolm Gladwell questions the very idea of measuring personality: 'We have a personality in the sense that we have a consistent pattern of behaviour. But that pattern is complex and that personality is contingent: it represents an interaction between our internal disposition and tendencies and the situations that we find ourselves in.'. . . .

But are Gladwell and Paul right to question the whole theory on which they are based? The history of psychometrics marches hand in hand with the history of IQ testing. Alfred Binet, the French psychologist, produced the first modern IQ test in 1905 and Walter Dill Scott subjected 15 engineering graduates to the first psychometric test in 1915. Both ideas were inspired by the conviction that there could be no reason why the human mind should be impervious to scientific investigation. . . .

Psychometrics works, but only if the tests are properly applied, rigorously interpreted and accompanied by traditional interviews. This means that they do not necessarily speed up the recruitment process. They might, however, help weed out unsuitables in advance, a huge benefit at a time when all companies are swamped with applicants for attractive jobs.

Source: Appleyard, B. (2007) Want a job? Let's play mind games. Sunday Times, 22 July.

6.5 Assessment centres

- The idea of the assessment centre grew out of the obvious shortcomings of the selection interview and other selection techniques.

- Assessment centres, usually provided by external consultants unless the firm is particularly large, allow the assessment of individuals working in a group or alone by a team of assessors, who use a variety of assessment techniques.

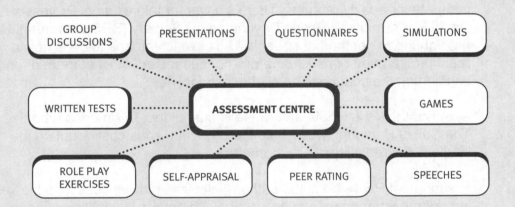

- Groups of around 6–10 candidates are brought together for one to three days of intensive assessment.

- The assessment centre can be designed so as to test the applicant's competencies against the criteria set out in the person specification.

Test your understanding 8

Explain why assessment centres are part of a competency-based selection process used by many major employers when recruiting staff for their graduate training scheme?

Drawbacks of assessment centres

- The assessment centre must be rigorous or else there is a temptation to select the person who just seems the most sociable or likeable.

- The cost of setting them up, administering them, staffing them and producing results can be extremely high.

6.6 References

The purpose of references is to confirm facts about the employee and increase the degree of confidence felt about information given during the other selection techniques.

Content of references

References should contain two types of information:

- Straightforward factual information. This confirms the nature of the applicant's previous job(s), period of employment, pay, and circumstances of leaving.

- Opinions about the applicant's personality and other attributes.

A standard form to be completed by the referee might pose a set of simple questions about:

- job title
- main duties and responsibilities
- period of employment
- pay/salary
- attendance record.

Problems with references

Opinions should obviously be treated with some caution. Allowances should be made for:

- prejudice – favourable or unfavourable.

- charity – withholding detrimental remarks.

- fear of being actionable for libel.

6.7 Employment offer and negotiation

- **Offer of employment** – once an eligible candidate has been found, an offer can be made, in writing or by telephone, subject to satisfactory references and medical checks.

- **Negotiation** – it may be necessary to reach a mutually agreeable compromise over some aspects of the employment contract, e.g. pay, hours of work or holiday allowance.

Offer of employment

An effective offer of employment must not contain anything that cannot be delivered and should contain the following elements:

- Must be a written document – a written statement is a legally binding document, which should help to seal the offer. A telephone call to break the good news to the successful candidate is fine, but should not go into too much detail about the offer in conversation.

- Must contain sufficient detail – must contain the job title and location with details of pay, benefits, hours of work, holiday as well as the terms and conditions of employment, including notice period, sickness payment schemes, pension scheme details, disciplinary and grievance procedures and an outline of the probationary period where one is in force.

- Should offer an opportunity to make further contact before a final commitment is made – a clear but informal opportunity for further discussion, which may lead to negotiation on terms and conditions of employment.

7 Induction

The purpose of an induction is to ensure the most effective integration of staff into the organisation, for the benefit of both parties.

The **benefits** of a good induction programme include:

- Quick and effective assimilation into organisational life

- A well planned programme will reassure employees. This will aid motivation and improve performance

- Increased commitment since it can provide a positive reflection of the organisation while the employee is still comparatively receptive and has not been subject to negative views

- Reduces staff turnover and associated costs

Induction programmes may focus on company wide issues, in which case they will usually be designed and run by the HR department, and/or focus on departmental practices and procedures, in which case they may be set up by the line manager.

Illustration 3

In 2013 the average UK employee turnover rate was 16.9% and the average cost of employee turnover was £6,300 for each employee. A major reason why employees leave within the first six months to a year is a poorly planned induction process. Therefore, there are significant savings to be made from implementing an effective induction process.

A good induction programme would typically include:

Pre-employment	<ul><li>joining instructions</li><li>conditions of employment</li><li>company literature</li></ul>
Health and safety	<ul><li>emergency exits</li><li>first aid facilities</li><li>protective clothing</li><li>specific hazards</li></ul>

Organisation	<ul><li>site map – canteen, first aid post etc</li><li>telephone and computer system</li><li>organisation chart</li><li>security pass and procedures</li></ul>
Terms and conditions	<ul><li>absence/sickness procedure</li><li>working time including hours, breaks and flexi-time</li><li>holidays</li><li>probation period</li><li>discipline and grievance procedure</li><li>internet and email policy</li></ul>
Financial	<ul><li>payment date and methods</li><li>benefits and pension</li><li>expense procedures</li></ul>
Training	<ul><li>discuss training opportunities and agree training plan</li><li>career management</li></ul>
Culture and values	<ul><li>organisation background</li><li>mission and objectives</li></ul>

8 Chapter Summary

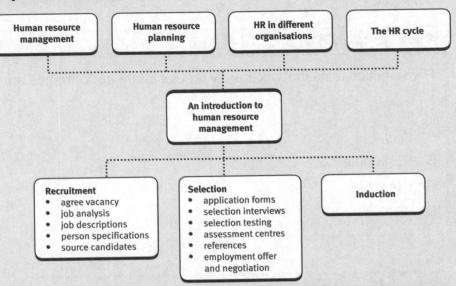

9 Practice questions

Question 1 – OTQ

HR selection tests that accurately predict future performance are said to be:

A   Valid

B   Equitable

C   Reliable

D   Stable

Question 2 – OTQ

An employer has decided to offer a job to a candidate following a selection process, but still has some doubts about whether the individual will be well-suited to the job. Which of the following options would be the most effective way of dealing with these concerns about the individual's aptitude for the job?

A   Making the employee redundant if he/she fails to perform well

B   Offering the job initially for a probationary period

C   Offering the candidate a low rate of pay until he/she has demonstrated the ability to do the job well

D   Dismissing the individual for incompetence if he/she does the job badly

Question 3 – OTQ

The use of standard questions in job interviews helps ensure:

A   fairness

B   validity

C   reliability

D   completeness

Question 4 – OTQ

The purpose of a person specification is to provide details of:

A   organisational size and diversity of activity

B   the types of responsibilities and duties to be undertaken by the post holder.

C   personal characteristics, experience and qualifications expected of a candidate

D   individual terms of engagement and period of contract

Question 5 – OTQ

Which one of the following is a part of the recruitment rather than the selection process?

A   Job analysis

B   Interviewing

C   Testing

D   Assessment centres

Question 6 – OTQ

Aptitude testing is most frequently used:

A   As part of a selection process

B   As part of an appraisal process

C   As part of a process of training and development

D   As part of an exit interview process

Question 7 – Middleregion (Case style)

Background

The country of Bigland has a democratically elected government which determines broad national policies. Local services such as education, social care and environmental services are the responsibility of the elected local government for the regions. These regions are funded by a combination of local taxes and government grants. The largest region is Middleregion, which is about to develop a new workforce strategy for its many local government employees. Recently it has received a report from its external auditor into its overall arrangements for achieving value for money.

Recommendations

The external auditor has made three recommendations relevant to human resources (HR):

- There needs to be greater clarity over the distinctive roles carried out by both Middleregion's Human Resources Department and line managers in developing and implementing HR practices;

- A new workforce strategy is a good initiative but planning will need to take account of a changing environment and be relevant to local conditions;

- Middleregion should consider moving to more electronically-based HR processes and systems (e-HR). e-HR includes using technology to improve HR services, such as recording and monitoring systems, automating administrative tasks like recruitment, and communicating HR information on the intranet.

Tasks:

(a) Discuss the contributions of both Middleregion's Human Resources Department and line managers in developing and then implementing HR practices.

(15 minutes)

(b) Explain, with examples, how Middleregion should plan a new workforce strategy that takes account of a changing environment and is relevant to local conditions.

(15 minutes)

(c) Explain the costs Middleregion should take account of when considering moving to e-HR.

(10 minutes)

(Total: 40 minutes)

Test your understanding answers

Test your understanding 1

- People resources are costly and should therefore be carefully planned.
- Knowledge, expertise and skill requirements are constantly changing and it can be difficult to keep up with these changes.
- Rapid social and technical changes also make planning difficult.
- All types of forecasting will be open to uncertainty.

Test your understanding 2

- By staying flexible.
- By taking greater account of external factors.
- By more sophisticated monitoring and control mechanisms.
- By planning in shorter time frames.

Problems in achieving plans might to a degree be predictable and in the past have also centred on:

- retention, especially when employees are well trained or have specialist skills
- slow promotion leading to staff turnover
- unexpected vacancies arising in senior positions or vital skills areas.

Test your understanding 3

- Effective recruitment depends on accurate job analysis, e.g. if the exact nature of the job is known, then it facilitates precisely worded adverts, which will assist in attracting a suitable field of candidates.

- It may eliminate the need for recruitment, e.g. the job may no longer be necessary or could be shared elsewhere in the organisation.

- To assist in determining the most appropriate method of selection.

- To help identify the need for training and the most appropriate training method.

- To establish differences between jobs so that wage and salary differentials may be determined.

Test your understanding 4 – OTQ

The correct answer is D

The competences an accountant needs include the following:

- Skills
  - Numeracy
  - Literacy
  - IT Literacy
  - Bookkeeping

- Knowledge
  - FRS, IAS, etc
  - Group accounts preparation
  - Hedging

- Attitude
  - Conscientious
  - Dynamic
  - Attention to detail

Test your understanding 5

- Finance Director required **(Title of the job)**

- At least five years post qualified experience **(special requirements)**

- Experience of a dynamic industry **(special requirements)**

- Understanding of investor relations and pre-floatation requirements **(special requirements)**

- Ability to manage change and form own department **(special requirements)**

- Role includes **(brief description of role):**
    - Planning, monitoring and control of business and financial strategy.
    - Reporting and accounting as per the legal requirements
    - Management of strategy for and liaison with stock market business press and the business analyst community

- Excellent package including competitive salary and share options **(remuneration)**

- Responsible for a growing team of 18 people **(number of staff directly supervised)**

- Report directly to the Managing Director **(responsible to)**

- Located in London with approximately 20% travel to other European locations **(location and special attributes, e.g. shift systems, willingness to travel)**

Test your understanding 6

Discrimination may be acceptable in certain circumstances, e.g.:

- Army soldiers must be fit, healthy and be able to carry heavy kit.

- Firemen must be a certain height so that they can reach the equipment.

- An Italian restaurant can choose to recruit only Italian waiters and waitresses.

Test your understanding 7

Shortcomings of selection interviews include:

* too brief to 'get to know' candidates.
* interview is an artificial situation.
* 'halo' effect from initial impression.
* contrast problem – an average candidate following an awful one will look very good.
* qualitative factors such as motivation, honesty or integrity are difficult to assess.
* prejudice – stereotyping groups of people.
* lack of interviewer preparation, poor questioning, poor retention of information.
* environmental factors, e.g. an unsuitable location, noise, lack of time.

Test your understanding 8

* An assessment centre uses a wide range of assessment methods and it is therefore argued that the approach is more thorough and therefore more successful than the more traditional approaches. If nothing else, the process takes longer and allows the potential employer to see the candidates over a longer period of time. The opportunity to get to know a potential employee could prove to be invaluable. This contrasts well with the very time-constrained, artificial interview situation.

* It has been shown that they are much better at predicting a successful match between the selected candidate and the employer. The wider the range of techniques used, the more successful the result in terms of reliability and validity.

* Avoidance of single–assessor bias.

* The development of skills in the assessors, which may be useful in their own managerial responsibilities.

Question 1 – OTQ

The correct answer is A

Question 2 – OTQ

The correct answer is B

Question 3 – OTQ

The correct answer is A

Question 4 – OTQ

The correct answer is C

Question 5 – OTQ

The correct answer is A

Question 6 – OTQ

The correct answer is A

Question 7 – Middleregion (Case style)

(a) **Middleregion's Human Resources Department**

Middleregion's Human Resources Department has a number of important roles to perform, some of which are listed below.

Ensuring alignment of HR to corporate aspirations

It should be the responsibility of the department to ensure that HR activities are aligned to the corporate strategy. The department should also make sure that new policies arising from the workforce strategy must support Middleregion's corporate strategy and broader organisational aims and philosophy. As such, the department will need a mature understanding of organisational requirements and will need to see the link to strategic and operational human resourcing.

Leading HR planning processes

As subject specialists, the department should take the principal role in matters of strategy development including leading the development of the new workforce strategy. The leadership it exercises should emphasise inclusivity and it must ensure that all key stakeholders, including line managers and employees are involved in the process. This involvement is important to ensure workforce commitment and successful implementation.

Bringing expertise to the planning process

The Human Resources Department can bring specialist knowledge and skills into the planning process. As such, it should keep abreast of any developments to service provision which could affect the workforce strategy and then be prepared to brief others on the implications for Middleregion. The department is also in the best position to suggest new initiatives and approaches. As such, it could use its contacts and professional association to find out what happens in other regional units of government, other areas of the public sector and best practice within the private sector.

Maintaining Middleregion's human resource asset

Human resources activities should be aimed at delivering agreed strategy. As such, it should assume responsibility for continuously developing the skills and capacity of the workforce. In particular the department should put in place measures to remedy skill gaps identified as part of the planning process.

Develop monitoring and review mechanisms

As a public body, Middleregion will need to demonstrate the impact the strategy is having on performance improvement. Middleregion's progress towards achieving its strategy means that targets and performance indicators are required, and the department should suggest and agree key performance indicators (KPIs) and other rubrics. Regular review and reporting mechanisms should also be formalised by the department.

Ensure adequacy of HR function

Senior HR managers will need to ensure that the function is capable of supporting and delivering strategy and fulfilling its organisational obligations. As such, they will need to make sure that it is staffed to an adequate level with those possessing the necessary skills and experience. The budgetary provision to operate the department will need to be adequate and, if not, a case should be made for additional funding.

Support managers

A key role of the department should be to help and support line managers in carrying out their role correctly and effectively. As such, it should find ways of providing advice and support in order to improve management practice. The department should be accessible to managers and should encourage communication and a dissemination of good HR practice within the organisation.

Middleregion line managers

Classically the role of management has been expressed as organising, planning, controlling and influencing. Middleregion's line managers are no different in respect of human resourcing issues. As such, their main role should include:

Organising: Strategy and policy implementation

Line managers need to recognise the potential impact they have on subordinates who are responsible for service delivery improvement and the achievement of corporate goals and strategy's objectives. These managers can play an important role in understanding and implementing the workforce strategy and people management policies. They do this by translating these into operational terms. In doing this, they may need to adapt and organise ways of working in order to fulfil the strategy requirements.

Planning: Participation in strategy and policy development

Whilst the Human Resources Department offers specialist knowledge and skills, line managers can complement this by bringing local knowledge and practical 'on the ground' experience to HR planning processes. This should help in having practical discussions of what might or might not 'work'.

Controlling: Monitor strategy achievement

Part of the management role is that of monitoring and control. Line managers should monitor how well employees they are responsible for are performing against the strategic targets. By way of example, managers may wish to compare their team's sickness and absence or staff turnover rates with overall organisational targets. As such, they may wish to determine (in conjunction with the Human Resources Department) local policies and measures to improve matters. More generally, line managers with their particular 'on the ground' perspectives will be in an ideal position to feedback issues that are getting in the way of achieving strategy or organisational policy.

Influencing: Communicate with and positively influence the workforce

Line managers represent the 'filling in the sandwich'; the link between policy makers and front line workers and, as such, they will represent the most direct communication mechanism for most staff. In terms of new initiatives, such as the proposed workforce strategy, they should look to gain the support of employees by:

- explaining its main features and its impact on individuals
- selling policies
- defending policies on behalf of the organisation.

Asking for guidance

The Human Resources Department should be seen as a source of guidance and support when dealing with people issues. Line managers must be willing to seek advice and support in order to improve management practice and deal with workforce problems and issues. The alternative of 'going it alone' or looking for quick fix solutions could be organisationally damaging.

(b) The external auditor has reported that a new workforce strategy will need to take account of a changing environment and be relevant to local conditions. Middleregion should plan a new workforce strategy that is mindful of these issues through:

- thoroughly analysing and understanding external factors
- thoroughly analysing and understanding internal factors
- planning collaboratively
- planning flexibly
- establishing review mechanisms and being prepared to adjust strategy accordingly.

Analysis of external factors

It is increasingly difficult for organisations to plan rationally when faced with a changing, and at times unpredictable, external environment. This means that there needs to be effort to analyse the environment within which an organisation exists, as part of the planning process. The macro environment is of great significance to Middleregion for instance:

– the likelihood of a change of national government may mean different funding or expectations

– funding comes from local taxes and government grants. Issues of national prosperity and employment levels have heightened significance.

In terms of planning for a future workforce, external data requirements will include regional employment trends and unemployment levels, demographic projections, skill levels and shortages, education levels, transport and planning proposals, labour mobility, and migration and immigration trends. This data can help in developing forecasts of people requirement where issues of future methods of production and technology usage and likely government levels of funding assume high significance.

Analysis of internal factors

It is important to understand the current and future local context facing the organisation when developing the strategy. This will help the strategy reflect the diversity of the workforce and key organisational challenges and changes. To this end, existing organisational strategy (possibly expressed as a corporate strategy) represents a first consideration. The whole purpose of a workforce strategy is that it focuses on human resourcing issues as a way of delivering overall organisational strategy.

It is also important to collect and analyse workforce planning data. A considerable amount of data, relevant to local conditions and internal issues needs to be collected and analysed. Some internal data requirements include employee analysis: numbers, gender, qualification, trade and job skills, experience, etc., categories of staff, staff suitable for promotion or redeployment, overtime levels and trends, labour turnover analysis and reasons, absence level by category and trends, productivity ratios and trends, comparison with national, regional and general public sector trends.

Issues of staff retention, turnover and absence need careful consideration in the light of issues such as:

- past retention, turnover and absence rates and those expected by reference to government targets and other units of government
- the rate at which staff are leaving and their reasons for leaving (based on exit interviews)
- numbers of employees retiring and likely future projections based on age profiles.

If a significant cause of turnover is due to a lack of promotion opportunities, inadequate training, low morale or poor management, then these problems need to be addressed within the strategy.

Problems in achieving future plans might to a degree be predictable and may well, in the past, have centred on:

- retention, especially when employees are well trained or have specialist skills
- slow promotion leading to staff turnover
- difficulties associated with putting succession planning into practice
- vacancies arising in very senior positions or in vital skills areas, etc.

Measures need to be incorporated into the new workforce strategy that anticipate these difficulties and counter them with positive actions.

Consideration should also be given to the organisation's ability to continue to attract suitable recruits into its various operations. Again, if there are difficulties these should be addressed through the HR plan. Having considered the existing supply of labour, an organisation will need to project a view of what the workforce will need to be like in the future in order to fulfil its strategic plans. The difference between the two projections of supply and demand can be made ('gap analysis') and plans developed accordingly. This might involve, for example, retraining, part time workers, use of consultants and contractors, overtime, computerisation recruitment, redundancy policy, etc.

Planning collaboratively

Workforce planning should not be seen as the job of Middleregion's Human Resources Department but should instead be a shared process involving a range of stakeholders from across the organisation in order that the plan ultimately is realistic, and workable. By adopting such an approach the strategy that emerges should more fully reflect local conditions and culture. In terms of the external environment, a wider planning group should also lead to better intelligence sharing and a more robust basis upon which to develop strategy. If it is felt that insufficient expertise exists to build a realistic picture then Middleregion might consider using specialist environmental scanners and strategy consultants to provide the necessary analysis.

Flexibility

The changing demands on Middleregion's service need to be reflected in its workforce strategy, so ensuring it is up-to-date and relevant. Since employees are probably the most unpredictable organisational resource, the best plans will be those that allow the greatest flexibility, this might be achieved in a number of ways, including:

- scenario planning and consideration of 'what if' options
- shorter planning time frames and cycles
- revisions to the strategy in the light of changing circumstances.

When the external environment is uncertain, complex and subject to rapid change, it may be impossible to develop a single view on environmental influences. In order to take account of 'what if' options or possibilities, plans might be constructed on the basis of both best case and worst case positions. Scenario planning builds on plausible views on how environmental changes might impact on the workforce and what might be done if this is the case. (This planning process might be assisted considerably by the use of IS and IT through spreadsheets and modelling applications.)

Middleregion should ensure that planning time frames are realistic. To that end, every aspect of the strategy will need to be fully reviewed on an ongoing basis. Most HR plans are developed on a rolling three-year basis, which means that forecasts for next year and the succeeding years in the cycle are updated every year in the light of this year's experience. Detailed plans for securing sufficient and suitable employees for current needs are made for a one year period, in line with current budgets. Less detailed plans are made for the three-year period, prepared in line with the organisation's corporate strategy.

Review Mechanisms and being prepared to adjust strategy accordingly

Middleregion could introduce more sophisticated monitoring, control and evaluation mechanisms. It is important to determine as part of the planning process how progress against the workforce strategy objectives will be measured. Once the strategy has been implemented, Middleregion will need to take measures to evaluate its success by considering what performance indicators should be used, what targets will be set, how success will be measured. Rather than being cast in stone, strategy might evolve and be adjusted in the light of ongoing experience and might lead to, for instance, resources being reallocated to accommodate changing circumstances.

(c) Middleregion should consider moving to e-HR by using technology to improve HR services, such as recording and monitoring systems, automating administrative tasks like recruitment, and disseminating HR policies and information on the intranet.

Software purchase or development costs

The cost of moving to e-HR will depend on what Middleregion requires the system to do. A system can be purchased or developed to undertake one task, such as the recording and monitoring of overtime levels, or can be integrated so that it supports a range of HR activities and is linked to other organisational systems such as payroll. Middleregion needs to clarify the HR services and information it requires. Once this is done, the scope of e-HR should be determined by considering whether these HR services and information needs are best provided in their current form or whether provision by e-HR would be preferable. Following this, costs might be estimated and a decision taken involving a weighing of costs and benefits. What is important is to articulate how e-HR will support and add value to the achievement of Middleregion's workforce strategy.

Associated costs

Middleregion will also need to consider related costs such as new hardware required as a result of e-HR, and running costs associated with maintaining the new system or systems. It is also conceivable that certain HR systems are computerised but need upgrading or scrapping which will have cost implications. If the newly introduced e-HR system is incompatible with existing systems or fails to meet user requirements, then additional development costs might be involved in order to bring about the necessary adaptations.

Cost of staff training and cost of disruption

New systems will involve employees undergoing training in their use. This may involve the cost of hiring external consultants and will also involve the 'cost' of the participants' time away from productive activity.

Opportunity costs

When making a decision to implement e-HR, Middleregion will need to carefully consider the objectives of the system and set out a clear specification for what is required, balanced against the budget available. Inevitably, the provision of a budget will represent an opportunity cost as there will be many other pressures and potential projects competing for budgetary provision. (An alternative situation may be that if Middleregion is highly reliant on manual effort at the moment, net cost savings may accrue through efficiencies implying a budget reduction).

Adjustment of business processes to fit software

There may be a need to adjust existing business processes to fit the software. Similarly, it will be necessary to review the current Human Resources function and if it is structured in a way that will not support e-HR, restructuring may be necessary possibly involving greater cost.

Middleregion should explore costs further by reference to the experience of other Regional Units who have introduced e-HR, the external auditors and potential suppliers of software solutions.

Appraisal, Training and Development, Motivation and Retention

Chapter learning objectives

Lead	Component
F1. Demonstrate the purpose of the human resource function and its relationships with other parts of the organisation.	(a) Explain the contribution of human resources to the sustainable delivery of the organisation's strategies. (b) Apply the elements of the HR cycle.
F2. Apply the tools and techniques of human resource management.	(a) Demonstrate the human resource activities associated with developing employees. (b) Demonstrate the role of the line manager in the implementation of human resource practices.

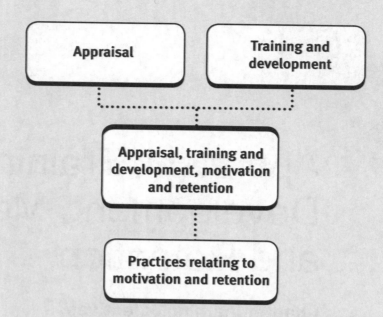

1 Appraisal

Appraisal is the systematic review and assessment of an employee's performance, potential and training needs.

1.1 Benefits of appraisal

Benefits for the employer	Benefits for the employee
• **Feedback and objective setting** – the appraisal is an opportunity for the employer to give feedback and to set the employee's objectives for the following period.	• **Feedback and objective setting** – the appraisal is an opportunity for the employee to receive feedback and to set the objectives for the following period.
• **Promotion** – it provides a formal system for assessing the performance and potential of employees, with a view to identifying candidates for promotion. This will assist with HRP.	• **Future prospects** – a formal appraisal system offers employees an opportunity to discuss further prospects and ambitions.
• **Training** – it provides a system for identifying training needs, in order to raise the level of efficiency and effectiveness.	• **Training** – appraisals can be used to identify and agree further training, to improve employee competence.
• **Improved communication** – if well managed, communication and hence working relations can be improved between managers and staff.	• **Pay and rewards** – the appraisal can be used as a basis for considering pay and rewards.
• **Career planning** – discussions concerning longer term development and career planning can be had and appropriate action taken.	• **Voice concerns** – appraisals can provide a platform for staff views and to voice concerns.

Effective appraisal systems

The following factors should be present in an effective appraisal system:

- Careful planning which ensures the purpose and objectives of the system are widely understood.

- Skill in carrying out the appraisal interview.

- Selecting the most appropriate method of appraisal.

- Setting challenging targets which the appraisee can influence.

- Adopting a participative system that enables those being appraised to have a meaningful input into the system.

1.2 The stages of performance appraisal

Stage 1: Identify the criteria for assessment, e.g. a number of objectives may be set based on job analysis

Stage 2: Manager prepares an appraisal report. Note: sometimes the appraisee prepares a report and they are compared

Stage 3: Appraisal interview is carried out between the job holder and the manager

Stage 4: Agreement of future objectives and solutions to problems, e.g. training needs are agreed and action points implemented

Stage 5: The manager's own supervisor reviews the assessment for fairness

Stage 6: Follow up – progress and success is monitored

1.3 Types of appraisal

Setting objectives as part of performance appraisal involves agreement on SMART objectives. A system of 'management by objectives' (MBO) is helpful if the employees are participants in their own objective setting.

A number of types of appraisal exist:

- **Self-appraisal** – this often takes place in preparation for a supervisor/appraisee meeting. This can save managerial time but the value of an individual appraising themselves may be questionable.

- **Supervisor/appraisee** – the manager or supervisor who carries out work or allocates priorities carries out the appraisal. In some cases where there are many workers this may not be possible.

- **180 degree** – often managers collecting anonymous or named views of colleagues can solve the problems of poor supervisor appraisals. This can also be performed in the open groups session with the emphasis on first how the group performed and then the individuals' contribution (or lack of it).

- **360 degree** – this is where the appraisee prepares feedback on the appraiser as well as getting 180 degree feedback from colleagues. Problems include potential conflicts, power, influence issues, time and bureaucracy.

Relationship between appraisal and the reward system

In many organisations there is a link between performance and pay. There are many problems in linking pay to performance including:

- employees concentrating on goals that have a definite link to the reward system

- inducing conflict when rewarding some employees more than others

- financial constraints due to recessionary factors, or poor company results

To overcome some of the difficulties of linking pay to performance it is necessary for those carrying out the appraisal to be well trained and skilled at carrying out the process. Schemes need to be uncomplicated, free from bias and subjectivity, and perceived to be fair by those who are to be appraised.

1.4 The barriers to effective appraisal

Lockett suggests that appraisal barriers can be identified as follows:

Confrontation	• Differing views regarding performance. • Feedback is badly delivered.
Judgement	• Appraisal is seen as a one-sided process – the manager is judge, jury and counsel for the prosecution.
Chat	• An unproductive conversation. • No outcomes set.
Bureaucracy	• Purely a 'form filling' exercise. • No purpose or worth.
Annual event	• A traditional ceremony, carried out once or twice a year.
Unfinished business	• No follow up. • Points agreed are not actioned.

1.5 Appraisal and career development

Appraisal has a clear link to career development. Career development sees the interaction of three concepts:

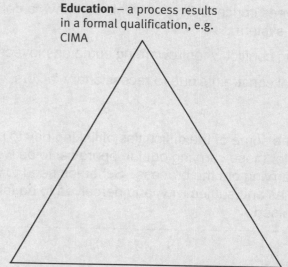

Education – a process results in a formal qualification, e.g. CIMA

Training – e.g. IT training required for the job the employee is doing now

Development – e.g. training in management skills for the job the employee may be doing in the future

Career planning and development

Career planning has traditionally been viewed as an organisation-driven activity that enables human resource managers to concentrate on jobs and building career paths so providing for logical progression of people between jobs. These career paths, particularly for people such as management accountants, have tended to be mainly within one specialised function and represent ladders on which individuals could progress within their functional specialism. Organisational career planning suffered severe setbacks from the layoffs during the recession of the late 1980s and early 1990s.

In addition these core concepts have increasingly been challenged due to a number of other developments including:

- Non-traditional organisational structures emerging. These flatter organisation structures have removed some career paths entirely and reduced opportunities in other areas. Additionally these structures imply a need for multi-skilling and teamwork at the expense of promotion 'ladders' found within traditional hierarchies. Increasingly workers are seeking to be 'multi-skilled' often developing a good understanding of more than one function rather than specialising.

- The development of general management skills and the concept of cross-functional career paths long been accepted as the norm in Japanese firms.

- Increasingly, career development has become led by the individuals themselves. An individual philosophy of building a portfolio of experience qualification and networks arose in order to develop a career outside a single organisational structure. This individual career planning focuses on individuals' goals and skills. It considers ways in which each individual might expand his or her capabilities and enhance career opportunities both within and outside a particular organisation. (Within the UK the Association of Graduate Recruiters recently warned that career paths no longer exist: only crazy paving that the individual lays himself or herself!)

Given this background, it is unsurprising that succession planning as an alternative to external recruitment may be seen as of decreasing HR significance. Problems have in any case always been associated with succession planning, including:

- Retention. Unlike other assets that have received investment, employees who are well trained (especially those who are were trained in anticipation of future developmental moves) are highly marketable.

- Individual failure. A failed assignment damages the individual, the company and the working relationships. 'Failure' may be attributable to one of a number of HR defects including poor control or managerial judgement, the over-promotion of individuals, and defective appraisal monitoring systems.

- Timing. One person failing to move because of personal circumstances can hold up the development of others unless some other kind of arrangement can be made. Slow promotion or development can lead to frustration and (for instance) graduate staff leaving shortly after becoming useful to the organisation. As the process depends on political expediency, many talented staff find that their present manager is reluctant to release them.

- Size of organisation. For a multi-national organisation, extensive relocation can be financially costly and for the family potentially distressing, demotivating and stressful. For many in small organisations a feeling of 'waiting for dead people's shoes' (as the old expression has it) may exist.

- Overseas postings. The issues of combining multi-cultural groups and three types of employee (the parent country nationals (expat), the home country nationals and the third country nationals) may prove problematic. Planning the correct combination of these staff is virtually impossible because of competing priorities and so many firms merely rely on the ability of all employees to 'mutually adjust' to each other and the new situation.

2 Training and Development

2.1 Introduction

Often the terms "training" and "development" are used inter-changeably. However, there are major differences between the two.

- While training focuses more on the current employee needs or competency gaps, development concerns itself with preparing people for future assignments and responsibilities.

- Development implies opportunities created to help employees grow. It is more of long term or futuristic in nature as opposed to training, which focus on the current job.

2.2 Learning

Learning is a complex process that underpins development, education and training.

Kolb's experiential learning cycle

Kolb suggests that learning is a series of steps based on **learning from experience**. He suggested that classroom learning is false and that learning should be an active process if it is to be effective.

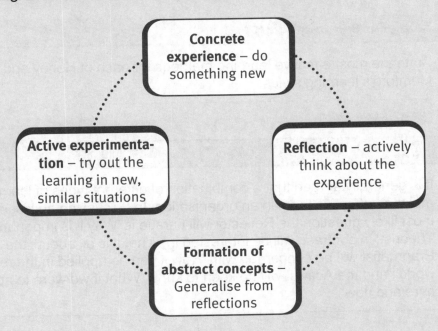

Honey and Mumford's learning styles

Honey and Mumford suggest there are four different learning styles:

Learning style	Explanation
Activists	Involve themselves fully and without bias in new experiences. They are open-minded, enthusiastic, constantly searching for new challenges but are bored with implementation and long-term consolidation.
Reflectors	Prefer to step back to ponder and observe others before taking action. They are in general cautious, may be perceived as indecisive and tend to adopt a low profile.

Theorists	Adapt and integrate information in a step-by-step logical way. They prefer to maximise certainty and feel uncomfortable with subjective judgements, lateral thinking and anything flippant.
Pragmatists	Are keen to try out new ideas, theories and techniques to see if they work in practice. They are essentially practical, down-to-earth people, like making practical decisions, act quickly on ideas that attract them and tend to be impatient with open-ended discussions.

Test your understanding 1

State the most effective learning methods for each of Honey and Mumford's learning styles.

Illustration 1

It is generally agreed that a combination of different types of learners will make an effective team in an organisation. In discussing an issue, the most likely question the Reflector will pursue is 'Why it is important'; the Theorist, in contrast, will be interested in 'What it is all about'; the Pragmatist will be concerned with 'How it can be applied in the real world'; and the Activist will be keen to know 'What if we were to apply it here and now'.

Effective learning programmes

The following general principles can guide the design of effective learning programmes:

- Participants should have both the ability to learn and the required skills/knowledge and the motivation to learn.

- It usually helps to provide an overview of the tasks to be learned before dealing with particular, specific aspects.

- The availability of timely, accurate feedback greatly enhances the effectiveness of most forms of training.

- There should be positive rewards or reinforcements when activities are carried out correctly. These rewards may be internal (e.g. a feeling of accomplishment) and/or external (e.g. the issue of a certificate, a compliment from the trainer, etc).

- Active involvement is usually associated with more effective learning rather than simply listening or reading.

- Most training will involve a learning curve which may be initially very flat as the learner struggles to acquire basic competence or in other cases quite steep when the skills required for modest competence are learned more quickly, but all learning will involve periods when there seems to be no improvement in performance (a learning plateau).

- Training should be as much like the job as possible to minimise problems of conceptualising theory to the workplace.

2.3 Management development

Management development (or simply development) is a realisation of a person's potential through formal and informal learning to enable them to carry out their current and future role. The process is seen as one of self-development.

Illustration 2 – Development

The importance of self-development is reinforced by the emphasis many professional bodies (including CIMA) places on continuing professional development (CPD), which recognises that being admitted to a professional body does not guarantee proficiency forever. Individual members of the profession must take responsibility for their own post qualification continual development and updating. In this way individuals can ensure they remain up to date in a rapidly changing world and can facilitate career planning.

2.4 Training

Training is formal learning to achieve the level of skills, knowledge and competence to carry out the current role (note the contrast with management development which focuses on the current and future role).

Training delivery can be provided:

- **in house** – e.g. through the use of on the job training, open learning (i.e. learning at a time, place and pace to suit the individual learner) or through using external trainers.

- **externally** – e.g. through local colleges, universities or specialist training companies.

Test your understanding 2

Identify the advantages and disadvantages of in-house training.

The use of IT in training

Information technology, and particularly the internet and intranet systems, has provided new opportunities for training and development at relatively low cost.

The stages of the training process

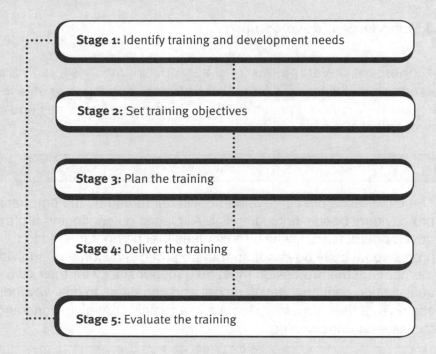

Stage 1: Identify training and development needs

Stage 2: Set training objectives

Stage 3: Plan the training

Stage 4: Deliver the training

Stage 5: Evaluate the training

To ensure training and development are effective, learning processes need to be evaluated (stage 5).

Donald Kirkpatrick suggested a four level model of evaluation.

Level	Evaluation	Description	Examples
1	Reaction	• How the delegates felt about the training or learning experience	• Feedback forms • Interviews
2	Learning	• The measurement of the increase in knowledge – before and after	• Assessment tests before and after • Interviews • Observation
3	Behaviour	• The extent of applied learning back on the job - implementation.	• Observation and interview over time
4	Results	• The effect on the business or environment by the trainee.	• Impact on existing KPIs

Since Kirkpatrick established his original model, other theorists and Kirkpatrick himself, have referred to a possible fifth level, namely ROI (Return On Investment), although it could be argued that ROI can easily be included in Kirkpatrick's original fourth level 'Results'.

Stages in training and development

- **Identifying training needs** – this could include an investigation into the organisation's current performance as well as mapping the corporate skills base. It should drill down to the level of the individual to target specific needs.

- **Setting training objectives** – as with all objectives these should have clear, specific, measurable targets in relation to the standard of behaviour required in order to achieve a given level of performance.

- **Planning the training** – this covers who provides the training, where the training takes place and divisions of responsibilities between trainers, line managers or team leaders and the individual personally.

- **Delivering/implementing the training** – a combination of formal and on-the-job training programmes will be used.

- **Evaluating training** – assessment of cost versus benefit using feedback forms, end of course tests, assessment of improved performance in the work place and impact on corporate goals.

2.5 Career/succession planning

Career/succession planning is the process for identifying and developing internal people with the potential to fill key business leadership positions in the company.

Traditionally, it was viewed as the process which allowed able employees to move up a pre-defined career ladder.

The advantage of career/succession planning is that it increases the availability of experienced and capable employees that are prepared to assume available roles. However, it is not without its problems:

- Operational issues – staff may feel that vacancies arise too slowly or at inconvenient times.

- Too rational – the high level of planning may not be appropriate in a fast moving business environment.

- Insularity – the policy ignores the possibility of more capable candidates outside the organisation.

- Career trends – the modern trend is for employees to take responsibility for their career development and to move between organisations.

- Emergence of flatter structures – this has removed some of the traditional career paths.

3 Practices Relating to Motivation and Retention

3.1 Reward systems

A **reward system** can help in keeping staff highly motivated in order to deliver high performance.

Types of remuneration structure	
Type	**Description**
Graded pay	A sequence of job grades against which a payment range is attached.
Broad banded	The range of pay in a band is significantly higher than in a conventional structure. The structure usually covers the whole workforce from the shop floor to senior management.
Individual job ranges	Used when the content and size of jobs is widely different throughout the organisation.

Job family structures	Consists of pay related to jobs in a function or discipline such as financial specialists.
Spot rates	Allocation of a specific rate for the job.
Pay spines	Consists of a series of incremental points extending from the lowest to the highest paid jobs covered by the structure. Pay scales or ranges for different job grades may then be superimposed on the pay spine.
Integrated pay structures	Covers groups of employees who have all been paid under separate arrangements. There may be one grading system which includes all employees.

The aims of a reward system:

- **Motivation** – the reward scheme should encourage desirable behaviour and should recognise that different employees will be motivated by different factors.

- **Quality of staff** – the reward scheme should help to attract and retain the best staff.

- **Consistency and fairness** – the reward scheme should provide a fair and consistent basis for motivating and rewarding employees.

- **Reward performance** – the scheme should reward performance, e.g. by promotion through developed pathways.

- **Recognise factors other than job performance** – the reward scheme should recognise other factors such as the level of responsibility or additional tasks taken on.

- **To control costs** – it is important that the reward scheme assists in controlling salary costs.

- **To achieve organisational goals** – the reward scheme should assist the organisation in achieving its goals.

- **To comply with legislation/ regulation**

An **incentive scheme** links pay to performance. It can be tied to the performance of an individual or a team of employees. The scheme should ideally link performance to organisational goals.

There are four main types of incentive scheme; profit-related pay, piece rates, performance-related pay and non-financial rewards. Each of these is explained below.

Profit-related pay

Payments are made to employees in the light of the overall profitability of the company. Share issues may be part of the scheme.

Profit-related pay schemes are not as popular as they once were. Briefly discuss the reasons for this.

Piece rates

A Taylorist philosophy based on paying employees on the basis of output alone.

This is suitable where output can easily be measured and mainly attributes to one individual.

Performance-related pay (PRP)

This is an appraisal based method where by the individual receives a bonus or an increase in pay based on achievements of the individual objectives (performance measures) set for them.

Performance measures for managers and employees should fulfil the SMART criteria:

- **S**pecific
- **M**easurable
- **A**chievable
- **R**elevant
- **T**ime bound

In this way, managers and employees will be aware of the levels of performance they need to attain with absolute certainty.

Illustration 3

The Organic Juice Company has three divisions, the Fruit Juice division, the Smoothie division and the Fruit Cordial division. The market for smoothies is expected to grow by 20% over the next year and the Smoothie division expects to retain its share of the market. No other changes are anticipated.

The manager of the Smoothie division has been set a target to increase gross profit by 20% year on year.

This target fulfils the SMART criteria in that it is:

- specific – gross profit to increase by 20%

- measurable – it is possible to measure the annual change in gross profit

- achievable and relevant – the target seems achievable and relevant given that the market is expected to grow by 20%

- time bound – a year on year target has been set.

Benefits of PRP	Drawbacks of PRP
• Increased productivity. • Method of rewarding and retaining most effective employees. • Should promote greater employee involvement and commitment to organisational goals.	• PRP not applied consistently. • Employees not aware of the level of performance they need to attain. • Subjectivity in assessment. • Financial constraints restrict the amount of reward resulting in employee resentment.

Non-financial rewards

The use of non-financial rewards recognises that employees are motivated by factors other than pay. For example, Maslow's needs from bottom to top are:

- Physiological needs such as a competitive basic salary.

- Safety needs such as a good pension scheme.

- Social needs such as work nights out.

- Ego needs such as an opportunity for a merit pay increase.

- Self-fulfilment needs such as a challenging job and achievement in work.

A **total reward package (TRP)** draws together all the financial and non-financial benefits available to employees.

Test your understanding 4

Identify the advantages and disadvantages of a TRP approach.

3.2 Flexible working arrangements

Flexible working arrangements can be used to increase employee motivation. Flexibility in work patterns can be achieved in many ways:

Flexitime	The need to work a standard set of hours but less restriction on when these hours are worked
Shift system	Working outside of normal working day patterns
Compressed week	Standard hours within fewer days in a shift rotation
Job sharing	Two employees share a standard hour week
Part-time	Fewer hours than the standard weekly number
Teleworking	Technology has enabled employees to work away from the office, usually at home.

Test your understanding 5

Explain the advantages and disadvantages for the **employer** of flexible working arrangements.

It is also important to consider the flexible working arrangements from the **employee's** point of view:

Advantages for the employee	Disadvantages for the employee
• Cost and time savings, e.g. because the employee works at home or does not travel to work at peak times.	• Increased costs, e.g. employees have to pay for additional utilities when working from home.
• Flexibility to fit work around family life and other commitments.	• Loss of social interaction, e.g. due to the flexible hours or working from home.
• Increased enjoyment of work since feel employer is listening to their needs.	• Lack of support, again due to the flexible hours or working from home.

3.3 Workforce flexibility

Flexible working arrangements encompass one type of flexibility within organisations. 'Workforce flexibility' is the term used to describe a much broader range of flexible working options:

- **Task or functional flexibility** – employees have the ability to move between tasks as and when is required. This will allow an organisation to react to changes in production requirements and levels of demand.

Achieving functional flexibility
Functional flexibility can be achieved by: • Training staff in a wide variety of skills. • Recruiting staff with a wider variety of skills. • Introducing a programme of job rotation.

- **Numerical flexibility** – the use of non-core workers allows the organisation to adjust the level of labour to meet fluctuations in demand. For example:
  - Temporary workers
  - Part time workers
  - Overtime

- **Financial flexibility** – this is achieved through variable systems of rewards, e.g. bonus schemes, profit sharing. By linking rewards to performance, a number of improvements in performance should be realised.

- **Flexible working arrangements** – as discussed in section 2.2. Arrangements that result in a variability of labour work time, e.g. flexible hours or a compressed working week, are sometimes referred to as 'temporal flexibility'.

Handy's Shamrock organisation

Handy suggested the idea of a 'Shamrock' organisation. People linked to an organisation are said to fall into three groups. Each group will have different expectations and it is important that they are managed and rewarded in an appropriate way. The groups are:

- **The professional core** – includes managers and technicians. They should be rewarded through a high salary and benefits since they are essential to the continuity of the organisation.

- **The contractual fringe** – contracted specialists, rewarded with a fee.

- **Flexible labour force** – part time and temporary workers provide flexibility

3.4 Arrangements for knowledge workers

Knowledge workers are people who create knowledge and produce new products and services for the organisation to sell. For example:

- Research staff
- Chemists
- Architects

As we move from a traditional manufacturing economy to a service economy, it is recognised that knowledge is a primary source of competitive advantage.

Implications for human resource management

- **Selection criteria** – employees should be selected for their skills, i.e. knowledge, as opposed to their ability to do a particular job.

- **Sharing of knowledge** – encouraged by:
    - Team working
    - Job rotations

- **Retention of knowledge** – this can be achieved by:
    - Filling vacancies internally.
    - Ensuring there is a well defined career path to increase motivation and hence retention.

- **Performance appraisal** – the appraisal must:
    - Prioritise the development of knowledge skills if the employees are to believe that the organisation takes these seriously.
    - Encourage employee input into their own development, skills and careers.

Commitment of knowledge workers

Key contributing factors to employee commitment are:

- The degree of flexibility and autonomy within the workforce.

- An emphasis on performance-related pay. Performance could be measured by, for example, the amount of quality information about a product published professionally on a web site that will help sell more of that product. The more motivated the knowledge worker is, the more quality information he or she will create.

- Appraisal systems that monitor and reward knowledge contributions and application e.g. knowledge turned into information, into documents, into content.

- Profit-sharing or equity-based forms of reward. Quality information about a product published professionally on a web site will help sell more of that product. The more motivated the knowledge worker is, the more quality information he or she will create.

- Career progression – make it clear that those who contribute quality information on a consistent basis will move up through the organisation.

3.5 Employee involvement

Employees should be given the opportunity to contribute to the organisation. **High performance work arrangements** rely on all employees for their ideas, intelligence and commitment to make the organisation successful. Increased motivation and positive financial benefits can be gained from:

- Greater employee participation in job design – job enrichment, enlargement and rotation can all result in increased motivation.

- Open and honest communication.

- Empowered, involved and listened to employees.

- A willingness for the employer to compromise and bargain with employees.

3.6 The psychological contract

The term **"psychological contract"** was first used in the early 1960s but became more popular following the economic downturn in the early 1990s. The psychological contract outlines the perceptions of the employee and the employer regarding what their mutual obligations are towards each other.

- Unlike the employment contract, the psychological contract is highly subjective, not written down and not legally binding.

- Key elements include the following:

	Employee	**Employer**
What do they want?	Want their needs to be satisfied	Want employee to work hard. Will have a set of expectations for each employee
What are they willing to give?	Will offer their energies and talents	Payment, benefits and other outcomes, e.g. a promotion

Implications for managers

- A psychological contract can exert a strong influence on behaviour because it captures what employees really believe they will get in return for what they give.

- If employees feel that the employer has broken promises, or violated the contract, employee reactions range from mild irritation or reduction in effort to handing in their notice.

- In order for managers to motivate and **retain** employees, they must understand the importance of the psychological contract.

Illustration 4

Kate has worked as a trainee accountant with the same company for the past two years. She is ambitious and enjoys her work. Her manager asks her to produce a report that is outside of her normal role.

The report turns out to be difficult and time consuming and she has to put in long hours to complete the report on time as well as carrying out her normal work.

She meets the deadline and sends the report to her manager. However, she receives no acknowledgement. The next day she finds out that her manager has successfully presented the findings of the report to his boss and has taken the credit for the report.

Kate is angry and has decided that she will never do any extra work for her boss again and has even started looking for another job due to the breach of her psychological contract.

Types of psychological contract

There are three types of psychological contract:

- **Coercive contracts** – which are not freely entered into and where a small group exercise control by rule and punishment. Although the usual form is found in prisons and other custodial institutions, coercive contracts also exist in schools and factories.

- **Calculative contracts** – where control is retained by management and is expressed in terms of their ability to give to the individual 'desired things' such as money, promotion and social opportunities. Most employees of industrial organisations 'enter into' such a contract.

- **Co-operative contracts** – where the individual tends to identify with the goals of the organisation and strive for their attainment. In return the individual receives just rewards, a voice in the selection of goals and a choice of the means to achieve such goals. Most enlightened organisations are moving towards such contracts but it must be emphasised that if they are to be effective, then the workers must also want them – if such a contract is imposed on the workforce, it becomes a coercive contract.

In all cases, the employees must know the results of their increased efforts and the management must understand the individual's needs.

4 Chapter Summary

Appraisal
- benefits
- stages
- types
- barriers
- appraisals and career development

Training and development
- learning
- management development
- training
- career/succession planning

Appraisal, training and development, motivation and retention

Practices relating to motivation and retention
- reward systems
- flexible working arrangements
- workforce flexibility
- arrangements for knowledge workers
- employee involvement
- the psychological contract

5 Practice questions

Question 1 – OTQ

When a performance appraisal scheme is ineffective, this may be due to:

A   a lack of objective criteria for the appraisal of personality

B   under-performing employees

C   excluding discussions about pay

D   a lack of objective criteria for the appraisal of performance

Question 2 – OTQ

One example of a flexible work arrangement is a compressed work week. A compressed work week involves:

A   working for longer-than-usual hours on some days in exchange for a day off work

B   working for some days at home instead of in the office

C   allowing employees to choose their hours of attendance each day, provided that they work a full day

D   allowing employees to work less than the standard number of hours each week

Question 3 – OTQ

Development can be defined as:

A   The creation and maintenance of an individual

B   The progressive alteration to the individual

C   Growth and change in the individual

D   The growth or realisation of a person's ability and potential

Question 4 – OTQ

Which THREE of the following are potential advantages of 360-degree appraisals?

A   Training is required to effectively implement and maintain

B   It depends on effective communication

C   It provides very large amounts of information

D   The concept of employee empowerment is embedded

E   It is an open system where employees see the feedback from all appraisers

F   It fosters continuous improvement of the employee

Question 5 – HR systems (Case style)

Background

A professional management body is funding a major research project into the relationship between certain HR systems and workplace motivation. As part of this project the University of S2013 has been engaged to investigate the use of staff performance appraisal systems in large organisations. The University's work involves a number of stages:

- **Stage 1**: questionnaires issued to all large organisations to understand the range of performance appraisal systems operating.

- **Stage 2**: initial results from stage 1 discussed with a group of senior managers (such as HR directors and chief executives).

- **Stage 3**: focus group meetings with employees at all levels within the organisations surveyed to understand employee motivations, attitudes and experiences.

- **Stage 4**: final report to the professional body and subsequent dissemination of findings.

Issues

Stage 3 has now been completed and a number of interesting issues have emerged:

- The use of formal performance appraisal systems varies significantly between sectors from 80% of financial service organisations to only 50% in the retail sector.

- Organisations not using an appraisal system do not feel that the potential benefits of a formal system justify the time and cost involved in operating it.

- Of the systems in operation, 90% involved an annual meeting between employees and their appraiser, normally their line manager.

- 15% of organisations used the outcomes from the system to help determine pay.

- There was little relationship between levels of motivation and the existence of a staff performance appraisal system. (Motivation was more closely related to issues such as organisational reputation and the operation of environmental action and sustainability programmes.)

- Employees were generally critical of their own organisation's system of formal staff performance appraisal.

Tasks:

(a) Describe the potential benefits of a formal staff performance appraisal system for a large organisation.

(15 minutes)

(b) Explain the possible reasons for employees being critical of their own organisation's system of formal staff performance appraisal.

(15 minutes)

(c) According to the research findings, environmental action by organisations and sustainability programmes are highly regarded by employees. Explain why this might be the case.

(10 minutes)

(Total: 40 minutes)

Test your understanding answers

Activists – they enjoy learning through games, competitive teamwork, tasks, role-plays and on-the-job training.

Reflectors – the reflector prefers learning activities that are observational such as carrying out an investigation or work shadowing.

Theorists – the theorist prefers learning to be structured, allow time for analysis and provided by other theorists, e.g. classroom based courses.

Pragmatists – the pragmatist prefers learning activities that are as close as possible to direct work experience. They will only engage in formal training, such as lectures or computer based training, if it reflects their actual job.

Test your understanding 2

Advantages	Disadvantages
• Course content and timing can be tailor-made to the organisation's needs.	• Participants are not exposed to outside influences.
• An organisation's specific technical equipment, procedures and/or work methods can be used.	• Participants may be called away at short notice to deal with work problems.
• Cost effective.	• Participants are more likely to withdraw at short notice.
• Easily monitored.	• Inhibits open discussion if immediate colleagues or bosses are present.
• Can involve expert sessions from senior managers or staff.	
• Can generate a team spirit and develop culture.	
• Can be linked to specific outcomes that are then monitored by participants.	
• Can be enhanced by incorporating work-based projects.	

Test your understanding 3

- The firm may 'massage' its year end profits.

- The tax implications of employee share schemes.

- Employees may resent the scheme if their actions do not directly impact the profit.

- Employees may resent the scheme if it is restricted to only a group of managers/directors.

Test your understanding 4

Advantages	Disadvantages
• Helps to retain and motivate high quality staff. • Method of attracting talented staff. • Recognises that a combination of pay and non-pay benefits are essential for motivation. • Flexible approach allowing employees to pick and choose the rewards to suit their needs. • Projects a positive image to stakeholders.	• Cost may outweigh benefit. • Wouldn't work in isolation e.g. if poor recruitment practices exist. • Staff may be suspicious viewing package as a way to keep pay down. • Costly failure if design flaws.

Test your understanding 5

Advantages

Flexible working arrangements may fulfil the needs of the individual resulting in:

- Increased employee motivation and productivity
- Increased commitment to the organisation
- Attracting talented individuals because of the availability of such conditions
- Reduced absenteeism and staff turnover.

In addition, the company may reduce costs, e.g. due to a reduction in office space if employees work at home or a reduction in the number of full time workers in favour of part time workers.

Disadvantages

Flexible working arrangements such as working from home or working non-standard hours may result in:

- Difficulties in co-ordinating staff
- Loss of control of staff
- Dilution of organisational culture
- Less commitment to the organisation.

In addition, some costs may actually increase, e.g. due to the extra cost of providing equipment for employees to work from home.

Question 1 – OTQ

The correct answer is D

Question 2 – OTQ

The correct answer is A

Question 3 – OTQ

The correct answer is D

Question 4 – OTQ

The correct answers are D, E and F

Question 5 – HR systems (Case style)

(a) It is apparent from the University's investigation of performance appraisal systems that a significant number of organisations choose not to operate such a system (as many as 50% in the retail sector). The reason appears to be the belief that the potential benefits of a formal system do not justify the time and cost involved. However, for a large organisation a number of potential benefits arise from such a system and these are described below.

Assist performance management

A good appraisal system would assist performance management across an organisation. Appraisal of performance is a vital part of the HR cycle and performance appraisal systems provide a convenient systematic method of linking overall corporate objectives to actual levels of performance. The approach also offers an opportunity to identify possible reasons for unusual performance, particularly where there is apparent 'underperformance'.

Provide individual workers with necessary feedback

Individuals need to be reassured that their past efforts have been worthwhile and are recognised by management. Individuals also need to know that their planned future activities meet with the satisfaction of their superiors. The activity associated with a staff performance appraisal system can contribute to the success of an organisation by providing such feedback and reassurance.

Identify training needs and maximisation of budget

A performance appraisal system could help provide a foundation for structured education, development and training for the workforce as a whole. The system could contribute towards:

- developing the abilities of employees by identifying training needs that support technical, professional and management development

- maximising the effectiveness of an organisation's training and development budget

- monitoring the effectiveness and results of past staff development activities.

Source of motivation

The University's findings suggest that there is little relationship between levels of motivation and the existence of a staff performance appraisal system. Other research suggests however, that an effective system of staff performance appraisal could, if properly administered, be a source of staff motivation. (The professional management body apparently believes this to be the case, hence the project). If the system offers an opportunity for staff to be listened to and helps foster an open, healthy atmosphere then it can only be beneficial.

A system for rewarding employees

Only 15% of organisations surveyed used outcomes from the process to help determine pay yet this represents a tantalising possibility. Increasingly organisations are trying to relate pay to performance (rather than status). The performance appraisal system could also enable the achievement of rewards other than pay such as promotion, opportunities for development, job enrichment and secondments, etc.

Focus on objectives

Central to performance appraisal is a dominant focus on objectives that:

- help achieve important organisational and individual objectives

- provide a mechanism to set individual objectives for the next period

- check attainment against existing targets.

A good performance appraisal system should also improve the opportunities for employees to contribute to organisational goals and objectives in a recognised fashion, A system of 'management by objectives' (MBO) is helpful in establishing a hierarchy of objectives so that individuals can recognise their own role within the wider organisational context. Objectives which can be set as part of appraisal involves agreement using SMART objectives (specific and challenging, measurable, but achievable, relevant and realistic and time-bound).

'Talent spotting'

It is sometimes healthy for a large organisation to experience some degree of staff turnover. However, this should be balanced against the need for continuity and retention of its most valued workers. A performance appraisal system could be a systematic and thorough means of identifying particular individuals for advancement, so allowing a degree of succession planning and reducing the loss of a company's most talented workers.

Develop relationships

A formalised system can help develop the relationship between a line manager and an individual subordinate by providing an agenda for discussion in a way that would not normally be possible.

Benefits to individuals

There are several benefits of a formal annual meeting for an individual employee. The annual interview can, for instance, provide an opportunity for genuine two-way discussion and feedback on:

- individual objectives and progress
- career and promotion prospects
- training needs and opportunities.

The meeting also offers an opportunity to formally voice concerns and forces individuals to reflect on both existing and past practice.

(Other benefits might reasonably be given including re-assigning staff to roles that are more suited to their strengths and interests, etc.)

(b) As explained in response to sub question (a) there are many potential benefits of a formal staff performance appraisal system for a large organisation. Employees in the research project however were critical of their own organisation's system and there are a number of possible reasons for this.

System feature: system is dated

Systems require periodic review in order to ensure that they are still robust and relevant. Whilst a system may originally have been fit for purpose it may now fail to reflect current organisational needs, and staff will be critical as a result.

System feature: Poor system design

A system may have a poor reputation amongst employees because it has been poorly designed. If there is an over-reliance on standardised procedures and paperwork then the system may seem too restrictive and unduly bureaucratic. Conversely, ill-defined processes and a lack of standardisation of paperwork may mean that the system operates haphazardly. Individual performance assessments should be supported by rational performance criteria (including performance indicators and measurable outcomes). Poor system design can allow undue levels of subjectivity which may undermine the scheme as a whole and render it unfair and ineffective.

System feature: Organisational 'fit'

It is also important that the nature of the system is 'right' for the organisation concerned. For instance, a 180 degree feedback scheme is better suited to an organisation that has a high degree of project team working or a matrix structure. If the organisation has an open, reflective organisational culture then 360 degree feedback might be even more appropriate.

System operation: faulty implementation

One reason for employees being critical of their own organisation's system of formal performance appraisal may be because of the way it operates rather than the features of the system itself. A failure to follow established procedure or lacklustre enthusiasm for the scheme can prove detrimental. If the scheme was introduced some time ago then employees joining an organisation after this date will miss out on the initial training that was given when the scheme was introduced and this may mean that they are not operating the system properly.

Lack of support by senior management

If the system is not taken seriously by managers then employees will also have little commitment to the scheme. Under these circumstances the system will be treated as a chore, a form of 'paper exercise' that is an unwelcome distraction from the 'real job'. For any scheme to work effectively it must be taken seriously by all parties with appropriate commitment to conducting formal appraisal interviews properly and completing all the necessary paperwork.

Lack of address of identified needs

For a system to be regarded as meaningful by a workforce, it requires an organisation to commit appropriate effort and resources to address the outcomes of the process. For instance, where training needs are identified a budgetary provision should be made. Similarly, it is unhelpful to formally note impediments to effective performance without attempting to address these matters.

Promotion policy ignores scheme outcomes

Decisions over staff promotions may be made without taking account of past performance. This would be very frustrating for an employee with a solid record of achievement evidenced by appraisal documentation being overlooked for promotion and would undermine the scheme as a whole.

Inadequate rewards attached

Only 15% of organisations surveyed used outcomes from the process to help determine pay, yet this represents a tantalising possibility. The performance appraisal system could also enable the achievement of rewards other than pay such as promotion, opportunities for development, job enrichment and secondments, etc. Divorcing rewards from the formal performance appraisal system may mean that the system lacks the necessary incentives to make it successful and well regarded by staff.

Adequacy of communication and training

Communication and training systems should explain the purpose of the system to the workforce as well as outlining ways to conduct appraisal interviews effectively. The organisations surveyed by the University may not have given sufficient attention to these issues and this is reflected in the dissatisfaction of the workforce that is expressed.

Ineffective appraiser technique and lack of planning

It is desirable that the system is participative and enables those being appraised to have a meaningful input. Poorly conducted appraisal interviews may frustrate this taking place. Insufficient training, nervousness, a lack of organisation or time may lead to poor appraisal interviews and negative staff experiences. Careful planning should be a feature of the scheme and it may be that either or both parties have failed to plan properly for the appraisal interview.

Inappropriate choice of appraiser and timing of appraisal meetings

Employees may be critical of the way in which performance appraisal is operated within their own organisation for two reasons that are contained in the research findings.

- Line managers invariably act as appraisers. Managers can misuse the time available in appraisal interviews by 'saving' bad news rather than addressing issues when they occur. A more developmental approach may be to have appraisals conducted by someone at the next tier of management in preference to line managers.

- Formal interviews tend to be annual. This means that vital dialogue and on-going measurement of progress towards objectives may be missed.

Inappropriate target setting

A system may be disliked by staff if performance targets are unrealistically demanding or beyond their individual influence. Otley's (1987) research into managers in the budget-setting process indicated that where objectives have been set inappropriately, motivation and performance can fall off dramatically once targets are 'missed'.

(Other factors might reasonably be given including delay between appraisal meeting and receipt of feedback, time involved in the process, etc.)

(c) The research reported in the scenario has indicated that motivation is more closely related to the existence of environmental and sustainability initiatives than to the existence of a performance appraisal system within an organisation. Action on sustainability and the environment are long term commitments involving an organisation in series of programmes, practices and policies which appear (from this research) to be important to its workforce. There are several reasons for this.

Giving employees a voice

Employees are likely to have many valuable ideas to contribute. If they are listened to then they will feel they are doing something tangible to further these agendas and this may provide a powerful source of motivation. Top management can be a little divorced from the 'action' whereas an organisation's workforce is closest to daily practices that can be improved upon to achieve environmental and sustainability agendas. By way of example, the greatest energy efficiency savings and performance improvements can come from focusing on the operation of an office building, warehouse, or manufacturing facility. This is where workers can make a contribution through close monitoring of temperature levels and questioning the need for lights to be lit and equipment to be left on stand-by.

Employer branding and enhancement of job content

Environmental action and sustainability programmes within an organisation may be well received by employees if they are given a role to play. According to Hackman and Oldham's job characteristics model, high levels of satisfaction and motivation follow critical psychological states of 'experienced meaningfulness of work', experienced responsibility, and knowledge of the results of their activities. All three states might be enhanced through participation in organisational environmental and sustainability initiatives.

Job security through organisational stability

Practices associated with sustainability include improved energy and water consumption and waste reduction, etc. Such practices can also ultimately lead to a lowering of operating costs. Sustainable practices will also offer opportunities to enter new markets and appeal to a different customer range, so increasing sales. In short, these programmes should provide a platform for organisational stability and success and so provide some reassurance of job security to individual employees, hence the levels of satisfaction that are evident.

Employee pride in the organisation they work for

There are many ways in which an organisation can tangibly demonstrate its social responsibility. For example, if it takes the trouble to measure its total carbon footprint this will allow it to take effective actions towards reducing the climate change impact of the business and its supply network. If actions such as these strike a chord with the personal values and beliefs of employees then this will instil them with a pride in the organisation they work for and will be better motivated.

Develop a positive culture

At the heart of an organisational culture is a shared paradigm. If environmental concerns and awareness of a need for sustainable practice are dominant features of organisational life and a shared world view this can help shape a positive organisational culture. A positive organisational culture and meaningful corporate agendas are likely to be valued by employees.

15

Employment Practices, HR Roles and Ethics

Chapter learning objectives

Lead	Component
F1. Demonstrate the purpose of the human resource function and its relationships with other parts of the organisation.	(a) Explain the contribution of human resources to the sustainable delivery of the organisation's strategies.
F2. Apply the tools and techniques of human resource management.	(a) Demonstrate the human resource activities associated with developing employees. (b) Demonstrate the role of the line manager in the implementation of human resource practices.

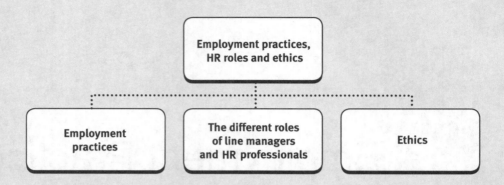

1 Employment Practices

There are a number of issues relating to fair and legal employment practices (e.g. recruitment, dismissal or redundancy practices) and ways of managing these. Two of these areas, dismissal and redundancy, will be explored below.

1.1 Dismissal

Dismissal is termination of a worker's employment with or without notice by the employer.

Dismissal without notice is usually wrongful because it breaches the contract of employment. When analysing whether dismissal is fair or a breach of contract, a number of issues are relevant:

- **Conduct** – a well documented and fair disciplinary procedure should be in place.
- **Capability** – the employer must demonstrate how the employee failed to meet the standards set for them and should detail formal/informal warnings and any remedial action it tried to take, e.g. extra training or transfer to another (more suitable) role.
- **Breach of statutory duty** – dismissal would be considered fair if continuing employment would breach statutory duty, e.g. health and safety legislation.
- **Some other suitable reason** – e.g. dishonesty, refusal to transfer within the organisation.
- **Redundancy** – see Section 1.2 below.

Constructive dismissal

This involves an employee resigning because the employer has made matters so difficult for them which equates with having in effect terminated their contract of employment.

1.2 Redundancy

A dismissal of the grounds of redundancy may be justified on any of the following grounds:

- cessation of business
- cessation of business in the place where the employee was employed
- cessation of the type of work for which the employee was employed.

In the UK, legislation demands that redundancies are fair and consultation must take place, e.g. with employees and trade unions. However, redundancy should always be viewed as the last resort.

Test your understanding 1

Identify the alternatives to redundancy that a good employer should consider.

Redundancy is unpleasant both for the individual and for the organisation. A good employer may consider:

- offering redundancy payments above the statutory minimum
- telling employees using the best method, usually face to face
- giving employees reasonable time off work to look for another job
- inviting local employment agency advisers to come to the premises
- providing good counselling service support.

2 The Different Roles of Line Managers and HR Professionals

2.1 Relative roles of line manager and HR professionals

There are a number of differences in the roles of a line manager and the firm's HR department. These distinctions can be summarised as follows:

Aspect	HR department	Line Manager
General approach	• strategic, longer term • based on the needs of the whole organisation	• more operational • focused on specific area of responsibility

Strategic role	• to help develop the HR strategy • to ensure that all HR activities are aligned to overall corporate strategy, aims and mission	• to implement strategy at a local level
Roles in the HR cycle	• to develop standardised documents (e.g. job descriptions, person specifications, etc.) • to design clear processes • to ensure legal requirements are met • to have fair and consistent HR practices	• to use standardised forms • to follow procedures • to adhere to systems
Areas of expertise	• specialist knowledge (e.g. employment law, health and safety requirements, industrial relations, etc.) • best practice (e.g. using professional associations and reading journals to find out what happens elsewhere) • may also offer payroll services	• will have specialist functional expertise (e.g. marketing) rather than HR expertise • hopefully have some experience of managing staff
Motivation	• develop organisation-wide policies relating to remuneration and bonus schemes • to make opportunities for worker participation and contribution (e.g. talent management schemes)	• to ensure staff know what is expected of them • to use non-financial motivators such as positive feedback, effective delegation, publicly celebrating successes, etc • to help set operational targets • to nominate staff for promotion/pay rises

The psychological contract	<ul><li>to ensure that the organisation keeps its side of the 'contract' by making payments on time, providing promotion opportunities, treating workers with dignity and respect, etc</li></ul>	<ul><li>can remind individuals of their obligations</li><li>provide feedback on performance</li><li>show respect</li><li>make the working environment pleasant and safe</li></ul>
Performance management	<ul><li>develop and communicate KPIs</li><li>set up systems, procedures and documents for annual appraisals</li><li>organise training for line managers if required</li></ul>	<ul><li>meet their own operational targets</li><li>set targets for subordinates</li><li>perform annual appraisals (perhaps with someone from the HR department)</li><li>adhere to corporate systems and practices</li></ul>
Grievance and discipline	<ul><li>to design clear processes (e.g. that a verbal warning must be given before a written one before...)</li><li>to ensure legal requirements are met</li><li>to have fair and consistent HR practices</li><li>to offer expertise in areas such as arbitration, advocacy, etc</li></ul>	<ul><li>to build a relationship with staff so issues can be discussed and resolved informally if possible</li><li>to use standardised forms and document all relevant facts and testimonies</li><li>to follow procedures</li><li>to adhere to systems</li></ul>

2.2 Specialist and generalist approaches to HR

As stated above line managers will often look to HR departments for expert advice on technical issues, such as employment law. This raises the issue as to whether or not people seeking to work within HR departments should aim to become specialists or generalists. The latter may be more attractive to smaller businesses while the former may be in demand if they have the skills needed given the economic cycle – for example, in an economic downturn firms may seek to downsize and so employee relations skills would be highly sought after.

2.3 Organising the HR function

An HR department may be organised into one of the four basic design models:

- **Centralised HR**

    In these organisations, there is a head of HR and reporting to this leader are the functional areas of HR: staffing, training, benefits, compensation, organization design, etc. These functional areas have responsibility for designing and implementing HR policies across the organization.

    This approach will result in greater standardisation of policies, greater efficiency and more integration. However, some would claim that it ignores local needs and stifles innovation.

- **Decentralised HR**

    Each separate business unit has its own HR department with a head of HR and dedicated functional specialists. Virgin in the UK and Tata in India are essentially holding companies where each business has a dedicated HR staff with very little corporate oversight.

    This approach will result in greater customisation of policies to local needs, greater effectiveness and more differentiation. However, some would claim that it can result in a loss of central control.

- **Shared services**

    Here a firm may try to get the benefits of both centralisation and decentralisation, perhaps by having centralised service centres for routine administrative tasks, together with centres of expertise, to allow local customisation.

- **Outsourced HR**

    Here HR processes are outsourced to external providers.

3 Ethics

3.1 Introduction

Ethics is a set of moral principles to guide behaviour.

Illustration 1 – Ethics and morals

'**Ethics**' is used interchangeably with the word 'morals'. However, it is worth noting that very occasionally there will be a conflict between moral judgement and ethical duty, e.g. a management accountant may have access to confidential information regarding big bonuses paid to the managers of a department that is under the threat of redundancy. Morally, the accountant may feel that they should inform employees/other stakeholders about these big bonuses but this would be a breach of confidentiality or professional ethics.

3.2 Dealing with ethical dilemmas

If you are faced with an ethical dilemma at work, then you should follow the following process:

(1) Obtain further information – do you have firm evidence to support concerns?

(2) Follow established internal procedures (e.g. whistle blowing help-lines)

(3) Consult with direct line management

(4) Escalate issue to higher levels of management

(5) Escalate to audit committee

(6) Seek advice from professional institute (e.g. CIMA ethics department)

(7) Finally, consider withdrawing from the engagement / situation.

4 Chapter Summary

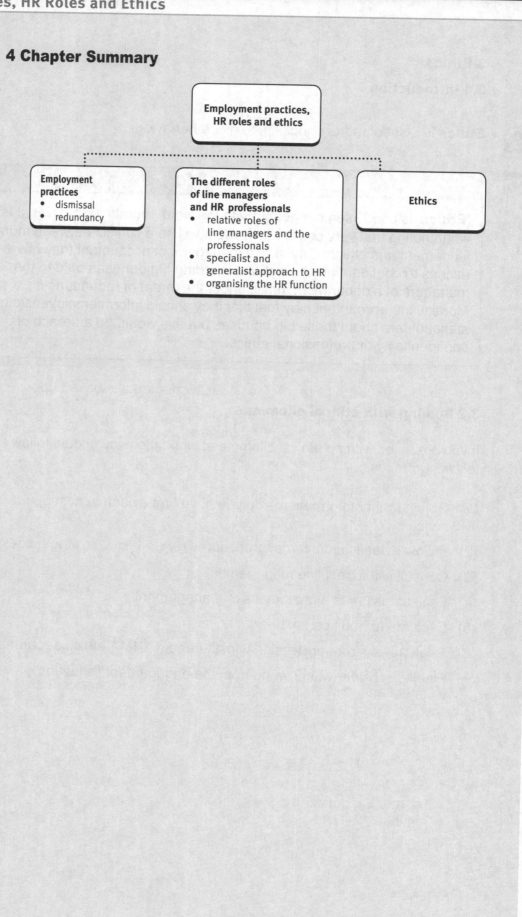

5 Practice questions

Question 1 – OTQ

Which one of the following may NOT be a justifiable reason for redundancy?

A   The type of work the employee does no longer exists

B   Refusal of the employee to transfer within the organisation

C   The business is about to cease trade

D   The part of the business where the employee works is being closed

Question 2 – OTQ

CIMA's Code of Ethics for professional accountants is based upon:

A   a scale of penalties for non-compliance

B   a framework of fundamental principles

C   sustainability principles and best practice

D   a framework of strict rules

Question 3 – Black Pearl Company (Case style)

You are a recently qualified management accountant and have just accepted a new post as management accountant in Black Pearl Co, a company specialising in the provision of credit and loans to wealthy individuals. You report to Mr. Sparrow, the senior management accountant and your duties involve performing credit checks on new customers through to the preparation of monthly management accounts and cash and profit forecasts for the company.

An initial review of the receivables ledger shows one debt from Miss Swan is quite old; there have been no loan repayments for the last six months, and the outstanding balance has risen to nearly $150,000 with accrued interest. When queried, Mr. Sparrow suggests not making a provision for this amount because to make a provision would decrease profit and cash flow by an unacceptable amount.

After leaving work for the day, you go for a drink at the Parlez wine bar with the junior management accountant, Will. After a few drinks, Will informs you that Mr. Sparrow is a personal friend of Miss Swan, which may be a reason Mr. Sparrow does not want to make a provision at this time.

Task:

Identify which, if any, of the fundamental principles within the CIMA ethical guidelines Mr. Sparrow has broken and describe possible actions that you should take in response.

(15 minutes)

Test your understanding answers

Test your understanding 1

Alternatives to redundancy include:

- reduced overtime
- limiting future recruitment for vacancies that arise or putting a total freeze on recruitment
- retraining for new roles
- transfers to jobs in other departments
- job-sharing between two or more people
- a shorter working week
- retirement
- more effective HR planning in the future.

Question 1 – OTQ

The correct answer is B

Question 2 – OTQ

The correct answer is B

Question 3 – Black Pearl Company (Case style)

Identifying the ethical dilemma

Mr. Sparrow appears to be basing business decisions on his friendship with other people. In this sense the following ethical principles may have been breached:

- Firstly, *Integrity* – members should be honest and straight-forward in all personal and business relationships.

- Secondly, *Objectivity* – members do not allow bias or conflict of interests in business judgements.

It certainly appears that Mr. Sparrow has been less than objective. Without the friendship with Miss Swan, it appears that the customer would have been sued by now to recover the outstanding money. The action also appears to lower the integrity of Mr. Sparrow because the level of trust you have in his actions will now be lower – you can no longer be sure of his motivations.

Action

You now have a possible reason for Mr. Sparrow not pursuing Miss Swan for the outstanding debt; although to be clear this is only hearsay and may yet be determined to be incorrect. To progress matters, you could ask Mr. Sparrow if there are any other reasons he can think of as to why the debt from Miss Swan remains unpaid – this gives him the chance to explain that Miss Swan is a personal friend.

If Mr. Sparrow denies knowledge of friendship, then there is simply his word against Will's – it will be difficult to report the case to CIMA's ethics committee for lack of objectivity because there is no breach of principles that can be proven.

However, there is still the issue of the outstanding amount from Miss Swan. You can suggest that a provision is made, although again Mr. Sparrow may reject this assertion.

Other options available to you therefore include:

- Reporting directly to the board on the issue,
- Taking advice from CIMA's ethics department.

It appears no further action can be taken due to lack of any firm evidence.

Index

Index

Index

Index